MW00781689

WONDERFUL WORLD
MY LIFE BEHIND BARS

By EMIL RICHARDS
WITH TOM DI NARDO

During a span of 55 years, Emil Richards has been a renowned presence in Hollywood soundstages, recording studios, jazz clubs and international touring venues. Considered a supreme artist on the vibraphone, marimba and xylophone, as well as a master of his world-famous collection of percussion instruments, Richards is renowned throughout the world for his versatility.

This book's lifetime of insightful and hilarious experiences include years with Frank Sinatra and George Harrison, as well as many anecdotes involving Burt Bacharach, Elvis Presley and Ravi Shankar, as well as most major recording artists.

Richards' chronology roughly categories the book's chapters into decades, with the 1960s mainly involving album recording, television shows in the '70s and films in the '80s and '90s. A parallel career means stories emanating through playing with George Shearing, Paul Horn, Stan Kenton and Roger Kellaway, as well as Igor Stravinsky and Richards' own group Calamari.

There are warm recollections of the great film composers, including Henry Mancini, Alex North, Jerry Goldsmith and John Williams, who ALL collaborated at finding a unique sound at Richards' warehouse before composing. Salad bowls used in "Planet Of The Apes," gongs lowered into fluid for space movies and many other unusual sonic effects will flash readers back to decades of favorite movies.

From an astonishing family history and grim days growing up in Hartford, Connecticut, through wild tours with Sinatra to Europe, Japan and Egypt, and visits to the Maharishi in India, Richards' entertaining, direct style perfectly complements this wealth of inside experiences.

Reza,
Enjoy this wild and wonderful life story that we hope inspires you to continue to be wild + free, creative! ♡
Camille & Family

WONDERFUL WORLD
OF PERCUSSION
MY LIFE BEHIND BARS

EMIL RICHARDS
with TOM DI NARDO

Wonderful World of Percussion: My Life Behind Bars
©2013 Emil Richards. All Rights Reserved.
No part of this book may be reproduced in any form or by any means, electronic, mechanical, digital, photocopying or recording, except for the inclusion in a review, without
permission in writing from the publisher.

Published in the USA by:
BearManor Media
P O Box 71426
Albany, Georgia 31708
www.bearmanormedia.com

ISBN: 978-1-59393-265-7
Printed in the United States of America
Book design by Robbie Adkins
Illustrations by Camille Radocchia Hecks

Contents

DEDICATION

Celeste Janene Radocchia, my helper, my partner, my saving grace, my wife.

I must thank Celeste for most of the good fortune in my life, my career, my family, and my success. We met in 1969 and became fast friends. I was working in the film and recording studios while going through a divorce, and Celeste came into my life just at the right moment. She didn't know music by notes, or in any technical way, but she had the means to know what I needed to become more successful in my chosen career.

She taught me the importance of listening to others and what they were trying to tell me about their film, their recording, or their music, and she helped guide me through meetings with composers and movie people.

I thought it was rare to find a soul mate, but I thank the heavens for bringing Celeste into mine. Everything I am, and have become, is because of what she has brought to my life though our marriage of over forty years.

Celeste, this book, my career, my life, would have been nothing without you. I dedicate this manuscript to you, for without you, your help, and your guidance, it could not have been a life worth much at all.

Thanks for sticking by me through it all. I am so very grateful, and so in love with you, beyond this life.

FOREWORD

Anyone who's seen a movie, watched a television show, listened to a song, gone to Disney World or reveled in a cartoon has been listening to Emil Richards—without knowing his name.

Emil's famous collection of over 700 percussion instruments, from all over the world, been heard in scores by famed movie composers like Henry Mancini, Alfred Newman, John Williams, Alex North, Jerry Goldsmith, Lalo Schifrin and Elmer Bernstein, all eager to collaborate with Richards in innovative sonic expression.

From the days of TV's "Mission Impossible" through "Lost," and from "The Diary Of Anne Frank" in 1959 all the way to the recent "Oz, The Great And Powerful," composers have counted on Emil to come up with original sounds. He has performed on over 2,000 film and television sessions, plus innumerable records for Frank Sinatra, George Harrison, Elvis Presley, Michael Jackson, Nat Cole and hundreds more.

But even more impressive is his generosity and willingness to share his imagination with three generations of percussionists. His clinics, seminars and teaching sessions pass on his 60 years of experience, and his ability to envision his art as a joyful inspiration to others may be his greatest legacy.

For over 55 years, I've seen and felt his spirit, enriched by his beloved Celeste, spread like sunshine over the long list who consider him a friend—and I'm proud to be one of them.

– Tom Di Nardo

"When I did the score for the 'Hellstrom Chronicles,' which was about insects, considering that we don't know what the insects hear, I decided to "invent" their audio world. In order to do so, I needed Emil Richards to provide me with many of his instruments. We decided to meet at his home, where most of those instruments were part of the décor of the house and the garden and hanging in the patio--for example, wind chimes, African bells, Korean thumb pianos, and many more. When I finished the project. Emil was telling everybody that 'Lalo is playing my house'."

– Lalo Schifrin

"Emil has had such a huge impact not only in the demanding and challenging art and craft of making music but on culture, creativity and the vitality of our humanity. His mind has alway searching for greater means of expression and invention. As a teacher and mentor he has ignited a wonderful passion for music and for meaning within the notes. I cannot think of a scoring session without him and his great playing and creativity. We are very rich and honored to know Emil as our collaborator, dear friend and point of light in a dark business."

– Ron Jones

"What can I say about my buddy 'Emilucci'?

One of the great gifts of my job is getting to work with my heroes. You have to understand that as a kid, I would listen intently to movie soundtracks and wonder to myself, 'What genius musicians are playing these instruments?' That I would then grow up to not only meet, but to work with these wonderful people was something that I never believed was in the realm of possibility.

Emil, to me, personifies the quintessential studio musician. He's a player who not only has the talent to play any piece of music you put in front of him, but also (and more importantly) the kindness and sense of humor to be able to work with anyone he meets. Emil is a true teacher, and a generous spirit who has been one of the great joys of my film scoring career. His advice and ideas have helped me look better then I deserve to look. I am a better musician because of him, and for that I will be forever grateful.

I have no doubt that if you have even the slightest interest in movies or music, you will find that his stories are as inspirational as they are funny and, most importantly, you will discover one of the greatest souls ever to grace the music industry."

– Michael Giacchino

"Throughout the many years of his long and distinguished career, Emil Richards consistently brought adventure, joy and discovery to all of his music making. His new book is a valuable addition to the documentation of a period of great creativity in American music."

– John Williams

"For all of the musical miles in our relationship, I will thank you, forever, for bringing your beautiful sound and spirit to all of our Cello Quartet and Quintet recordings.
You are Blessed,"

– Roger Kellaway

"Emil and I both grew up in Hartford and I was fortunate to do some wonderful sessions with Emil, the most helpful guy to newcomers and on our Wrecking Crew team, and the greatest percussionist in Hollywood. Emil had the most toys and sound effects known to mankind, and he used them all when called upon to do so. He was always a happy camper on sessions, partially because he had the beautiful and caring Celeste to look after him. I am grateful for his friendship and brotherly love."

– Hal Blaine

"As a young man, I was pretty obsessed with ethnic musical instruments and the music of Harry Partch and percussion of all kinds in general. In the first musical-theatrical troupe I was in, I spent many days building marimbas and our own home-made Balinese gamelans. I dreamt of becoming an ethnic percussionist. but that wasn't what fate had in store for me.
Then, in 1985, Tim Burton hired to me out of the blue to write the score for 'Pee Wee's Big Adventure.' That was my first time in front of an orchestra, and the lead percussionist in that orchestra was Emil. Someone told me 'that guy actually played with Harry Partch'... I was really impressed and, after some time, Emil invited me to see his amazing collection of instruments. I realized at that point Emil was what I had dreamt of becoming in another reality.
Now, nearly 28 years later, Emil has played on .... I have no idea, maybe 60 or 70 scores of mine. He never disappoints and continues to amaze me. When it comes to percussion, Emil has always and always will be an irreplaceable original. ...The Man! ....The One and Only.
With love and admiration,"

– Danny Elfman

"Emil Richards stands 5 foot something, but he is one of the biggest men I know. A Giant of a legend, not only in his music which spans almost three-quarters of a century, but as an example of spiritual evolvement. He is a master in music and Trancendental Meditiation, and has shared his vast knowledge of both with me. Emil has probably played more notes than our National Debt! And everyone has most likely listened to his playing in every medium and style of music imaginable. Now enjoy the 'notes' of his incredible life."

– Robert Davi

It was always a secure feeling to have Emil in the studio with me. He was very creative, with a wonderful attitude.

– Burt Bacharach

My first impression of Emil Richards came via Frank Zappa in 1966, when Frank was writing 'Lumpy Gravy' for Capitol Records. During the discussions concerning the contracting of musicians for the recording dates, it became clear that Frank already had a working knowledge of the top session players in Los Angeles. So he was able, for his first solo album, to name some of those guys and cross his fingers; one of them was Emil Richards, who was on a very small list of his heroes in music. The idea that with a phone call (and whatever the unions dictated) you could get this actual guy to show up, and actually play, was right there at the top of his list of Wildest Dreams.

In rock-and-roll, the guitar player of the group heavily relies on the bass player and the drummer--the rhythm section. But in the world of composing for an orchestral event, this composer, at least, relied on the percussionist. At the ripe old age of 25 he wanted the best, and that is what he got. I guess it all comes down to beating it with a stick, whether it be a mallet or a baton. The two of them together remain Ambassadorable in the world of music to which I was introduced all those scores—and scores of years--ago.

– Gail Zappa

Emil would like to say *"My dear friend George Harrison, whom we all miss, shared these kind words for my CD 'Wonderful World Of Percussion' 20 years ago:"*

"Famous people come and go, where they go and I don't know. All I know is clear, Emil's still here... As wild, wonderful and original as one can hope for, I love Emil Richards - check him out and smile."

– George Harrison

Illustrations

CHAPTER ONE:
ROOTS — 1912-1930

from my seventy-fifth year, when I began writing this book, until my eightieth, when it was completed, I've asked myself many questions about the meaning of my journey: why did I choose the life of a musician, why was I meant to travel the world and meet people with so many messages, and how did it all begin?

The answers flow from the source, the Italian village of Pescosansonesco, high in the mountains above Pescara, where the rich farms produce the famous grapes and olives of the Abruzzo region. The year was 1912, and my father Camillo Radocchia and his friend Nunzio Aprile were beginning their first year of high school, a light-hearted time for most fifteen-year-olds. But Nunzio was obsessed with the recent loss of his mother Josepa, believing she had died of a broken heart.

The cause was a steamy affair between Nunzio's own father Antonio and the adjacent property owner Concetta DiBella, who was trying to run her farm and look after her four siblings after her parents died. Josepa had ignored the rumors she heard in the village, until the day she took her homemade bread to Concetta's farm and found her in bed with Antonio. Refusing to eat or even speak, Josepa died in her sleep in a matter of months. Nunzio told young Camillo, "I'm not sure how, but I know that *puttana* is responsible for my mother's death, and someday I will kill her."

On a Tuesday in May 1912, Camillo and Nunzio took their usual short cut home from school through Concetta's farm. Nunzio saw Concetta sitting in the shade of an olive tree beside a sickle, which she used to cut the weeds around her grape vines—and which Antonio continually sharpened as an excuse to visit her. He picked up the sharp sickle, ran up behind her and yelled, "Puttana, you are responsible for my mother's death, and now you will die!" Then Nunzio swung the sickle at the back of Concetta's neck with such force that her head came right off her body, rolling at Camillo's feet with the eyes and mouth opening and closing as if gasping for breath. Camillo was too frightened to move or stop looking at the slumped, headless torso of Concetta, jerking and twitching as the blood poured out from her neck. He heard Nunzio yelling and running toward the school, away from their homes, but Camillo seemed frozen until finally, Concetta's torso came to rest. Her mouth stopped moving, and her eyes stared up at him in panic. Suddenly, reality jolted him into overwhelming fear and guilt at what he had just seen, as if he had been the murderer. He started to follow Nunzio, running as far away from that horrible scene as he could imagine, and as far from his family as he had ever been.

For two months and over 900 miles, existing only by scavenging, begging, and sometimes eating grass from the fields, the two boys made their way through Switzerland, Germany, and Holland to Amsterdam. Finding a ship bound for an American port, they stowed away without being certain of its destination. Through the long days and nights, Camillo relived the haunting image of Concetta's body and head twitching and gagging for breath, and ached with longing for his parents, Domenico and Domenica, whose faces he might never see again. The rough seas sickened them, even when they found food down in the ship's storage lockers, and only the constant fear of discovery and their consuming hunger allowed a respite from their bitter thoughts.

They landed in Quebec seventeen days later, but Camillo and Nunzio remained hidden for another two days until they were certain it was safe to sneak off the ship. From Quebec, they walked through the fields of Canada and across the border into the United States, and then through the state of Maine. Camillo's only hope was to make his way to Hartford, Connecticut, where his oldest brother Augustino lived, so he and Nunzio hopped an empty freight car heading south from Maine. The train stopped in the middle of the night, and Nunzio jumped off to find some food.

Suddenly the train started up again, with Camillo shouting to Nunzio, but even though Nunzio grasped the ladder with one hand, the train accelerated too rapidly for him to climb back on. The screaming Camillo saw Nunzio recede into the dark night, and for the first time in his young life, he sat down and cried. He knew he would never see Nunzio again and he was consumed with loneliness and guilt, as though he were to blame for the events of the last few months. The train's final destination was Providence, Rhode Island, and the end of Camillo's journey came a few days later when he finally reached Hartford.

Augustino lived in the black neighborhood called "the bottom," about the worst section of Hartford, but to a village boy like Camillo it seemed like a large, modern city. Scarlet fever had taken Augustino's wife Francesca just three weeks earlier, but he was happy to see Camillo and hoped they could both visit the old country again. Camillo was afraid to return, fearing that he would be arrested or implicated in Concetta's death, so he was relieved that Augustino did not have enough money for both of them. He only told Augustino that he had stowed away on a ship, both as an adventure and to find a better life in America, being careful not to mention the incident or his companion.

Augustino's shop sold fruit and vegetables to the blacks in the Windsor Street area, and to all the Italian and Sicilian immigrants in the Front Street neighborhood. In the next few weeks, he introduced Camillo to the customers and neighbors, instructed him on the details of selling produce, and finally left to take his voyage back home.

The produce business wasn't very profitable, so Camillo also had to work long hours at the Hartford provisions slaughterhouse, carrying heavy quarter-sides of beef on his shoulders to the local butcher shops. The slaughterhouse was adjacent to the railroad tracks, and seeing the steer and pigs brought in from as far away as Chicago made him dream of having his own butcher shop.

Fillipa Tillona, who had been born in the mountain village of Licodea Eubea, near Catania and Mount Etna, had come to America from Sicily with her parents Maria and Emilio when she was three years old. She went to school in New London, Connecticut, where her father was a barber for the Navy as well as a classical flute player, but she had to drop out at age fifteen to assist her family of three siblings financially. Her excellent English made Camillo feel inferior, as he was always ashamed of his accent when speaking English and felt more comfortable speaking Italian whenever he was around his countrymen.

One day, Camillo was showing one of the new workers how to run one of the machines as Fillipa happened to walk by. Camillo greeted her with a *buon giorno*, but in his instant of distraction his hand moved closer to the machine, which severed the middle finger of his right hand. The girl who Camillo was training let out a shriek. "My God, you're bleeding," cried Fillipa, who took her apron and wrapped Camillo's hand in it until the ambulance arrived. All Camillo could say to her was, "This is the happiest day of my life. Can I have permission to call at your home?" Two years later, the twenty-three-year-old Camillo and his seventeen-year-old bride were married.

In 1921, a year after their marriage, both Camillo and Fillipa became American citizens. Times were hard and prohibition had been in effect for two years, but the key to the young couple's dreams—seemingly so far away—happened to be close at hand.

One night, Camillo happened to hear about a twenty-six-car freight train, filled with grapes, that would be passing through the Windsor Street slaughterhouse train yards. The train derailed as it was making its way through the yard, leaving all twenty-six cars of grapes rotting on the tracks. The owner of the grapes offered to sell the whole trainload, from Massachusetts orchards, for $19,000. It seemed like the opportunity of a lifetime, because the Italians and Sicilians would buy the grapes to make home made wine during prohibition; many drank wine with their meals every day, and Camillo hoped he could sell all the grapes before they spoiled.

But he also knew that borrowing from a loan shark meant owing forever. In desperation, he asked Emilio DiLoretto, the owner of the slaughterhouse, for the money, promising to pay back the $19,000 plus ten percent interest within six weeks. To his surprise, Mr. DiLoretto said, "Here, give me your hand. I don't want your ten percent interest, and I don't need to have you sign any papers, just bring me back my nineteen thousand dollars in six weeks. I've watched you since you were sixteen, carrying beef on your shoulders for me in my business, so I know you are an honest and fair man, and I have seen how you have helped the people in this neighborhood. So go and sell those grapes before they rot on the tracks." And he handed him the $19,000, in the year 1921, on a handshake.

Five and a half weeks later, Camillo repaid Mr. DiLoretto and opened his own butcher shop in the black Windsor Street neighborhood, selling fresh produce as well. Camillo and Fillipa were finally making a good living, and the grapes continued to sell all through the prohibition years.

Their first child, Domenico, named after my father's father, was born in July of 1929, only a few months before the stock market crash. The imminent depression affected every part of the world, but Camillo continued to think of his family as fortunate.

"Whatever we can't sell in the store, we can eat at home," he said, "so at least we will never go hungry."

CHAPTER TWO:
THE 1930*S*

was born three years later on September 2nd, 1932, and named Emilio after my mother's father. Roosevelt soon became president and ended prohibition, and my mother applied for, and received, the first liquor license in the state of Connecticut. She made the front page of the Hartford papers, and alongside her picture and headline was a grim headline reading, "Hitler Burns Books in Berlin Today."

Other people applying for a liquor license complained that Phyllis (as she was called in English), a mother of two small children, shouldn't be eligible to sell liquor. And because the liquor commission was very strict, Camillo was determined to keep his life above board. She retained her license, but had her mother Maria apply for a license as well to insure that she would stay in the liquor business and that the store would remain open.

I remember my maternal grandmother Maria (or Nana) well, as she lived with us until her death in 1947, but only slightly recall my maternal grandfather and namesake Emilio. He died when I was three years old, but I can still remember him playing an old wooden ebony flute around our house. After his death, Nana moved into our house permanently and since she spoke only Sicilian, I also spoke, and still understand, the Sicilian dialect.

In 1933 Pa, as we called Camillo, bought the property on Windsor Street in the black ghetto where we lived above the shops. On the ground floor were Ma's liquor store, Pa's butcher and grocery store, and a tavern run by a friend of Pa's, George Tossi, that served beer, wine, and hot meals. There was never a dull moment on Windsor Street, and we witnessed a stabbing, shooting, or some form of domestic violence just about every day.

When I was six and my brother was nine, in 1938, Pa decided it was time to allow my brother Domenico to play the accordion. Domenico had begged Pa for over a year, so they went to the music store and Pa made the mistake of taking me along. As Pa was signing the papers for purchase of the accordion, I kept pulling on his pant leg, insisting, "I want an instrument too! I want an instrument too!" Pa kept saying, "No, stop, be quiet." But I would not stop, and kept repeating, through my tears, "I want an instrument too!" Just then Pa said, "What do you want?" I wanted to pick out something quickly before Pa changed his mind, so I immediately pointed to the first thing I saw, which happened to be the biggest instrument, and the closest, and said, "I want that."

I didn't even know what it was, but it turned to be a two-and-a-half octave xylophone supported by placing it on two chairs.

For sixty-five dollars, I got the xylophone, a pair of mallets, and six months of weekly lessons.

My first teacher's name was Mr. Wilson, and I can't remember much of what he taught me those first six months. Luckily, my mother came with me for every lesson and she learned to read music, so she was the one who taught me how to read music and begin to play my first instrument. I stayed with Mr. Wilson for another six months before moving on to Adolph Cardello, who was the most renowned drum and mallet teacher in Hartford. He was also the biggest drum dealer in Connecticut, so all the band drummers that came through Hartford stopped into Cardello's shop to get drum heads, sticks, and other supplies; I remember seeing Gene Krupa, Cozy Cole, and Buddy Rich at his shop. During my years with Mr. Cardello, he helped me to read music and stressed the importance of reading a new piece of music every day.

Since we came from a very rough neighborhood, it would have been easy to fall into a life of crime. Some of my friends in the hood, June Bug, Stinky, Beans, Snake, Kong, Hook, Rocco, and Quino were pretty tough. Most of them were stealing cars just to take joy rides, and to show the other neighborhood kids that they could drive. Others were breaking into homes or grabbing the purses of women who were walking down the street. A favorite trick was to go to G. Fox, the big department store on Main Street, just up the hill from our neighborhood. While a man was having a new pair of pants fitted with the tailor, they would go into the men's dressing room and take his wallet or money from his other pants. This was all common in my neighborhood but I decided that I wanted to be a musician, and that meant staying home and practicing a lot. Music is truly what saved me from choosing a life of crime.

On my first day of second grade, in 1939, I noticed a big crowd in the school-yard watching a boy playing drumsticks on the sidewalk. He was very accomplished, and the kids showed their appreciation of his talent by clapping. After he finished I introduced myself. "My name is Joe Porcaro," he said, "and I live on Front Street in the Italian neighborhood. Come to my house and let's play sometime."

That first meeting with Joe, who we called Skinny back then, initiated a close friendship and professional partnership that remains strong to this day. We started to chum around and practice together, and soon began to play for weddings and feast-day celebrations with a clarinet player from Joe's street named Joe Bonitto.

The people in these neighborhoods didn't have much money, so they were thrilled to get our trio to play for their christenings, weddings, and other affairs in exchange for feeding us and then passing the hat around for tips. It was a good feeling to play for people and make them happy, and it gave us the enthusiasm to memorize as many standard songs as we could.

CHAPTER THREE: THE 1940*J*

n my eighth birthday, Pa bought me a four-octave marimba. Since it was too tall for me to reach the bars, he built a large step for me to stand on, cutting it down every year as I grew. Just over a year later, as my brother and I were coming out of the movies at about 6 p.m. on a Sunday, we heard about the attack on Pearl Harbor. It was snowing, and they were selling an extra newspaper which read "Japanese Attack," but we didn't even know where Pearl Harbor was. From then on we would have air raid drills and I would hide under the marimba to protect me from a bombing raid, because that's how big it still seemed to me. That marimba still stands proudly in my home.

At nine years old with new marimba, 1941

My brother and I would play duets, accordion, and either marimba or xylophone, for our parents and for different radio shows around the state. I still have some of those performances on the original old 78rpm records. Shortly after this, though, my brother gave up the accordion and Pa made me take accordion as well as marimba lessons. I didn't like the instrument that much but it was easier to carry around than the marimba, so I used to take it into the Italian neighborhood and practice with Joe Porcaro. The mob guys would have craps games and poker games, and would pay me to practice accordion on the roof—and watch out for the cops. If I saw the cops coming, I would play the Star Spangled Banner as a warning to the crapshooters, getting in my practicing and making a few bucks on the side.

Joe's neighborhood was a different world. Cab drivers would leave people off at the top of the hill, because people were afraid to go down into our neighborhood. They said that blacks scared a lot of people, and I never quite understood this because I had lived there my whole life, but it was so. Many of the men would work for a while, then go on welfare and bring my mother their whole check for booze. My mother would say, "You take some of the money from this check and buy food for your family," rationing how much liquor they could buy with their checks to be sure they always had enough to buy food next door at Pa's meat and grocery store to feed their families.

My brother and I also had to help Pa in the grocery store. I vividly remember a man in rags coming in and begging for a piece of salami and a loaf of bread. I refused him, but my father ran after him, and gave him a loaf of bread. He said, "You don't have to give him meat or other foods, but do not refuse anyone a loaf of bread."

Many storefronts on my street had Baptist church revival meetings in them, with a piano or organ, guitarist, drummer, and a bunch of tambourine players. Joe and I used to beg my mother to take us into these storefront churches to hear the great swinging music that these worshippers made. We would go in and you would hear the preacher say, "Liquor and gambling are works of the devil, so stay far away from them." Ma would put some dollar bills in the collection tambourine, and the preacher would say, "Liquor is evil, but if you must drink, go to Miss Phyllis's to buy your liquor because she has a good soul."

In 1942 Father Toscano, the priest from Saint Anthony's church in Joe's neighborhood, decided to form a dance band for our CYO dances. Joe played drums and we had two sax players, a guitar, two trumpets, two trombones, two clarinets, my xylophone, and Father Toscano on piano to form the CYO dance band. I was only ten years old, but playing in my first big band.

We used to rehearse at the parish hall, and every kid who wanted to play in the band—or attend the dance—had to go to confession and take communion. Joe and I also now had a small five-piece group for playing weddings and street fairs, and his dad became our manager and even drove us around to all of these jobs. We even played for the servicemen at Windsor Locks Air Force base. It was surprising to see a lot of Italian war prisoners there, and we used to sneak them cigarettes and candy every time we went there to play.

My father had developed severe ulcers, and every winter he went to Florida as the warm climate seemed to help him. I would accompany him for three months every winter from the time I was ten until I was fourteen, when the war ended; I enrolled in school in Miami, and Pa took the xylophone down each winter so I could still practice. He also found me a great teacher, Vincent Motte, who was a percussionist with the Miami Symphony and also had his own percussion store.

At 13, playing a concert, 1944

In 1944, when I was twelve and helping my father in the store, a black man named Charley Harold, who worked for my father, was in the walk-in freezer getting some meat. I heard him singing the same song that was playing on the store's radio, so I opened the door, and said, "Charley, how can you hear the song that's on the radio in here?" He said, "Come in here and shut the door." So I went in and he gave me a joint of marijuana. It did open my ears and seemed to make my hearing better–or so I thought at the time.

In July of 1944 the Ringling Brothers, Barnum and Bailey circus came to Hartford as they did every summer, and the train cars would unload near where we lived on Windsor Street. I went to the circus with Ma the first day they were in town. My brother and I had tickets for the matinee a few days later, but Pa said we couldn't go because he was busy in the store and couldn't take us; he also said he needed us to work in the store and, since I had already gone, I had to stay home and practice for a recital I had coming up. My marimba was in our living room just over Ma's liquor store and Pa's butcher shop. They could hear me practicing, and whenever I stopped they would bang on the ceiling with a long broom handle to let me know I hadn't practiced enough.

Suddenly, we heard fire engines and saw great clouds of smoke coming from the circus grounds. A bulletin came on the radio saying that, if you were a doctor or nurse, your services were needed at the circus grounds. We soon found out that the main tent had caught fire; 167 people were killed and several hundred people were severely burned. After Pa closed the store that night, he went to the state armory to help out with the bodies. He got home late the next morning and couldn't sleep for days after the horror of so many charred bodies. The circus never came back to Hartford while I lived there, or for many years thereafter.

At the top of Windsor Street, near Main Street, was the State Theater, which claimed to have the largest ground-floor seating capacity of any stage-show theater in America. All the big bands would come through to play the State, and whenever Lionel Hampton came through, Ma would pack me veal cutlet sandwiches on homemade Italian bread with roasted peppers and provolone cheese and a jar with Zinfandel wine to take along. The wine went every where with me, even to school, since Dr. Georgio said I was anemic and needed liver pills to enrich my blood, but Ma knew wine would do the trick. I would get to the theater at ten in the morning and catch Lionel's shows at one, four, seven, and ten, and even though I would have to sit through the same Charlie Chan movie four times, I got to catch Hamp play vibes. I did this for a lot of the bands that came through, and dreamed that I could play that well some day. I was all

right as long as I got home before Ma closed the liquor store, which was open until 11 every night except Sunday.

The war ended and the peace agreement was signed on my birthday, September 2, 1945, V-J Day. That following summer, Pa took the whole family to Italy to see his family in Abruzzo. For a fourteen-year-old, it was a thrilling experience to go two weeks on a ship to a foreign land and find so many people, who you had never met, hugging you and loving you.

Pa's mother and father were both dead, but his oldest brother Augustino was still alive, as were his two sisters,

Pa and Emil's brother Dominico in Abruzzo, 1946

Filomena and Maria, and his youngest brother, Pietro. Pa also had another brother, Giovanni, who had come to America and settled in Wakefield, Massachusetts. Since Pa hadn't ever returned to Italy since he had run away thirty-three years earlier, it was a great summer for him, as it was for all of us. When we went to visit Pa's parents grave, he fell on his knees, the first time my brother and I ever saw Pa cry. He sobbed, "I'm sorry Papa, I'm sorry Mamma, I didn't mean to run away, it wasn't my fault, I didn't do it." We didn't understand what he meant. But when we got back to America, my brother and I asked Pa, "What did you mean when you cried and said those things at your parents' grave?" He then told us the incredible story of Concetta's murder and his adventure with Nunzio.

When I returned, Joe Porcaro and the other guys were still playing with Father Toscano and the CYO band, so I rejoined them. Joe was also playing with another orchestra that had five saxes, three trumpets, three trombones, and a rhythm section, but didn't have arrangements for a xylophone in the band, so I formed a quartet with guys from Windsor Street: Al Guerrera on guitar, Nick Franco on bass, and Tony Cursio on drums. We played summer camps and parties and called ourselves the Tempo Four.

I found a new marimba teacher at this time named Florence Schaeffer. She was a senior in High School, but she had studied with the great Clair Omar Musser and had played in his fifty-piece marimba band. I was her first pupil, and she showed me everything that Musser had taught her.

My parents never gave me any money, but I was able to keep all the money I earned. Nana used to ask me for a quarter or fifty cents every week for church, and when she died in 1947 she left me and my brother five hundred dollars each that she had saved from all the quarters and halves we used to give her. With my five hundred I put a down payment on a vibraphone, and my parents surprised me by paying for the rest of it, and I went back to playing with Joe on drums.

We didn't know at the time that our piano player, Dave Mackay, had retinal degeneration and had gone totally blind. Dave and Joe were a year older than I was, and our bassist, Fred Mace, was even older. Ma's brother, Uncle Jimmy, got us a job at the Oak Grill after we lied about our age, and we played in the bar for dancing three nights a week for the next three years. Fred encouraged me to change my name, as a lot of musicians were doing at that time. Fred's brother Tommy, who played tenor sax, clarinet, and oboe in the New York recording studios and for Broadway shows, had changed his name from Mesamace to Mace, and he changed Fred's name too. From Emilio Radocchia, I chose Emil Richards. I never changed my name legally, as Pa would have freaked out, but our group became known as the Emil Richards Quartet.

I have kept in touch with Fred Mace in LA since 1959, and last saw him in 2007.

We used to drive from Hartford to New York in two and a half hours, and we would go with Fred to Birdland, the Embers, and the Hickory House to hear jazz groups perform. I loved to hear Red Norvo and Adrian Rollini play vibes.

Tommy played oboe on the "Charlie Parker with Strings" record, and that was a real thrill for us. We all wanted to be studio musicians when we grew up, to have the great musician's life that Tommy had, and he made me think that being a professional musician was a real possibility. It only took two and a half hours to get to Boston, and we would go to the Hi-Hat and the Savoy to hear Miles Davis, Dizzy Gillespie, and Milt Jackson play. I was still pretty young, so I had to wait till my folks were asleep before leaving the house at midnight to get to New York at 2:30 in the morning. The bands played till 4 a.m. and we would get home by six-thirty, just before our parents got up. My brother Domenico was a great big band fan, and he would always play the latest big band albums for me.

In 1947, when I was in high school, I first met Betty Meyers. She used to come to a lot of the dances that I played for, and we started to hang out together.

When I was in tenth grade, Arthur Fiedler, conductor of the Boston Pops Orchestra, came to town to conduct six concerts with the Hartford Symphony. Joe Porcaro was already an extra percussionist with the orchestra, and we were both studying timpani with Al Lepak, who was the orchestra's timpanist. After the first rehearsal, Maestro Fiedler said, "In the next few months there will be a lot of pieces with xylophone parts, so I want a good xylophone player in this orchestra." So I got called, and I became a percussionist with the Hartford Symphony orchestra at sixteen years old.

Fiedler was an honorary fire chief with the Boston Fire Department, and still conducting for the Boston Pops orchestra when he came to conduct the Hart-

Joe Porcaro and Emil, 1949, before Hartford Symphony concert

ford Symphony. It normally took two and a half hours to drive from Boston to Hartford, but after Fiedler finished rehearsing the Boston Pops, he would put on his fire chief hat, and with his station wagon's siren blaring, he would make it to Hartford in an hour and ten minutes. For the six months I worked under him, he did this every week.

At the first rehearsal, we were playing Leroy Anderson's "Juke Box Jingle," and my part called for a clunk on the cowbell to signify the coin being dropped in the jukebox. Fiedler asked, "Is there some thing else you can use to hit the cowbell with?" After trying various things, a silver dollar dropping inside the cowbell was the sound Fiedler liked best.

Three days later we were ready for the first concert, and I wore my new tails with white bow tie and vest. My girlfriend Betty and my mom came to the concert, and I had lots of xylophone parts on the second half of the show. The only thing I had before intermission was in the final piece in the first half, a triangle on the very last note of "Clair De Lune." Betty and my mother saw me just sitting there through the first half of the program, doing nothing until the very end of the last piece where I finally got up and, on the last note of the piece, tapped the triangle. Both my mother and Betty let out this wild laugh, as their eyes had been on me the whole first half, wondering when I would get up and play.

The second half of the program began with "Juke Box Jingle," and I was ready with the silver dollar in one hand, ready to throw it into the cowbell, which I held in my other hand. Fiedler gave the down beat, which I was watching so closely that the silver dollar missed the cowbell, hit the French horn player seated in front of me to my left, and rolled down the riser right down to the Maestro's feet. He picked up the coin and carried it all the way back to the percussion section and handed it to me, saying, "Shall we try it again now?" of course, I was embarrassed, but learned an important lesson in my career: to use peripheral vision to watch the conductor. Over the years it taught me to lower my music stand, so that it would be closer to the instrument that I might be playing, and to keep my vision distributed between the music, my instrument, and the conductor.

The rest of the concert had a lot of xylophone parts, which I played with no problem at all. I played with the orchestra for those six concerts with Fiedler and stayed on for five years, playing under Moisha Parinoff, George Heck, and Fritz Mahler, who was the nephew of the composer Gustav Mahler. During that time Joe Porcaro and I also played with the Fairfield Symphony Orchestra under Andre Kostelanetz, playing with guest artists like sopranos Risë Stevens and Lily Pons, as well as the Connecticut Pops Orchestra, with Daniel Sadenburg. We both worked on weekends playing Dixieland with Dave Mackay on piano and John Giuffrida on bass (he would later play with Tony Bennett). We were the nucleus for many guest artists, including Bobby Hackett, Vic Dickerson, Joe Marsala, Ralph Sutton, Wild Bill Davison, and Jack Teagarden.

While still in high school, I had two vibe teachers who taught me the most about the vibraphone: an optometrist, Dr. Quinn, and Lou Magnano. Dr. Quinn loved Red Norvo and showed me a lot of his music. I used to go to his eye clinic, after his working hours, and we would jam for hours. This was the essence of my lessons with him. Lou Magnano had a lot of the George Hamilton Green studies to show me, and he also shared his skill in chord voicing with me as well as how to really play bebop.

I also studied theory at the Hartford School of Music with Asher Zlotnik.

When I was studying mallets in those years there were not very many studies for vibes or marimba, so I read a lot of violin and flute studies. Zlotnik taught me how to make up my own scales and exercises, and I have some great mallet studies that I have published through the years as a result of the Schillinger techniques he showed me. Zlotnik had studied with Joseph Schillinger, who had also taught his theories to George Gershwin. Schillinger had told him, "You cannot make a musician out of an untrained ear." So Asher would emphasize sight singing to me, and make me find three songs for every interval going up and coming down at least an octave. "Find the first two notes of a song that started with a perfect octave going up, like "Over the Rainbow,"" he would say, except that I couldn't use any songs he mentioned. So it took a long time to find three songs for each interval that I knew, but it made me want to learn as many good songs as I could; it opened my ears and helped my sight singing and reading as well. I later realized that his point was not so much to find the song that started with the interval you were working on, but that you were singing that interval all day every day. Whether you found three songs that started with that interval or not, you were learning to sing that interval. He also taught me Schillinger's techniques for re-harmonizing a piece of music and reading rhythms. Using his technique, you would never run across a rhythm figure that you couldn't read.

Joe and I also jammed at the Elks Club with all the black players from Windsor Street. There was another club on Windsor Street, but we weren't allowed because the owners were strict about anyone under twenty-one being in the club. Their house trio consisted of Horace Silver on piano, Joe Calloway on bass, and Walter Bolden on drums. The bandstand was at the front of the club, and the owner would let us listen with our ears to the glass. Stan Getz came to the club for two weeks, finally taking the whole trio with him to New York, and that's how Horace first left Connecticut for The Apple.

Many years later Horace came in to have dinner at a club where I was playing with my quartet, Calamari, and we talked about those early Hartford days. We also discovered that we both had the same birthday, the second of September, though Horace has a few years on me.

CHAPTER FOUR:
THE 1950*J*

I graduated from Hartford High School in 1951, having written the class song and been voted the class cutup. Besides my academic courses at Hilliard College, I continued music theory classes with Asher Zlotnik at the Hartford School of Music, as well as snare drum and timpani lessons with Alexander Lepak at the Hartt School of Music.

In 1952, while I was still earning my A.A. (Associate of Arts) degree from Hilliard, Betty and I were married. I continued to play with the Hartford Symphony, the Fairfield Symphony and the Connecticut Pops Orchestra, along with club dates three nights a week and Sunday jazz sessions at a club called the Matarese Circle.

During those years, I knew that I'd be drafted into the Korean conflict if I didn't continue with school. After graduating, I decided not to enroll in music school or college the following fall before doing my Army commitment, so I could get on with my life.

Joe Porcaro and his wife Eileen had their first son, and Joe asked me to be godfather to Jeff, their firstborn. Jeff grew up to be a great drummer and, along with brothers Mike and Steve, would launch a very successful group called Toto. I was very proud to be a godfather, and I used to go by their house often to see little Jeff. After Jeff became such a great drummer, everyone wondered how he had acquired such a great sense of time. I would explain to anyone who asked, "When he was a baby his mom, Eileen, used to burp him by tapping his back to the cymbal beat—spang-a-lang spang-a-lang. That's why Jeff never had indigestion and man, did he have rhythm!"

In the fall of 1954, during the Korean War, I was drafted into the U.S. Army. During basic training in Fort Dix, New Jersey, my captain was from Hartford, so he gave me passes so I could get home and play jazz clubs with my quartet on weekends.

It was difficult to get into an Army band since, in those days, everyone claimed to be a drummer or percussionist. Fortunately, I was selected for the First Cavalry Division band after my three months of basic training, and was sent to Sapporo, on the northern Japanese island of Hokkaido. I was in my glory because the band had a vibe chair; I played timpani with the concert band, glockenspiel with the marching band, and vibraphone with the jazz band and orchestra. We were stationed so high up in Hokkaido that on a clear day you could see Siberia, and after three hot summer months, we were lucky to move down to Sendai, just above Tokyo on the main island of Kyushu.

My band members included Stu Phillips, who now writes music for movies and TV, Joe Battaglia, who now runs the New York Big Band, and drummer/vibe player Curry Tjader, vibist Cal Tjader's brother. Stu was also writing charts for the Sauter-Finegan Orchestra, a hot band at that time.

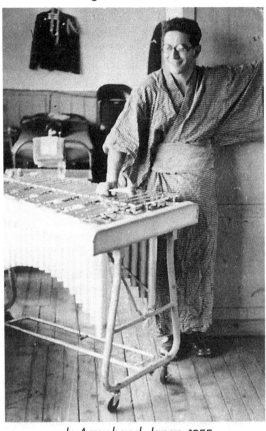

In Army band, Japan, 1955

On my first visit to Tokyo, I thought I heard a Bud Powell record playing before I realized the music was coming from a basement club. It was my first contact with a girl and an alto sax who sounded a lot like Charlie Parker—Toshiko Akiyoshi on piano and Sadeo Watanabe on alto. Since there was a vibe on stage that another group used, I jumped up and just started playing with them. For the rest of 1954 and 1955, I was able to travel to Tokyo on weekends and play with her band and drummer J. C. Heard's as well. When I had accrued forty-five days leave, I was able to travel all over Japan with Toshiko's band, and she booked us into some great clubs with very enthusiastic audiences.

Though I had only been in the Army for two years, I was promoted to the rank of sergeant and assistant to the bandleader. He was very obese, and the whole band had a very sloppy look. One day we played to welcome a gung-ho, war-zone general who had flown in from Korea. He immediately yelled at the bandleader, "I've never seen such a sloppy bunch of soldiers, and you are even fatter and sloppier than the rest. I will be here for two weeks, and I want to see your band exercising out on that parade field every morning." Of course, the bandleader assigned the detail to me. The parade field faced company headquarters, so the general would watch us from his office window as we jogged by every morning. I would lead them to the farthest end of the parade field and have them practice conducting so, from that distance, it would look as though we were doing heavy calisthenics. Between this practice and leading the band, I really got my conducting chops together.

Betty and I had grown apart while I was away, so when I returned on New Year's Day 1956, we started divorce proceedings and I moved to New York City. Stu Phillips called me to play vibes on his album *A Touch of Modern*, my first professional recording, and I even wrote a couple of the charts. Terry Snider, the session drummer, took a liking to me and turned me on to recordings and TV specials with Perry Como, Mitchell Ayres, and the Ray Charles Singers.

Every week I would meet drummer Ed Shaughnessy at his gig on the Garry Moore Show to give him vibe lessons, and played on weekends with him, Flip Phillips on tenor, and Charlie Mingus on bass. Because I had done so much practicing in the Army, I tended to play a lot of notes in my solos, and Mingus would yell out "Breathe! Breathe!" to remind me to save some space in the solo. "To use space in your playing is as important as all those notes you played," he would say, and it was an important lesson for me. Mingus gave me another tip when we played "Cherokee:" "During the solos, play the first 32 bars and when you get to the (16-bar) bridge, just keep playing those 16 bars over and over. When you are through soloing on the changes to the bridge, then play the last 16 bars and take it out." That was a real challenge between his bass, Shaughnessy's drums, and ridiculously fast tempos, and I would practice improvising on that bridge at home for hours at a time.

When Shaughnessy's quartet wasn't playing, I would play for singer Chris Connor in New Jersey, where I befriended pianists Ray Bryant and Junior Mance. There were other gigs with bassist Oscar Pettiford, and lots of jingles— music for ads—that I was fortunate to get into as well.

During this time Betty also moved to New York and, since she didn't have a place to stay, she moved in with me. Drummer Ed Thigpen had just gotten off the road after a long stint with Billy Taylor, and started studying vibes with me since he wanted to be with his family in New York. The best chance of getting some visibility was to be out on the road, but the only band at that time with vibes was George Shearing's quintet, so I was surprised to get a call from Shearing's manager John Levy (who had been his first bass player), asking me to fly up to Boston and audition for the quintet. I had heard a lot of his records and after playing a couple of songs, Shearing said, "We open in Detroit next week, can you fly there and start?" So I replaced Johnny Rae and joined the band. When I got back to New York that night Ed Thigpen called to say he had just turned down the drum chair in Shearing's band to study vibes with me. I had to tell him, "Gee, Ed, I just took the vibe chair with his band and I leave next week."

After several months George said, "We're going to be in Los Angeles for two months, and we're all bringing our wives out with us. You are married, aren't you?" and I said, "Yes." Betty flew out to meet me and, one afternoon, we went downtown to City Hall and became remarried.

The band consisted of Jean "Toots" Thielmans on guitar, Al McKibbon on bass, Percy Brice on drums, Armando Peraza on congas, George, and me.

George could hear everything, and whenever anyone made a mistake he would clear his throat to let you know he caught it. We did live remote broadcasts three nights a week for a coast-to-coast radio show called "Monitor," and even on the air, George would clear his throat when anyone goofed.

We toured with many other bands, and one in particular with the whole Count Basie band was heaven. I'll never forget another, in the dead of winter, with Miles Davis' band when he had John Coltrane, Cannonball Adderley, Paul Chambers, Wynton Kelly, and Philly Joe Jones. On another we traveled with Gerry Mulligan and drummer Chico Hamilton, and I befriended Paul Horn, who played flute and reeds with Chico's band.

When our drummer Percy Brice came down with the flu during an epidemic, Chico took over for a night, then he got sick and Donald Bailey, from Mulligan's band, got the bug. Philly Joe played drums in all the groups for a couple of nights, and sometimes because of that killer flu we ended up putting together all the healthy players to make up just one band. It was tough, but I was thrilled to be able to play with some of the finest jazz musicians on the scene.

George used to take most of the solos in the band, so the rest of us would tell him that there were requests for "Jordu" or "Joy Spring," because we soloed on those tunes. George wrote a song that featured me called "From Rags to Richards," and I used to say someone requested it every night. He knew there really weren't any requests for it, because we hadn't even recorded it yet—although we would in my third year with the quintet.

In 1957 we traveled to Texas and for the first time, really felt the power of prejudice. We were booked to play for a millionaire's party in Lubbock, Texas, for a group of ex-cattlemen who had struck oil on their property. We were checking into an exclusive $200-a-night hotel, and the clerk said that our three black musicians in the band could not stay there. Armando Peraza, who spoke with a very thick Cuban accent, began to argue with the hotel owner who said, "You're not black, you're Spanish, so we can give you a room." Armando became even more furious, because his complexion was darker than Al McKibbon or Percy Brice. We couldn't believe people could be that stupid, but Al, Percy, and Armando reassured the rest of us that they'd be all right for one night, because there was a black motel in town. The next day, we learned that that motel had no vacancies, and they had ended up getting rooms in an all-black hospital. I was upset and acted rude to every one of the so-called millionaires at that night's party. One gentleman, who asked me why I was so bitter, was very sympathetic and invited us all to stay at his ranch, but I refused, though we had three days off until a three-week gig in Chicago. Then he said, "Please let me make up for the bad experience you all have had, stay at my ranch and I will fly you all in my private plane to Chicago." It was a nice gesture from a kind person, but we told George we would never work with him in Lubbock again.

In another incident, our limo broke down and we had to take a train on our way to Los Angeles. We met Dizzy Gillespie at the Dallas train station and, as we were waiting to board the train, Dizzy saw this white guy drinking water from a fountain marked "Whites Only." Dizzy went over to the man and said, "Hey, mister, how's that white water taste?" We all cracked up laughing, but it wasn't really funny.

While recording at Capitol Records in Los Angeles I met Billy May, who wrote all the string and brass parts for George's albums. Another contact was Manny Klein, whose two brothers were music contractors, and he told me to call him if I ever decided to move to LA

After our gig, we took the first coast-to-coast jet on American Airlines from Los Angeles to New York. The plane flew higher than any of the other commercial flights up to that time, so the pilot kept lowering and retracting the hydraulic landing gear over several major air fields. Over Chicago, because of the temperature and the altitude, the landing gear froze, and the pilot announced that we were making an unscheduled landing in Chicago. We hit the runway on our belly, and we could see the men in protective suits shooting chemical foam onto the field. After spinning, slipping, and sliding all over that field, we finally came to a safe stop. George, being blind from birth, was the most shaken. He refused to fly after that, and bought the band a huge Chrysler limo for traveling.

George used to take my arm to come out onto stage, and I would direct him to the piano. After a concert in Champaign, Illinois, we were chatting with friends without realizing that the place had emptied out when the lights were turned off. George grabbed my arm to be led out of the hall, but I told him that I couldn't see a thing. He grabbed my arm and said, "Come on, you blind bastard, follow me and I'll get you out of this place." I held his shoulder as he snapped his fingers and listened to the snaps bouncing off the walls, and we soon were outside. That was a great experience, and when we told the rest of the band they said maybe George should be leading us around!

Armando Peraza introduced me to Mongo Santamaria and Willie Bobo, who were playing with Cal Tjader's band, and I played a session in San Francisco with Mongo as leader. There was another great Cuban band in Chicago, and we used to go to an 11 a.m. Sunday morning brunch with Armando, hear this great Cuban music, and eat Cuban food.

My son, Emilio Junior, was born in the Bronx while I was out on the road in Milwaukee. Ray Mosca had joined the band on drums, and Jimmy Bond on bass. We were working fifty-one weeks a year and, during that time, traveled about twelve times from coast to coast.

One cold and snowy night, while we were playing at the Embers back in New York, Billy May stopped in to say hello. I told him I was thinking of getting off the road and settling down, but didn't know whether to settle in New York or LA He said, "I decided years ago that, if I've got to scuffle, I might as well scuffle where the sun is shining most of the time."

His words made sense, and in 1959 I left the band, packed up my wife, little Emilio, my vibe and marimba, and drove to Los Angeles. I called Paul Horn and Manny Klein on my first morning in town, a Friday. Paul said, "You're playing with my band Friday and Saturday nights at the Renaissance club, starting tonight." We played 3 nights a week there for the next five years, working with blues singer Jimmy Witherspoon and opposite comedians Lenny Bruce, Lord Buckley, and Paul Mazursky (who became a noted film director). Lots of aspiring actors like James Coburn, Kim Novak, Sal Mineo, and Dennis Hopper hung out at the club; Hopper would talk to me for hours about how much he missed James Dean, who had just died, and how talented he was.

Manny Klein also called back immediately with good news. "Emil, we're doing a Lawrence Welk album this afternoon at 2 p.m., and there will be three more sessions next week." So I went to work my first day in town, playing marimba plus tambourine and triangle, which I had to borrow.

Musicians would go the union hall to pick up a check two weeks after a studio session. Right across the street was the Professional Drum Shop, and another store called Drum City was just a few blocks away. I made the decision that every time I picked up a check, I would buy the instruments that I had been asked to play on the sessions. That was the beginning of my collection of percussion instruments.

Through the years I played on all Lawrence Welk's recordings, and he was very friendly to Pa when he was in town visiting. Lawrence even asked me to do his TV show, but I was busy with other dates. The other reason was that, since I wasn't into his kind of music, I didn't want other musicians to see me on TV as a member of his band.

My first movie session was at Fox in 1959, under the legendary Alfred Newman, for *The Diary of Anne Frank*. Some people warned that he would be yelling at everybody, but it didn't turn out that way. In fact, he treated me very gently and with real respect. His orchestra was the most famous in Hollywood, and it's no wonder.

My first house in the San Fernando Valley had a pool, but also had a first, second, and third mortgage. Pa went with me to the bank, and told the vice president of the branch that he wanted to pay off my second and third loan. When the official said there were penalties for an early payoff, Pa got very angry and said, "You think-a you gonna smoke a cigar on me? Here's the cash, take it or leave it, with no interest penalty." Of course, they took the cash and only the first mortgage remained.

I remember Pa saying to me, "You think-a you own this house? You're just the janitor for the bank. You take out the garbage and you mow the lawn. You just miss one payment and you'll see who owns-a this house." This was another example of Pa's wisdom.

Pa also gave business advice to my brother Dominic, and as a result he now owns a chain of twenty-six stores all over the East Coast, as big as Costco, and owns the land they occupy as well.

CHAPTER FIVE:
THE 1960∫

efore long, I had played sessions with the Beach Boys, Jan and Dean, the Everly and Smothers Brothers, the Mamas and the Papas, Elvis Presley, and the Jackson Five, and was averaging fifteen sessions a week. At nights I played with Paul Horn's quintet at Shelly's Manne Hole and with Shorty Rogers' big band at the Crescendo on the Sunset Strip. And, in addition, there were the jingles and the live TV shows that I played when I first got to town.

One session was a jingle for Frank Sinatra, which he was doing during Senator John Kennedy's campaign for the Presidency. It was based on "High Hopes," with words adapted by Frank and lyricist Sammy Cahn.

In 1960 I did my first live TV show with Sinatra, with Nelson Riddle conducting, and was amazed at how fast he worked. He didn't believe in a lot of rehearsing and often said, "Come on, me and the boys are getting bored, so let's go before we lose the groove." I only learned to really understand what he meant in the years to come. Sinatra's drummer at the time was Bill Richmond, who later became the writer for many of Jerry Lewis' shows and movies.

Nelson began to call me for all Sinatra's live TV specials, and I sometimes played for Sammy Davis, Jr., Dean Martin, Bing Crosby, and Nat "King" Cole. One day during a live TV show, an NBC security guard kept trying to get my attention and I didn't find out until after the show that I was the proud father of another baby boy. Betty and I named him Claudio, after one of my cousins whom I had met in Italy.

On my first road tour with Sinatra, in 1961, we traveled to Atlantic City, Mexico City, and Acapulco. The band's other members were Sol Gubin on drums, bassist Joe Comfort, Paul Horn on sax and flute, Al Viola on guitar, and pianist Bill Miller. When we played at Skinny D'Amato's 500 Club in Atlantic City, I witnessed for the first time how everyone, from the newsstands to the card dealers at the nearby casinos, made money whenever Frank appeared. Even the police made more money, as it took more of them to handle the crowds around Frank, and Skinny actually directed them and told them how to control the crowds as if they worked for him.

During the Atlantic City engagement, Frank said, "I have a real treat for you all. We're going to a place for dinner you're not going to believe." I went in his car, the others went with Skinny, and we ended up in a tiny place near the ocean that seated only eight people. A sign on the door said, "If it's raining, I'm open, otherwise I've gone fishin'." "You're in for a treat," Frank promised, because he had arranged it with the owner, who cooked us a meal fit for a king. A large safe sat on the counter and, at the end of the meal Frank said, "OK, open the safe." Inside was a cheesecake made with ricotta, the best cheesecake anyone had ever tasted. Frank said, "His cheesecake is so famous, he keeps it in a safe so no one will taste it and steal his recipe. But we need an extra hour to digest it." We went on an hour and a half late for the next show, but it was all right because Skinny was with us.

When we got back I started to do all the acts that came into the Greek Theater in the evenings, and do record sessions during the day.

In 1962 then-President John Kennedy asked Sinatra to do a tour to benefit underprivileged children of the world, under the auspices of the State Department, and to raise enough money to build children's hospitals in every country that he visited. Frank said that he would pay for the tour himself, and the President agreed to have us met by the U.S. ambassador in each country.

Billy May and Nelson Riddle condensed the big-band arrangements down to a six-man band, and we rehearsed at Sinatra's house for a few weeks before we left in May of 1962, which was quite a thrill. I got to really get to know him and the other guys in the sextet. He had first asked Red Norvo to do the tour, but since Red had firm commitments in Las Vegas, Frank handpicked a sextet of people who had worked with him: Bill Miller, his long time accompanist, on piano, Irv Cottler on drums, Ralph Pena on bass, Al Viola on guitar, Harry Klee on sax and flute, and me on vibes.

What a swinging band, and what a swinging tour! I believe Frank sounded the best he ever did in his whole career on that tour, and the proof of it is on the CD *Sinatra Live in Paris, 1962*.

Then-head of Paramount Pictures Howard Koch, and Prince Romanoff both accompanied us on that trip. Howard and I became close friends, and though he was an important producer he was the most humble and one of the nicest people I have ever met. Whenever he saw me at Paramount through the years, he always stopped me to ask how I was doing and where I was playing. Sometimes he invited me to lunch on the lot just to talk about that Sinatra tour.

Frank had invited Prince Romanoff and his wife out of gratitude for his generosity. As the story goes, before he became so famous, Frank would wine and dine all his friends at Romanoff's restaurant—at the Prince's expense.

When the ambassadors met us in each country, they would process our passports and get us right through customs. So I was able to fill the belly of Frank's plane with percussion instruments from Hawaii, Japan, Hong Kong, India, Israel, Greece, Italy, Monaco, and England. We didn't perform in India, but we stopped in New Delhi to refuel Frank's jet, and there was a reception for us there. There were a lot of beautiful women dressed in saris who met the

In Tokyo with Frank Sinatra, world tour, 1962

plane, which was typical wherever Frank appeared.

We did ten days in ten different cities in Israel, and raised enough money to build a hospital right on what was, at that time, the Israeli-Arab border. When the bus taking us to the Tel Aviv concert broke down, Sinatra had to do stand-up comedy at the theater as he waited for us to show up. We were so late, and so nervous, that Irv Cottler dropped all the music as we came on stage. Frank even came over and helped us pick it all up and said, "Take your time, it's okay." It was typical of how kind and considerate he always was to us, and he intro-duced us as great jazz and recording artists wherever we went.

After the concerts we would jam with the local musicians from each country. We don't know how he found out, but most of the time Frank would show up with his tour guests and hang out with us. He was looking forward to getting back together with Ava Gardner, who was living in Spain, and every night he would sing, "Some like the perfume in Spain--YEAH!!" He gave us all ten days off when we reached Athens, Greece, so he could go see Ava. We did the con-cert there at the Acropolis, and at rehearsal Frank kidded, "Gee, maybe we can raise enough money to put a roof on this joint."

After the last concert in Greece, he called us all up to his hotel suite and said, "I'm leaving for Spain now, and I have something for you guys in the other room. Please clear the bed off and have a great ten days vacation. Goodbye."

We went into his bedroom and looked on the bed, which was loaded with a pile of drachmas; he had been embarrassed to hand us so much money.

I took off for an island called Hydra and studied some odd time rhythms with the drummers from that island, getting into the Greek rhythms of seven and nine from the local players. There were some young American and European artists living on that island that had done some awesome paintings. I'm not a lover of still life paintings, but one American had a painting of potatoes on a velvet cloth that made me cry.

A few days into my vacation, a beautiful yacht showed up in the harbor, sounding a very loud horn. It kept blowing until I was close enough to notice Sinatra standing on deck and when he spotted me, he yelled, "Come on, we're leaving Greece," so I grabbed my belongings and took a ride on Porfirio Rubirosa's motorboat to the yacht. Frank said, "Come on, we have to gather the rest of the guys and fly to Italy early." When we got back to Athens, his jet pilot told me "He and Ava had a big fight." Frank had showed up at Ava's villa in Spain with the two pilots, Rubirosa, and three of his friends, plus Howard Koch and the Romanoffs. Ava evidently said to Frank, "I thought you were coming alone to see me." While everyone was being fed by Ava's cook and housekeeper, she left for a nearby taverna, where Frank found her with a bullfighter. He and Ava must have had a serious argument, because he came back and told the pilots to get the plane ready to go back to Athens; I believe this was the last time they were ever together. Now for the rest of the tour whenever Frank would do "I Get A Kick Out Of You," he would sing, "some like the perfume in Spain-YUKK!!" You can even hear this on the *Live in Paris* CD. I don't think he ever got over Ava.

Before we left Athens, Frank said, "I'm taking everybody to a grocery store for dinner tonight." We drove an hour out of Athens and ended up at a grocery store near the sea. There was one long table in the store, and owner started serving us twenty-two courses of fish dishes. They were all delicious, and the very last one was a fish soup to wash down the meal; I thought this odd, as soup is usually the first dish in most cultures. But, in every country we visited, Frank loved turning everyone on to great and unusual food.

We arrived in Italy four days early and Frank gave me some time off to visit my father's brothers and sisters, who I hadn't seen in sixteen years, so this was a great return trip for me. They didn't own a television then, so I talked the local coffee house into letting all my relatives watch the commercials we made with Frank in Rome for Perugina chocolates. While we performed in Rome, the commercials were shown throughout Italy all day long.

Our last concert was in London at Albert Hall for her Majesty, the Queen. The concert was at midnight, and in the front row of the sold-out Albert Hall sat Judy Garland, Anthony Quinn, Elizabeth Taylor, and Robert Wagner. Frank sang for two hours, and it was the best I ever heard him sound. I have a treasured video of that, our last concert of the tour.

When we got back home, composers began calling to ask what percussion instruments I brought home, so they could see them and start to write for them. This was the beginning of my collecting frenzy.

I also started doing cartoons for Hanna-Barbera, and most of the music was written by Hoyt Curtin (the uncle of actress Jane Curtin). Some of the shows were *Huckleberry Hound, Yogi Bear,* and the *Flintstones,* with *Scooby Doo* and *The Smurfs* coming years later. In addition, I also recorded my first album as leader that year, called *Yazz Per Favore,* on the Del-Fi Label. It was a Latin jazz album, with Al McKibbon and Francisco Aquabella as two of the players on those sessions. Cuco Martinez, one of the Cuban musicians Armando Peraza had introduced me to in Chicago, was the timbale player.

Most people remember what they were doing the day President Kennedy was killed. I was on my way to a recording session for Dick Van Dyke, who was doing a comedy album with narration and some very funny music, when I heard the announcement on the car radio. At the studio, all the musicians were standing around in disbelief, talking about the news that the President was dead. Dick Van Dyke came into the studio looking very teary eyed, and said, "I'm sorry, fellas, but I just don't think I feel very funny today. If I must, I'll pay every one for the session, and we'll schedule coming back another day next week, but I just can't record a comedy album tonight." We all agreed to postpone the sessions without charging for the cancellation, as we all felt the same way. We all just went back home and felt the sorrow that hung in the air.

Around this time, I began to work on a few movies with composers Alfred Newman, Jerry Goldsmith, and David Raksin, who wrote the standard "Laura." Raksin wrote music that made me feel like I never played my instruments before. His music was really difficult, and at the first run-throughs it often sounded as through there were a lot of mistakes in the orchestra. Every one would have questions about the notes they were playing, and Raksin would say, "No, those notes are right, just play your part *forte.*" By just changing the dynamics, the music would sound right and beautiful. It's only one of the reasons he was quite a unique composer.

I also met the American composer Harry Partch, and immediately fell in love with the man, his music, and his instruments, which had 43 tones to the octave. To be able to hear bass marimbas and his diamond-shaped marimba play tones closer than quartertones was a thrill, and a new experience for my ears. Harry was living in an abandoned chicken hatchery in the northern California town of Petaluma. We began corresponding by mail, and it wasn't long before I helped to sponsor his move to LA with all his instruments. Many percussionists formed an ensemble to play all of his music, and some composers like Jerry Goldsmith and Frank Zappa came to see him, but Harry hated the Hollywood scene and settled further south in Encinitas. I continued to give him support by buying materials to make a few more instruments, and by bringing a lot of great percussionists around to rehearse and play his music. He was working on what turned out to be his last major work, "Delusion of the Fury," which we performed in its premiere at Royce Hall at UCLA and later recorded for Columbia Records.

Two instruments used in that work were the Quadrangularis Reversum and the Gourd Tree, which I commissioned him to make. The Quadrangularis Reversum is similar to Partch's Diamond Marimba but the bars are placed in reverse, meaning that instead of the higher tones being on top and getting larger in tone as you go lower, the lower tones are on top and, as you go lower, the tones get higher. There are also extra bars on each side of this amazing instrument. Harry had found these square bamboo resonators, which were very rare and which he had never seen before, so I bought them for use in the making of this instrument and was the first player of this instrument in that premiere.

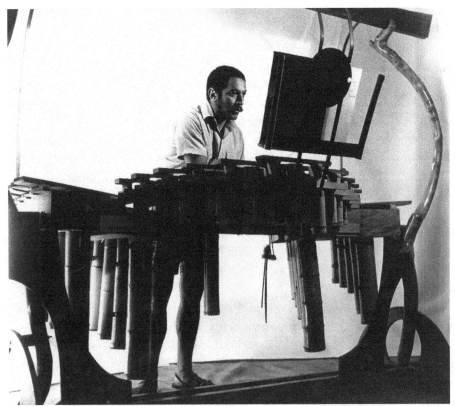

Emil playing Quadrangularis Reversum, 1965

I am proud to say that I was a disciple of Harry Partch and his music from 1963, when I first met him, until his death in 1974. Before his death, he called and asked me to come to his house, where he was writing his will. He wanted to leave half of his instruments to me and the rest to Danlee Mitchell, who kept the instruments at the University of California in San Diego where he taught percussion. Harry thought I was the right person to house and maintain his instruments; I told Harry that I was honored, but that I didn't think his instruments should be separated. Besides, my collection of percussion instruments was growing and I didn't really have room for them. Through Harry I also met Irv Wilson, who built–and helped me build–the microtonal instruments in my collection with thirty-one tones to the octave.

In the early 1960s, I formed a group of experimental players called A.H.A. (the Aesthetic Harmony Assemblage). Joining with me and my percussion instruments was Don Preston, who played piano with Zappa; Mike Craden, who became a founding member of the percussion group from Canada called NEXUS; Paul Beaver, who made a series of new sounds on a Solovox and became the first serious electronic instrument musician in LA; and Rowena Preston, Don's wife, who worked with film. Craden was a great painter who would create pictures while we played free-form music well before that movement started.

During one session at Columbia Studios, I found work prints of an orbiting John Glenn in a trash can. Rowena used them with spliced sections of other films, and we would play free music to the film of space shots and her other images. We went to psychics to have readings of former lives, and see what we could find out about the correlation between music and color, as well as our purpose in this lifetime. The answers we received were meant to help raise the vibrations of humanity, so we held concerts with that goal in mind. We had all kinds of reactions from our audience: some disliked our approach and were physically and emotionally upset and others were pleased, but everyone would eventually come up afterwards and thank us for the 'release.' It seemed as though we had discovered a new way to get our audience really involved in our performances. Unfortunately, because I started to get very busy with studio calls, we never pursued this direction after its first year.

When I first started working in the studios, I noticed that the reed players got a 'double' for every instrument they played. A double was 50% of your basic scale for the first double, and then 20% for every double after that. If a sax player played clarinet, he received 50% extra, if he played flute, he received 20% more, and if he played piccolo, he received yet another 20% more of his basic scale. But a percussionist could play xylophone, vibes, marimba, bells, and chimes, which were all considered "mallets," with no doubles. Timpani were separate,

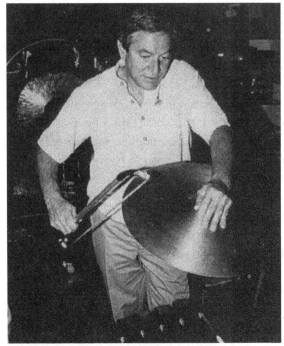

At Universal Studios, 1960s

and drums, all percussion and Latin were lumped into a category called "traps." I didn't think this was fair, so I had meetings at my house with every drummer and percussionist working in the studios, and set up a doubling list that was more in line with what the other sections of the orchestra were getting. Some players thought I was making waves, and should back off, and my answer to them was: "I wish some one would have taken care of this before I got to town." So I went into negotiations with the studio heads, and this is what we ended up with in our contracts:

-Xylophone, bells, and marimba were the "mallet category."
-Vibraphone became a separate double.
-Chimes became a separate double.
-Timpani became a separate double.
-Drum set became a separate category.
-The "Percussion" category consisted of anvil, bamboo wind chimes, bell plate, bird whistles, boat whistle, brass wind chimes, bulb horn, concert bass drum, concert snare drum, cow bell, cricket clicker, cymbal(s), duck call, field drum, fire bell, fight bell, glass wind chimes, jingle sticks, piatti, piccolo snare drum, pop gun, ratchet, ship's bell, siren whistle, slapstick, sleigh bells, slide whistle, tabour, tambourine, tam tam, temple blocks, tom-toms, triangle, washboard, and wood block.
-The "Latin" category consisted of au-go-go, cabasa, castanets, cencerro, chocalho, claves, conga drums, cuica, guiro, quijada, maracas, maraca sticks, pandero, puelli sticks, reco reco, sand blocks, timbales, and vibraslap.
-If a percussion instrument was not on these lists, then each one will constitute a separate double, such as tabla, steel drums, cimbalom, bass marimba, etc. In some cases, the instruments are so highly technical that performance on them warrants an agreement between the individual player, management, and/ or the contractor.

The studios finally agreed to this, and it has been honored in our contract for all these years. I am proud of these accomplishments, benefiting all my fellow players.

In the mid 1960s I finally talked my dearest and oldest friend, Joe Porcaro, to move out to LA with his wife and four children. It was a little scary for him, but I knew he was a great player and would be able to work. There was enough work for everyone in the 1960s so if you could play, and you were good, you could do all of the studio recording work you could handle.

His first session was a TV show with Jack Elliott, who knew Joe from Hartford, and Allyn Ferguson, who wrote the themes to many shows, including *Charlie's Angels*, together. None of the musicians knew Joe as yet, and I wanted a way to introduce him to everyone. When there was a cue with nothing for Joe to play, I asked him to go out to the lounge and bring me a cup of coffee, and while he was gone I marked a gong note with a triple forte at the very end of my music. When he came back into the studio, I said, "Joe, put the coffee down very quickly and take this gong mallet. They need a gong hit very loudly at the very last note of the cue." The music was real quiet, and I was playing vibes. At the very last note of the piece, it's real quiet, and Joe came in with this enormous gong crash! Of course it wasn't really in the music, but it made the whole orchestra turn around and glare at Joe. I said, "Hey, everyone, say hello to Joe Porcaro, he's my good friend and the new guy in town." Every one laughed, and Joe turned all red at his introduction to the Hollywood studios. Joe, as well as his talented sons, continue in very successful careers on the West Coast.

With Joe and Dave Mackay, two old Connecticut buddies, we formed a group and recorded two albums under my name for Uni—*New Time Element* and *New Sound Element*. For the *New Time Element* album, I took all current songs and recorded them in odd time rhythms with one exception: Dave Brubeck's "Take Five" was already in 5/4 time, so we played that one in the standard 4/4. In the second album I wrote original compositions for each month's birthstones, playing all the melodies on the Moog synthesizer—the first album using the Moog on the West Coast.

Nat Cole was rehearsing a show to take to Broadway with Barbara McNair, and he asked Paul Horn and me to play the show, where I befriended Nat's drummer Lee Young, brother of the great sax player Lester Young. I played the road show in San Francisco for four weeks, but came back to LA to do live TV shows with Frank Sinatra, Judy Garland, Danny Kaye, and the Smothers Brothers. There were also plenty of record sessions with Ella Fitzgerald, Sarah Vaughn, Lena Horne, Dean Martin, Henry Mancini, Sinatra, and a long list of others.

Whenever we recorded with Sinatra he would come in and say, "Let's go, it's past post time, and I want out of here." He would make one take and say,

At Western Studios for Dean Martin, 1965

"Okay, did you get that on tape? Then let's go on to the next one." He knew that whenever an engineer or the producer is given a chance, he would record each song over and over; Frank knew the band would get tired and bored, so everyone was on their toes and recorded the first take as well as possible. This made the electricity happen, and that's one of the reasons why Frank's recordings are all so great. Of course, he would vocalize while Billy May or Nelson Riddle was rehearsing the band, so that his voice was warmed up for recording those one-take sessions. Nat Cole also worked that way, and the only time we ever had to make a second take with Nat was when he blew a word. We made sure the music was always perfect the first time.

I was still doing mostly record sessions in 1967 when I was called to do a session for Frank Zappa's first big record, "Lumpy Gravy." There were a lot of heavy musicians on that session, and some said the parts were impossible, but I loved it because it was one of my biggest challenges since arriving in LA The music was good, and I loved that the music was hard to read and play.

Zappa said to the musicians who said the parts were unplayable, "If I play your parts on guitar, will you try again?" Of course Frank played every one's part perfectly, and I gained total respect for him; we became close friends throughout his life.

We also premiered his composition, "200 Motels," with a select group of players augmented by the LA Philharmonic. As a result of my playing with him and the orchestra, I got called to play percussion with the LA Philharmonic under Zubin Mehta whenever they needed to augment the section.

With Frank Zappa, Lumpy Gravy sessions, 1967

With Frank Zappa, Lumpy Gravy sessions, 1967

In 1968, bandleader Stan Kenton decided to get off the road and form a larger orchestra in LA called the Stan Kenton Neophonic Orchestra. I was a member from its beginning, and our timpani player was Frank Carlson, who had played in Woody Herman's "First Herd." Kenton had a thing about black socks; if you wore anything but black socks on the bandstand, he didn't care how good you played - you were gone, because appearance was very important in his orchestra.

Kenton hired all the major composers in LA to write for his orchestra, and we performed about two concerts a month. You can imagine the great music we performed, with three or four composers like Lalo Schifrin, Dave Grusin, Oliver Nelson, or Michel Legrand writing for each concert.

A new guitar player named Glen Campbell, full of energy, showed up at one record session. There were usually about eight guitar players on every session in those days and besides Glen, who stayed in the studios until he hit it big and had his own TV show, the regulars were Tommy Tedesco, Barney Kessel, Howard Roberts, Mundell Lowe, and Dennis Budimir, just to name a few.

After Frank Sinatra bought Reprise Records, I played for everyone who recorded on his label, including Sinatra, Bing Crosby, Rosemary Clooney, Dean Martin, Sammy Davis, Jr., Doris Day, Bobby Darin, John Denver, Lou Rawls, and many more. Sinatra helped his daughter Nancy get started in a singing career, and we recorded a duet with her and Frank called "Something Stupid;" I also played on her big hit, "These Boots Were Made for Walking."

With my old pals Joe Porcaro and Dave Mackay, we had formed another group we called the Microtonal Blues Band. In 1969, we recorded a live album called *Spirit of '76* for Impulse (ABC) at a club called Donte's, where we played after studio sessions from 1964 until 1970.

Sinatra decided to go into retirement as a singing performer, and I started to play fewer record sessions and more TV shows, like *McHale's Navy, Mr. Ed, The Munsters, Gomer Pyle, Hogan's Heroes, The FBI, Starsky and Hutch,* and *The Addams Family.* Some of these shows still play in reruns on TV, and it's fun to hear all the kooky percussion sounds I made for those series.

It was a busy few years. I was doing *Mission Impossible, The Mod Squad, My Favorite Martian, I Spy,* and *I Love Lucy* at Paramount in those days. We used to also play live for an audience in between set changes during the filming of the *I Love Lucy* show. At M-G-M, we did *Bonanza, Little House on the Prairie, Daktari,* and *The Waltons.* At Universal, we worked on *Kojak, The Bionic Woman, Columbo, Streets of San Francisco, Charlie's Angels, Quincy, SWAT, CHiPs,* and *Murder, She Wrote.*

I also played all of the xylophone parts on *Yogi Bear, Huckleberry Hound, Lassie,* and *The Flintstones* at different studios around Hollywood, besides working on many TV specials recorded at Disney Studios. I remember doing *Harlow* with Neal Hefti, Jerry Lewis' *The Nutty Professor,* and Truman Capote's *In Cold Blood,* when I first met and worked with Quincy Jones. Since I didn't keep accurate records until 1970, I have only mentioned major shows which many readers may still remember.

I now started to study East Indian rhythms with Harihar Rao, and discovered that a trumpet player by the name of Don Ellis was studying with him as well. After our Indian rhythm lessons, Don would say, "Let's jam on the blues in seven." I had not played the blues in seven before and, since he took it so fast, I really had trouble with it. I went home and practiced for hours and said that this would never happen to me again.

The next week after our lesson I said, "Hey, Don, let's play the blues in seven." This time Don said, "No, let's play the blues in five." Once again I had a slight problem keeping up. After that, I practiced playing the blues in every odd time meter there was so I would never be caught off guard again.

We formed a group called the Hindustani Jazz Sextet, playing mostly at Shelly's Manne Hole jazz club in Hollywood and at Royce Hall at UCLA. I was also a member of the Don Ellis Big Band during this period.

Around this time Herb Alpert approached a few of us to form the Baja Marimba Band. We did some concerts in LA and the records sold very well, so Herb wanted us to take the band out on the road. I was too busy in the studios, so I recommended Julius Wechter, who had played on some Martin Denny records with me, and my old army band buddy Curry Tjader; that band went on to have many hit records.

John Williams, Sr. was the drummer and percussionist at Columbia Studios. He had come to LA many years before with Jerry Colonna, the pop-eyed, mustached comedian who had originally played trombone. When I came to town John Williams, Jr. was a pianist in the studios, and when he became a movie composer his dad played timpani on his sessions. When he was conducting and had something to say to his dad, he would say, "Oh, timpani, in bar seven make that a forte on the timps." Two of John's other sons are also percussionists in the studios, and they told me that on Christmas, John Sr. would send John Jr., the composer, a card signed, "Love, Mom and Timpani!"

Dave Grusin was another pianist in the studios before he became a film composer, as was Artie Kane before we began to play his music for *Wonder Woman* and *Love Boat*.

I had seen an old Hungarian instrument called cimbalom, and bought one in 1966 for my growing collection. It was played with cotton-wound mallets striking strings, and was the predecessor to the piano; it had a very strange keyboard and was quite difficult to play. Since there are so many instruments in our field, it becomes a near-impossibility for any percussionist to master them all. I'm not referring to the multitude of standard percussion instruments, but rather the stranger ones that film composers seem to want to hear and write for, like tabla drums, steel drums, udu drums, dulcimer, boo bams, and so on. Eventually I discovered that most of the good cimbalom players did not read music, but played their folk-Gypsy music flawlessly on the instrument.

Early in 1969, Robert Craft contacted me about an upcoming April concert for Igor Stravinsky's 87th birthday, with surprise sketch performances of *Svade-bka-Les Noces* in French or, in English, *The Wedding*). Stravinsky scored his four-tableau masterpiece *Les Noces* in 1917 for 40-piece orchestra, and made a final version in 1923 (though a four-piano reduction is occasionally played). But in 1919, he had also begun another version for the unusual combination of two cimbaloms, harmonium, mechanical pianola, and percussion. Since he regarded

Cimbalom

the synchronization of the pianola to be impractical, he completed only the first two tableaux and began work on *Pulcinella* without ever hearing his music played on those instruments.

For the next four weeks, between recording sessions, I spent every free moment preparing for this, and Craft found another percussionist who was preparing the second cimbalom part. It was interesting to me that some of the music that appeared impossible on paper seemed to lie very comfortably on the cimbalom.

After the wonderful concert in Stony Brook, New York, Stravinsky was guided up to the stage in a wheel chair, and congratulated me for being one of the few dwindling musicians preserving the playing of the cimbalom. I said later that I was fascinated with the instrument, being a mallet player, and asked, "Maestro, the music and interval skips that you wrote for the cimbalom look very difficult on paper, yet lie very comfortable on the instrument. Did you play the instrument yourself?" Stravinsky replied, "Yes, I had all three instruments in Morges (Switzerland) where I lived in 1919, and I spent time playing and tuning them to become more familiar with them while writing the music." He felt that the cimbalom's sound could not be duplicated in any artificial way, and hoped a foundation would someday be set up to retain many of these early instruments.

One important recording was with Sergio Mendez and the group Brazil '66. This was the beginning of the bossa nova wave in the U.S., and Sergio's band was at the forefront of that movement. He taught me about the Jakebo rhythm, popular then in Brazil, which was a bossa nova beat played in 5/4 time. Over twenty years, we would record again with Brazil '88.

This was at the height of my record date era, and I got to record for just about anyone making an album at the time in LA The complete list is enormous, but some artists I worked with were Joan Baez, Petula Clark, Sam Cooke, Vic Damone, Bobby Darin, Doris Day, Blossom Dearie, John Denver, Donovan, The Fifth Dimension, Simon and Garfunkel (that's me on bells on "Scarborough Fair"), Gladys Knight and the Pips, Frankie Laine, Steve Lawrence, Peggy Lee, Julie London, Johnny Mathis, McGuire Sisters (with Sam Giancana at every session), and the Righteous Brothers. One of the jazz artists was Benny Golson, who stayed in LA for a few years and worked on radio and TV sessions.

One memory demonstrates just how important music is to a film. In one 1967 session, we recorded music for a movie called, *Oh Dad, Poor Dad, Mama's Hung You in the Closet and I'm Feeling So Sad* starring Rosalind Russell and scored by George Duning, one of the heavy older film composers. In the story, a rich couple is preparing for a large dinner party and after the husband commits suicide in the closet, the wife keeps coming upstairs to pretend to talk to her husband. It is supposed to be a comedy, but whenever the wife came to the closet Duning's score got so mysterious that you would get goose pimples watching it. But this wasn't what the producers had in mind, so they called in Neal Hefti to do a tongue-in-cheek score so funny that you can't help but laugh at that same moment. It's a great example of how powerfully music can affect the mood of a film.

I had heard about Maharishi Mahesh Yogi in 1966 and started to become involved in Transcendental Meditation. There were some people in LA who also got into it quite early, like Paul Horn, as well as Robby Krueger and John Densmore from The Doors. The four of us used to go to Maharishi's lectures and spent a week together with him in Lake Tahoe, jamming with each other between his lectures.

Maharishi had studied to become a physicist, and found a very scientific approach for teaching meditation. In his lectures he would say, "When you water a tree you don't water the leaves, you water the root. Just like that, through meditation you dip into your being. You do not try to clear the mind of thoughts, you use the natural tendency of the mind, which is to wander. When you are aware of the mind wandering, you replace it with the thought of a Mantra, which is a word or sound that has no meaning to you but, at deeper, subtler levels, its results are very powerful and useful in your every day life." Besides meditating, I wanted to know how a mantra was chosen for a person, and how to teach these principles to others.

In October of 1969, I decided to visit India to have long meditations and learn how to impart this technique. The Beatles, Mia Farrow, and Donovan had gone for studies with Maharishi just before me; Nigel Bruce (who had played Dr. Watson in all the Sherlock Holmes movies with Basil Rathbone) and Ellen Corby (Grandma Walton in *The Waltons* TV show) were at the course I attended.

On the way to India, I stopped to visit my father's family in Italy once again. It was wonderful to renew our relationship since I had not been there since the 1962 Sinatra tour. After Italy, I stopped in Iran where I studied the santur, played with mallets on its strings. I bought one made by a master builder from Isfahan, as well as other wonderful percussion instruments, and did another buying excursion in Istanbul, Turkey.

My first stop in India was Delhi. India was like nothing else I had ever experienced before, and I immediately loved the music and the whole feeling of the country. I bought as many instruments as I could find, and had them shipped home before my meditation studies. The instruments were not that expensive, though it cost just as much to buy them as to ship them home. But it was my only option, because I bought as many instruments as I could find, and this time I did not have the luxury of Sinatra's plane and duty-free status. We first went to Kashmir, and studied with Maharishi on a houseboat for a few weeks, then went high up into the mountains to Palgam. This was the most spiritual experience for me, and the beginning of deep meditations and enlightened feelings.

From there we went to Rishikesh, where Maharishi's ashram stood at the foothills of the Himalayas by the sacred Ganges River. We would meditate in our small rooms during the day, and attend Maharishi's lectures in the evenings. At this course I gained insights that I have used through out my life, and I continue to meditate for a half-hour every morning and when I can, in the early evenings as well.

My batteries were fully charged when I left India, first stopping in Thailand to obtain a complete set of Thai gamelan instruments and bamboo angklungs. I studied the Thai xylophone techniques before heading for Bali, which is the most beautiful country I have ever been to. Music is a part of everyday life there, with musical gatherings for births, deaths, weddings, and even crop harvesting. I bought some of the instruments and gamelans from there, traveling to many villages to record music from each region until I didn't want to leave. The final stop was Australia, once again meeting many wonderful musicians and buying a few instruments.

I returned home on Christmas day, and immediately began to receive calls from almost every major film composer. They asked what new percussion instruments I had brought back, and were interested in new and different sounds for their scores. Very soon, however, I did another album for Impulse (ABC) called *Journey to Bliss*, a narration about meditation using many of the instruments from my trip.

There were more TV jobs because things were shifting in popular music. Self-contained groups were becoming the big sellers, and the record sessions began to dry up. Playing with these groups meant a "record date mentality," meaning that you could no longer see, feel, or hear the performers–except through very inferior headphones–because of the baffles separating us from each other. In most cases, the percussionists were even placed in a separate room. It was a musician's nightmare and an engineer's dream, because they could now isolate each section and fix any mistakes with mixing. Many of these groups felt that, since they were given such large budgets, they needed to stay in the studio forever until each song was perfect. But since most of them didn't really know what they were doing, they would keep playing the same song over and over, *ad nauseam*, for days. The studio musicians would say, "We'll get it right if it takes every penny they've got!"

What those so-called musicians, and many engineers, didn't realize was that studio musicians pride themselves on playing the music perfectly on the very first run-through. There is a spark and a challenge for us that is hard to explain. We are all up for it, and we do our best as a team to play it with the best feeling and energy that we have that first time. After that it's anticlimactic, and to keep doing it over and over gets very boring, yet most engineers never even turn on the machines on that first take.

Sometimes there are minor mistakes in the band, but the feeling is there–and it's hard to recapture. Now I knew what Sinatra meant at sessions when he said, "Let's go before me and the guys get bored." This is why I was glad it was time to move on to other areas of recording.

CHAPTER SIH:
THE 1970ſ

The decade began with plenty of movie soundtracks, as well as the Jo Stafford/Paul Weston live TV shows. *I Spy* with Bill Cosby and Robert Culp was a big hit, and the adventures began to expand into different countries every week. Earle Hagen, the composer for the show, would call and say, "We're in Hong Kong this week, so bring some Chinese instruments." I worked with Earle on many shows before I discovered he was the composer of the great standard "Harlem Nocturne."

Though I had never been to Africa, there were great sources for African instruments in LA, and another in New York. Whenever these collectors would acquire something new, I would immediately buy it if it was unique or had an unusual sound; even if it was an ordinary instrument, I would still buy it if it wasn't already in my collection.

Many of my percussion instruments were used on *Kung Fu*, which ran for about four years; I played on every one of those TV shows.

But my busy schedule had taken its toll on my home life. Betty was so used to my being away that we just parted ways and filed for divorce in 1970. This was very painful, because my two sons were so important in my life, and from that moment I made sure they knew I would never stop loving or supporting them. I believe I have fulfilled that intention all of their lives.

On the day I moved out, I went to the realtor who had sold me the third house I had bought in LA, informing him that I needed a large rental house because of my vast and still-growing collection of musical instruments. He said, "Meet my assistant, Celeste Robinson, she will show you some houses that are for rent." Seeing Celeste was like being struck by a Sicilian lightning bolt, and I knew immediately that she was going to be my partner for the rest of my life. Though I was busy working night and day in the studios, I still wanted Celeste to be with me every minute of every day. We have been married over forty-one years, and I still feel the same about her today; if I am asked to do a clinic at a college, or a concert out of town or out of the country, I will not go without my soul mate by my side.

Considering the time and money invested in my collection, it was very gratifying to me when composers would come to see them and ask about how they were used, how to notate for them, and what rhythms were used in the areas where they came from.

Here's one example: composer Maurice Jarre, a percussionist from Paris, called me because I had played a score he remembered called *The Collector*.

He was assigned a major movie, and wanted to see my cimbalom and some other instruments in the collection. That film was *Doctor Zhivago*. Maurice used a full Russian chorus, four harps, a balalaika string orchestra, and as many as 25 drummers as well as a hundred-piece orchestra. This was the beginning of the big-budget movie scores, and Maurice had the largest budget for a film score up to that time.

Elvis Presley kept us in the studio from early morning until late at night on *Fun in Acapulco*, ordering the finest food so we would stay and keep recording. Elvis was fun to work with, as he loved good food and good jokes. He was loyal to his musicians, and kept his original musicians in addition to all the Hollywood studio players for the length of the scoring sessions, whether we were involved in every cue or not. I got to play all the marimba parts in addition to the other standard percussion instruments on that job.

A normal session is three hours in length, and a double session six hours with a break for lunch; film scores take anywhere from four to seven days of double sessions to complete. The complete list of movies is in my appendix, but some of the more famous during this period were *The Sand Pebbles, Guess Who's Coming To Dinner, The Outlaw Josey Wales, Forty Carats, Cool Hand Luke, Divorce American Style, The Deer Hunter, Defiance, Ensign Pulver, Klute, Funny Girl, The Wild Bunch, Papillon, Summer of '42, Magnum Force, Star Trek* and *Patton*.

There were also TV shows like *Hawaii Five-O, Mork and Mindy* and *Laverne and Shirley*, plus the Looney Tunes cartoons. TV shows are usually recorded in a three-hour session for a half-hour show and a double session for an hour show. Cartoons are the hardest shows to play, because the music follows the action on the screen and is often left-handed and erratic, with strange rhythmic devices to fit the antics on the screen. I would usually play all the great xylophone parts, which I loved because the xylo was my first instrument.

Some films from the 1970s would end up being remade, and I would eventually play for the same film with different actors and composers years later like *The Thomas Crown Affair, Ocean's Eleven,* and *Planet of the Apes*. On one Barbra Streisand movie called "Up the Sandbox," David Shire was the original composer, and Streisand almost drove him into a nervous breakdown. Then Dave Grusin wrote a great score, but she kept saying, "That's not quite what I want. Just let Emil watch the screen and freak out hitting stuff in certain places." Dave agreed, but I said, "Wait, Dave, you get the big bucks for writing the score, you tell me exactly what to do because I don't know what Barbra wants." Well, he didn't know, and neither did she, so his score was rejected too.

Next came Billy Goldenberg, who came in and did everything Barbra told him to do, and that was the score she used. (Billy was the son of Moe Goldenberg, the noted percussionist from New York. Billy had also been the musical director for the great early TV show *Kukla, Fran and Ollie*.) I worked on all three scores, and once again said to myself, "We'll get it right if it takes every penny they've got!" But I later learned that almost every major composer in Hollywood has had the experience of a rejected score at one time or another during a career.

In the early 1970s, my biggest thrill was working with composers I had heard about through my first theory teacher back in Connecticut, when we played those soundtrack LPs and then analyzed their scores. The list included such masters as Alfred Newman, Frank Skinner, Elmer Bernstein, Walter Scharf, Hugo Friedhofer, Ernest Gold, and Alex North. Another was Bernard Herrmann, whose last score of *Taxi Driver* I was fortunate to play on; he passed away the day after we finished the score, Christmas Eve 1978. Alex North, who worked on many John Huston films, was another composer I worked with closely and one who became a dear friend. He was very aware of percussion's potential, and often came up with sounds that were unique and exciting.

Roger Kellaway formed his Cello Quartet with Roger on piano, Chuck Domanico on bass, Edgar Lustgarden (who had once played in the NBC Symphony with Arturo Toscanini) on cello, and me playing marimba and other woody percussion sounds. This high-level quartet gained the popularity of jazz as well as classical audiences, and we recorded our first album for A&M in 1970.

I learned a lot from Hugo Friedhofer, who I had met through Earle Hagen. Among many other things, Hugo had done the orchestrations for many of the legendary scores by Erich Wolfgang Korngold. Hugo had great ideas, like a fast chase with running sixteenth notes, with a triplet at the beginning of a bar. "That's how to slow the whole orchestra down in a hurry," he would say.

In a surfing movie originally called *Stoked, The Wave People*, I finally wrote my own score, with a small group playing my jazz compositions and a free-form jam for the surfing scenes. (Unfortunately, I lost track of the director and the movie, and have tried in vain to discover if it was ever released, or if its title was changed). This music seemed to work well together with the film and Hugo, who came to those sessions to give me moral support, really liked the different approach I took in writing this score. He was one of the all-time great film composers, and having him there for my sessions was a thrill and an honor.

In February 1972, Celeste and I were married at the Self Realization Temple. Pa came out to L.A. for the wedding and Joe Pass (born Joseph Passalaqua), the late, great jazz guitarist, surprised us by playing classical guitar solos as people were entering for the ceremony. We took three-and-a-half months off for a long honeymoon with an open, around-the-world ticket, and we bought instruments, went to music festivals, and studied ethnic instruments. Celeste didn't play music, but she learned the function and history of each instrument I bought and studied. We went to Hawaii, and I bought all the Polynesian, Samoan, and Hawaiian instruments that I didn't already own. While there, I met Celeste's long time friend Sanford Lung, who has remained our friend, attorney, and part of our family for most of our lives.

Next on our instrument-buying trip was Japan, and in Kyoto we bought all the religious bells, gongs and drums we could find. The man selling the bells spoke no English, and my Japanese was rusty, but we were able to communicate through music. I had found the lowest pitch bell and was trying to find pitches that kept ascending higher, so the three of us hit all the bells until we made up a bell tree without speaking a word.

We visited the house of Sadeo Watanabe, my friend from Toshiko Akiyoshi's band during my Army days in the 1950s. Back then, he had lived in a small Japanese-style home with his mother. I told Celeste that she would see an authentic Japanese home, with all the rituals. So I was surprised to find that things had greatly changed in those twenty years–Sadeo was now married and living in a high-rise building with an elevator and all Western-type modern furniture.

We next traveled to Kuala Lumpur to meet Hans Hoffer and Star Black, a couple I had met during my 1969 visit to Bali. Hans had written a book for the government called *Road to Bali*, and now he had his own publishing company and was writing all the guidebooks for all of Asia and Southeast Asia. His main office was now in Singapore, and we went there with him next to study some Indian drone instruments. Next we went to Jakarta, Java, where I studied and bought some of the gamelan gongs from that region.

Next came Bali, where Celeste fell just as much in love with the island as I had. We ordered a lot of bamboo xylophones and angklungs from a shop in a village near Ubud. As we were riding bikes to a remote village far from Ubud one day, a man stopped us and said, "I am making the Joged bumbung, bamboo xylophones, and angklungs that you ordered in Ubud." (Though Joged bumbung is a type of Balinese music, the local musicians also referred to a bamboo marimba, like the one he made for me, as Joged bumbung). But how he knew the instruments were for us remains a mystery.

We went to a village high in the mountains where every one in the village played bamboo jaw harps, an instrument I was studying which originated in many different countries. I brought some made of metal and the villagers, who were fascinated to see them, traded some for their bamboo versions. We stayed in Bali for quite some time, as we were both enthralled by the island; in addition, Celeste couldn't fly because of an ear infection. We stayed until we received the joyful news that Celeste was pregnant.

On a stop in Hong Kong we slipped into Red China, buying cymbals, gongs, drums, and wood blocks that we shipped home. We stayed at the Peninsula, the same great hotel I remembered from the 1972 tour with Sinatra, and were picked up at the airport by the hotel's Rolls-Royce. We also went to Taiwan, where we found even older Chinese drums and blocks, since many people had left mainland China and taken many of their family's older possessions. In Thailand we went to the floating gardens, where all the angklungs were sold. My theory is that the xylophone and marimba did not come from Africa originally, but originated in China and worked its way through Southeast Asia in the form of the bamboo rattles known as angklung and Joged bumbung before ending up in Africa.

Our next plane stop was in Rangoon, Burma, a strange place to be in the early 1970s because it was Buddha's birthday, known as the water festival. We bought many versions of a bell-like instrument called Kyeezee, which was copied years later by the Zildjian company, which now sells a smaller version of these very large, beautiful bells shaped like the top of Burma's pagoda temples.

There were beautiful instruments in Katmandu, Nepal, as well as signs reading "Best government hashish shops," with maps and directions on where to buy it legally. Because of that, a lot of American and European kids had dropped out and were there just to be stoned. What a wasted existence, we thought, and a bad image for a lot of our young people.

We rented bikes to reach some Tibetan villages, but there were two instruments that Celeste would not let me buy. One was a prayer drum made out of the skulls of a male and female under the age of fourteen, and the skin was made from their human skin; the other was a trumpet made out of the thighbone of a grown person. Celeste felt these two instruments carried a strange vibe, so I settled for a prayer drum made of wood, and passed on the trumpet.

India was extremely hot, and after three days we left Calcutta for New Delhi. We were able to stay at the home of one of my many friends, who had servants to help us find instruments. One day, in old Delhi where the crowded and noisy streets were full of cows, buffalo, and even elephants, I had to crouch near the floor to hear the sound of a set of bells made of glass. Celeste called my attention to a man at the front door amazed at the strange position I was in, but I thought he looked just as weird considering he was wearing a fifteen-foot long snake draped around his neck.

In beautiful Beirut, Lebanon, we visited relatives of Hollywood friends who served us raw lamb tartar; we didn't think we could handle it, but it was delicious. Many years later, when we were watching the CNN news reporting on Beirut, Celeste said, "Look, there's the very balcony where we stayed." It was hard to forget, because we had set the camera's self-timer to take our picture kissing on the balcony. Suddenly we watched the balcony explode with a direct hit, and the whole side of the building blew up right before our eyes.

We then met with some acquaintances in Iran's city of Tehran, which was quite beautiful in those days. After buying some drums and studying the odd time rhythms in five and nine from that region, we tried to go to Israel. But since Israel would not accept our entry directly from Iran, we first went to Cyprus—where we found no instruments and stayed only a day.

Since I had spent ten days in Israel on the 1962 Sinatra tour, some of the musicians remembered me, and we also traveled to Bethlehem, Nazareth, and Jerusalem among the many religious sites. In Tel Aviv, we found music from many countries, as Hebrews from all over the world brought their ethnicity with them to Israel. A real highlight of that visit was the opera *Aida* with, of course, the famous opening aria *Celeste Aida*, so it was a treat for Celeste. The orchestra was also outstanding, with one of the greatest string sections I had ever heard.

Celeste enjoyed the joke at the Acropolis about Sinatra raising money to put a roof on it, and we left Athens for the island of Hydra, where I had spent part of my vacation on that tour. After such a long journey, Celeste loved it because there were no cars and not much to do except wait for the fishermen to come in at night with your fresh fish supper. But there was a little time to study the Greek nine-rhythm with a local drummer.

The next stop was Italy with a special visit to Abruzzo to visit Pa's relatives, who treated Celeste warmly. They disconnected the refrigerator as they said the motor noise would affect her pregnancy. After that came Paris, a short stay because there were no instruments to buy, and then London, where we went to many shows and even found a Chinese shop which had some instruments I had overlooked in China.

We spent a few days in New York before heading to Connecticut to see my folks. Pa had met Celeste at our wedding, but this was the first time she and Ma had met, and Ma fell in love with her from the start. Finally we returned back home, though the instruments took months to drift in from so many countries.

Celeste was three weeks overdue, so I stayed very close to home. I took her with me to an evening record session with Barbra Streisand and Michel Legrand, and naturally all the musicians came over to say hello. Lyricist Marilyn Bergman came over and said, "I'm sorry, Emil, but Celeste is distracting Barbra and she wants her to wait outside the studio." I told her that if she had to leave, I would have to leave too, considering her condition. When Barbra overheard our conversation and realized the situation she apologized, doing everything she could to see that Celeste was comfortable.

On December 30, 1972, our daughter Camille was born, and Pa came out from Connecticut again. She was named because neither of my two boys or my brother's three boys were named Camillo, which pleased Pa very much.

Some of the younger, hip writers for film that I worked for in the early 1970s were Ralph Burns, Billy Byers, Dave Grusin, Michel Legrand, Russ Garcia, Paul Glass, J. J. Johnson, Oliver Nelson, Lalo Schifrin, Allyn Ferguson, Michel Columbier, and Quincy Jones, who I worked on with *Hot Rocks* and *Roots*. With Bill Conti we did the *Rocky* pictures and later, the *Karate Kid* movies; with Allyn Ferguson, I did all the early Johnny Mathis record sessions.

The Roger Kellaway Cello Quartet did another album in 1973, and Camille was on the cover with us; I don't think she was quite two years old at the time.

In January of 1974 Sinatra came out of retirement, and I played on *Old Blue Eyes Is Back*. After this album, Frank asked me to join him in his comeback opening in Vegas with Ella Fitzgerald and the Count Basie band. This was a thrill for me, as I got to play a lot of solos with the band behind Frank. He was on the stage when we arrived, and Camille ran right up to him with her arms outstretched; Frank picked her up and said, "Look, she's star-struck at two years old."

Frank was very gracious to Camille and Celeste. His daughter Nancy was having a baby, and he wanted the bodyguards to get ready for the baby's arrival by watching over the two of them. Several months later, Celeste brought Camille to a Joni Mitchell record session, and Joni could not put Camille down, holding her all through the recording while she was singing. She began to know all the artists I worked with, and they all enjoyed having her around.

Just before we went on stage, we were in Frank's dressing room at Caesar's Palace when Frank received a telegram from Elvis Presley, who was opening at the International. The telegram read, "Dear Frank, have a great opening, welcome back, and thanks for the overflow. Signed, Elvis." Frank took it as a mark of respect, saying, "What class that kid's got. He's the hottest act on the planet, and he says thanks for the overflow." As it turned out they both had sellout crowds every night, and we had to add a 4 a.m. show every night we were there.

Frank used to introduce me as Emil Richards, and one night two mob guys grabbed me in the elevator, put a knife to my throat, and asked, "What's your real name?" When I replied, "Emilio Radocchia," one said, "Are you ashamed of your Italian heritage?" I said, "No, it's just an easier name for a musician to use." They were dead serious, and they reminded me of how Pa had reacted when I told him about my stage name.

Though Sinatra's temper was legendary, his friends could do no wrong. Once, in Vegas, when Don Rickles wanted to impress a girl, he asked Frank for help and Frank told him to bring the girl over to his table. Later on, Rickles asked Frank to come over to HIS table, as it would impress his date more. Frank agreed, and when he finally went over and said hello, Rickles yelled, "Don't bug me, can't you see I'm busy talking?"

Of course, Frank cracked up.

One more example happened some years later. After a landslide pushed the home of Frank's longtime pianist Bill Miller off a cliff, killing his wife and pushing him down a ravine, I visited Miller in the hospital. He said that Frank was there when he woke up. Frank had to tell him that his wife didn't make it, and that his daughter was all right. He said they had moved everything salvageable out of the house, and had bought him a condo and a wardrobe. Frank even had his lawyer investigate the ruptured city water tank that caused the landslide, which ended in a big settlement for Bill. That's just the way Frank was.

Back in LA, Frank did another live TV show with guest dancer Juliet Prowse. She came to a record session shortly after that and Frank told us to watch our language and be on our toes, because Juliet's parents were flying in from South Africa and he wanted to impress them.

That same week, I was able to play on an album with the alto sax player Johnny Hodges, a great player and wonderful man from Duke Ellington's orchestra. And, after Frank became a partner with Warner Brothers and was in the movie business, I worked with Nelson Riddle on *Robin and the Seven Hoods* and *Ocean's Eleven*.

On yet another trip in 1974, Celeste and I acquired all the Latin instruments and marimbas we could find in Mexico City, then traveled to Guatemala City where I studied—and then bought—the marimba grande.

We wanted to hear a seven-piece marimba band, though we found that they only played in the local cathouses. Naturally, we went to one, and I even got up and played with them. But they were not really impressed, and their expressions seemed to say, "So what, almost everyone here plays marimba!" We offered to buy them a drink, and one player said, "Please, senor, we would rather have the money for our families." So our money went for their homemade raw rubber mallets and for tela, the membrane which is placed on the resonator hole that makes the instrument buzz.

Our next stop was Bolivia, 17,000 feet above sea level at Lake Titicaca. Celeste bought one of the derbies that all the local women wore, and the locals really got a kick out of seeing Celeste with their local hat. Potato was a staple in almost every dish they served and, unsurprisingly, the women were all quite large which, in this region, was a sign of beauty.

In Peru, where I finally located the drum called Guerre Di Bamba, we were shocked by a terrific earthquake. We rushed to our hotel's lobby and asked the manager why the building was not evacuated. He said, "Senor, we have earthquakes every few hours and sometimes minutes apart this time of year. Do you want us to trouble you all day long?"

With Cat Stevens and Brazil 66 drummer Chico Batera, Rio, Carnival 1974

My brother Domenico and his wife, who had flown down from Connecticut, met us in Rio De Janeiro for Carnival, which we celebrated with Cat Stevens and Chico Batera. Chico, a native of Rio, was witnessing the Carnival for the first time, because his family and perhaps 150,000 residents leave Rio for the influx of 300,000 tourists. Naturally, I bought many Brazilian instruments and saw all the great percussion bands that played and danced in the streets during the Carnival parades. The best drummers we heard were the most unschooled drummers, who had no technique and played with stiff arms. To me, this is what makes the Brazilian snare drum beat really lope, with that laid back, great feel.

The four of us stopped at Caracas, Venezuela, where our cousins Claudio Di Vincentis and Stefano Di Bartolomeo lived. My brother and I first met these cousins in Abruzzo after the second war, on our first trip to Italy with Pa in 1946. There was great harp music and maraca playing here, and I brought back many pairs of maracas. A relaxing week in Aruba was a delight before coming home, and Domenico had been spending one to three months every year there since then. He now lives there with his wife permanently.

In 1968 I had worked on a score with sitarist Ravi Shankar for a film called *Charly*, which won an Academy Award for Cliff Robertson. When we got back home, Ravi introduced me to George Harrison, and we all worked on an album called *Ravi Shankar and Friends*. The studio was A&M, named for its owners Herb Alpert and Jerry Moss, and we worked there a lot in those days. I used to go into A&M's business office, where a very sweet young woman named Olivia

Arias worked, to obtain stickers from A&M artists which I put on twelve trunks carrying small percussion instruments I used in studio sessions.

One day, during the Shankar sessions, Olivia came into the studio asking to meet George Harrison, not realizing that George had just come into the room behind her. I said, "Sure, turn around. George, say hello to Olivia, she would like to meet you." I like to think I was responsible for their meeting, and they were inseparable until his death.

In 1973 I was given the Most Valuable Percussionist Award by the National Academy of Recording Arts and Sciences (NARAS), and won it again the next three years; in 1977, because I was no longer eligible, I was given the Emeritus award. I was very honored to be chosen so often, and it was especially gratifying since the award was voted on by my peers.

George Harrison decided to do a U.S. tour in 1974 with fifteen musicians from India, plus a band consisting of Tom Scott, Robin Ford, Billy Preston, Jim Horn, Andy Newmark, Willie Weeks, Chuck Findley, Jim Keltner, and me. Tom Scott and I played with this band, and with the fifteen-piece band from India with Ravi Shankar and tabla player Alla Rakha as well. I learned a great deal from Ravi-Ji about melody, ragas, and the complex rhythmic structures known as te-his. I made sure to sit next to Alla Rakha on the plane and when he would wake up in the middle of the night and start reciting rhythm cycles, I would write all these te-hi rhythms down and come home with a wealth of information on Indian music.

There were many exchanges on different sounds with two percussionists with Ravi Shankar's band, primarily film studio musicians from Bombay. Many people may not be aware that India is the second largest movie making capital in the world, making films primarily for domestic use. Though they did not speak English, we somehow communicated through melody and rhythm. When Rij Ram, one of the percussionists, heard a new sound that impressed him, the look of joy on his face was indescribable; the only English word he knew to describe his pleasure was "correct!"

George and Peter Sellers had the same manager, so Sellers joined us often on this tour.

While we were in Philadelphia, I dined at an Italian restaurant in South Philadelphia with Tom Di Nardo, a longtime pal who I had met back in Boston in 1957 while playing with George Shearing. Thirty-three years later, knowing Tom was an arts writer for a Philly paper, I asked him to help me in the preparation of this book.

When I was six years old and just starting to study the xylophone, my grandmother had taught me how to crochet, and I would help her make squares for her tablecloths and bedspreads. While on this tour, which was in the dead of

Crocheting a hat for Peter Sellers, Dark Horse tour, 1974

winter, I crocheted a hat for every one of the twenty-six people traveling with the band.

Gerald Ford was president during this tour, and his son Steven was attending college at Utah State. After our concert there, he came backstage accompanied by Secret Service agents. He asked us where we would be playing in late December, and George told him that we'd be playing Washington, D.C. and staying at the Watergate.

When we arrived, we found an invitation to the White House for an informal Christmas party, and Steven met us when we arrived in our limos. Bill Graham, the concert tour manager, scolded one of his roadies for wearing jeans, and told him to go back to the hotel and change. Steven was wearing jeans and said, "Hey, man, this is the White House. It belongs to all of us, so you can come in as you are."

The President and Mrs. Ford were not at home, so we were allowed to go upstairs and check out their private quarters, and I was surprised at how small their living quarters were. We then proceeded to the ballroom, where pianist Billy Preston accompanied our Christmas carol sing. I kept looking at this huge crystal chandelier over our heads, thinking that it must have a really beautiful sound.

Finally, I asked Bill Graham to lift me on his shoulders so I could rattle it and see how it sounded, but Celeste told him not to do it. When I thought no one was watching, I walked down to the end of the ballroom, then took a long running jump at the chandelier and got a good smack at it. It sounded great but continued to sway, and I thought for sure it was coming down. When Celeste came over and said, "Emil, what did you do?" I began praying it wouldn't fall, and it didn't. Celeste said, "Didn't you see that Secret Service agent go for his gun when you came running across the ballroom?" I hadn't seen him, and he finally came over and said, "That was a dangerous thing to do, as I was starting to aim at you."

With George Harrison, Harrison's Dad and brother Peter, Dark Horse tour, 1974

Well, I did get to hear the wonderful sound of that crystal chandelier, though Ravi Shankar and all the Indian musicians couldn't stop laughing.

While on this tour, we never had to check into a hotel. When our private jet landed at an airport, we would be greeted at the bottom of the landing with a limo and our hotel key. We were already checked into the rooms and we would have a list of everyone's names, what rooms they were in, and which floor the hospitality suite was on. George had an Indian cook making vegetarian meals at all times for us. He always had a guitar in his hands, and would play and sing constantly. At each city that we played, Bill Graham and George played some kind of trick on one of the guys in the band. Bass player Willie Weeks had mentioned that he hated shellfish, especially crab and lobster. When we got to Seattle and Willie went into his bathroom, we heard him let out a bloody scream. Bill Graham and George had arranged for his bathtub to be filled with salt water and live lobster and crab.

I wasn't exempt from the tricks. Celeste didn't come with us to Milwaukee, and I mentioned getting up early to catch a flight to Chicago to meet her and our daughter Camille, so when I opened the door to my room in Milwaukee there were six live roosters on my bed. In Washington, George wanted to get up especially early the day we were going to the White House, and Bill put fifty alarm clocks under his bed.

It was also the birthday of Chuck Findley, the trumpet player, who was a little bit lonely since his wife couldn't be there to meet him. None of us knew she was coming to surprise him, so when she walked into his room they found blow-up dolls in his bed, under his bed, in the dresser drawers, and even two stuffed in the refrigerator.

Only wives and children were allowed on the trip, but Robin Ford insisted on bringing his girlfriend along. She complained about everything, every day, all the time. When they reached their room at the Plaza Hotel in New York, they could not turn the lights on. All the bulbs had been removed from the whole room, and there were no rugs on the floor, no shades or curtains on the windows, no phone, no chairs, no bed, nothing! The room was completely bare, and Robin's list of room and phone numbers were deliberately wrong. Everyone was so tired of his girlfriend's complaining that they thought they would really give them something to complain about.

Near the end of the tour it was Christmas time, and when George and Olivia entered their room at the Plaza, they could barely enter because Bill Graham had placed floor-to-ceiling Christmas trees in every inch of their room. This is the kind of fun we had in between the great music we played for that tour.

Celeste and Camille traveled on our private plane for most of this ten-week tour, starting on the West Coast and ending up at Madison Square Garden on Christmas Eve. On the last tune of the last show, all the wives and children came on stage and picked up small percussion instruments, and played the encore with us. The music was great, the band was hot, the memories are eternal, and George remained a close friend through the years.

When I got back, Sinatra had married Mia Farrow, and we were doing a special with him at NBC. Mia and I talked about the Maharishi and our time spent in Rishikesh, India studying Transcendental Meditation, which she had done as well. Frank had a big seller in George's "Something," and because he knew I had been on tour with George Harrison, wondered if George would write a song for him. He liked George's writing, and wanted to record more of his music.

One night after the tour was over, George Harrison, Peter Sellers, and Jim Keltner came over to my house, and we stayed up just talking and having fun until ten in the morning, when they left to pick up Ringo. Later, Jim told me that they ran out of gas on the Sunset Strip. A big tour bus full of people looking for movie stars' homes drove right by, and never noticed Ringo Starr, George Harrison, and Peter Sellers pushing Jim's Mercedes to the gas station.

George invited Celeste, Camille, and I to join him and Olivia in Kauai for a break. He rented a large house right on the beach that came with a cook, a butler, a maid, and a chauffeur. George paid them all off and sent them home. He and I did the cooking and the girls did the cleaning. It was a great rest after the hectic road tour we had just finished. George even let me cut his hair on that vacation.

When we got back to LA, I got busy again working on movies most of the time. Before every big project, composers would call and ask, "What's new, what new percussion instruments do you have that I haven't seen or heard?" They would come to the warehouse where I stored all the instruments, to see what I had. In the early days I made the mistake of showing them almost everything I collected, and found that a return trip was always necessary to show them just the specific instruments required for their project, as they got overwhelmed hearing too many instruments. It was better to pin a composer down to what specific instruments he might be interested in, what country the film would be shot in, were there funny scenes or scary scenes, questions like that which made it easier to limit the number of instruments and steer them in the right direction.

It's common for many composers to use one percussion instrument's sound right out front, not realizing that their individual qualities can be married and mixed together to create quite new unusual sounds. I try to encourage them to mix the woods, with the metals, the skins, the bamboo, and the glass to come up with colors that even synthesizers can't produce.

But many of the composers do an amazing amount of homework, especially about percussion instruments, sometimes adding to my own awareness of the field.

One day Henry Mancini called, wanting to know what I had in the way of Eskimo instruments for a picture called *Ice Station Zebra*. I told him there wasn't very much except for a hoop drum with walrus skin, played by hitting the rim while rotating it to make the drumhead vibrate with a wobbling sound. Mancini said all he was able to find was a lot of vocal music, and he had a bullroarer made out of walrus bone that he played for me, which we used on that sound track. I didn't know the Eskimos had or knew about bullroarers, so this was something new for me.

Although the bulk of my work was movies, there were plenty of record dates as well. Some particularly memorable ones were with Jack Jones, Neil Diamond, and George Duke, who had left Zappa and was recording jazz albums on his own. There were also some with Marvin Gaye, Mel Tormé, Cleo Laine, Carmen McRae, Irene Kral, Diana Ross, Carly Simon, and Morgana King, who played Don Corleone's wife in *The Godfather* movies.

Frank Zappa called to tell me that Ruth Underwood, his percussionist, was leaving the band, and that he intended to start a new band without percussion. Frank talked with a foul mouth and loved to use swear words, but in contrast he was a excellent parent; his children were well-behaved at home and he and his wife Gail disciplined them as good parents should. Besides, Frank was very strict about no one having drugs in his band and was a man to be respected for his principles. I said, "Frank, you write too well for percussion. You must keep percussion in your band." He said, "You come out on the road with me or find me another girl percussionist like Ruth, with big boobs!"

He ended up with a male percussionist in his new band, and invited me and Celeste to his opening concert at the Santa Monica Civic Auditorium. When we arrived we fell on the floor laughing, as in front of the music stand of Ed Manne, his new percussionist, was a flagpole with a huge black brassiere hanging at half-mast in honor of Ruth, his former percussionist. The band was great, and Frank introduced the composer, writer, and theorist Nicolas Slonimsky to come out on stage. He sat at the piano and improvised on all his wild scales to the accompaniment of Zappa's music for an incredible evening.

For the movie *Congo*, Jerry Goldsmith wanted to use all authentic percussion instruments from the Congo, as the director had faxed him pictures of all these instruments which were actually in the shots. When Jerry showed up at the warehouse, I had already placed all my Congolese instruments on the floor. It was gratifying for me, as I had an instrument to match every picture that Jerry had brought from the director, plus several more that he didn't have as well.

It became harder and harder to find new percussion instruments, so Celeste and I put together two books called *Making Music around the Home and Yard* and *Tune In, Making More Musical Sounds*. My godson, Jeff Porcaro, did the illustrations, and he spent his fee for drawing these characters to buy the drum set he used on the Sonny and Cher show.

These books showed how to make authentic sounding instruments from objects found around the kitchen and other rooms of everyone's home and yard. We came up with four great different sounds one can make with just spoons. I used stainless steel mixing bowls for Jerry Goldsmith for all the chase scenes in the original *Planet of the Apes*. If you struck these bowls on their rims, they made the most beautiful bell like sounds. But if you struck them on their bottoms, they made a high-pitched boing-ing sound, which is what Goldsmith wanted for that movie.

Celeste and I started to go to schools to do clinics, showing parents, teachers, and kids how to make great sounds from common objects they used every day, and I continued to use these sounds in the studios as well.

Many teachers would ask, "Now that we know how to make instruments, and become aware of all these great sounds around us, how do we play them?" So we came up with a third book called *Musical Compositions for the Very Young and/or Unmusical*.

In 1976 Celeste and I took Camille, now four years old, to visit at George Harrison's castle in Henley-on-Thames in England. Before we arrived there, we stopped in Sicily to visit Licodea Eubea, in the mountains of Catania, Sicily, the little town where my mother was born, and the region where the maranzano (jaw harp) was played. We met a few close cousins of my mother's, but most of her family had migrated to the United States.

Playing at home, 1975

We bought many sizes and shapes of the jaw harp there and found out about my great-grandmother, who had been murdered when a local man tried to rob her. He panicked, and smothered her with a pillow when she cried out for help; he did not mean to kill her, and only spent a short time in jail. He was now dead, but his family thought that we had come back for revenge, and there was a lot of tension while we spent the day with Ma's cousins in that little town. This is still the way of the peasant peoples of Sicily. The cab driver would not drive through this town, and left us at the edge of the little village to walk to my mother's place of birth. When we left, her cousins drove us out of town to meet the cab driver, saying it was not safe to walk back through the town. It was a strange experience, but wonderful to meet some relatives and to find some jaw harps.

We then went to England and, while in London, met the famous percussionist James Blades, who wrote the definitive book on percussion instruments. We became fast friends, and he had a copy of my catalog of over 300 percussion instruments in my collection as of that time. (My collection now exceeds 750 percussion instruments listed in a catalog I publish called *Range Finder for the Percussion Seeker*, which includes the ranges of the instruments, and is added to this book as Appendix 5.)

I asked James if he had ever heard a spoon or fork tied to a piece of string. You wrap the two ends of the string around your index fingers and put your fingers in your ears. I had him try it and told him he wouldn't believe how much it sounded like Big Ben. He was a very interesting man, laughing as he mentioned that Big Ben, the famous clock, chimed in 5/4 time.

Every day during World War II, he had played the four opening notes of Beethoven's Fifth Symphony (DOT DOT DOT DASH) on timpani over the BBC and, depending on what note he dampened on the timpani, provided a coded message to the Allies all over Europe, the only code never broken by the Germans throughout the war.

After London, we went to visit with Olivia and George Harrison in Henley. George had a guitar in his hands all the time we were there, loved writing lyrics and music, and was prolific in coming up with new songs all the time.

There were also some TV gigs in the mid- and late 1970s. Some were the *Mary Tyler Moore Show, Night Gallery, Love Boat, Lou Grant,* and *The Hulk.* I also recorded an album with Louis Bellson, the first time I had worked with him, though we had met in the mid-60s through Remo Belli. Remo, the inventor of the plastic drum head that revolutionized drumming, still has a huge factory in Valencia, California. Louis was doing a Latin album with Alex Acuna from Peru, Cuban bassist Israel "Cachaio" Lopez, Manolo Badrena, a great Brazilian, Cuban Francisco Aquabella on Bata drums, Wilfred Reyes Sr. and Jr. on percussion, Bellson on drums, and me on marimba. I got to write a composition right at the studio for this session we called "Sentido En Seis" ("Six Feeling"). The album was called *Ecue Ritmos Cubanos,* and has been re- released by Pablo records on CD.

Louis Bellson is one of the warmest wonderful human beings on the planet. I said, "Louis, those crotales are beautiful, and that gong is very different. I never heard a gong from Italy before." The next day the crotales and that Italian gong showed up at my house. Louie has been that way his whole life, and a few years later I was able to return the kindness when he heard a snare drum that Irv Cottler used on Sinatra tours in the 60's, and I had the honor to present it to Louis for all the generosity he had shown me through the years.

I joined Frank Zappa's Electric Orchestra for concerts and recordings in 1977, and two of the compositions I remember were entitled "Bogus Pomp" and "Gregory Peckery".

Throughout the 1970s, I played on over 300 movie scores, some mentioned previously. I worked on *Shaft* and *Shaft in Africa* with Isaac Hayes, and played with Dominic Frontieri on a lot of John Wayne movies like *Rio Lobo* and *Rio Bravo.* When Jerry Fielding was alive, we worked together on all the Clint Eastwood movies, like *High Plains Drifter, Play Misty For Me, Magnum Force* and *The Outlaw Josey Wales.* Clint Eastwood, who has become a friend through the years, always comes to the scoring sessions, because he directs and produces most of his movies and he also loves and plays jazz.

In 1979 I became one of the founding members of the New American Orchestra, comprised of 85 of Hollywood's leading musicians. We played concerts twice a month for the next four years under the leadership of Jack Elliott and

Allyn Ferguson. We also played for the Academy Awards Show with this orchestra from 1979 to 1982, and marked the start of my playing at least 26 Oscar shows under Jack Elliott (three times), Henry Mancini, John Williams and Lionel Newman (twice each), Burt Bacharach, and Bill Conti (17 times).

The Gong Show was popular on TV for a while, with amateurs doing unusual acts. Once in a while they would run out of people to put on the show, and I got a call to come on and do something strange. I found a twenty-five foot pipe, filled it with buckshot, got goofily dressed, and used my real name (Emilio Radocchia) on the show so no musicians would recognize me. They did five shows a day, so I waited around for hours with very serious contestants who really wanted to win. I was there to get gonged, have a laugh, and go home, but if some of these participants got gonged, they would either cry or get angry enough to want to kill. After they called the contestants for the fourth show and I wasn't called, which meant I would have to wait till the last show, I called Celeste and said, "I think I'm going to just leave and come home. These people are really serious, and I'm bored waiting to go on." Celeste said, "Have fun with it. Just think, Ma and Pa will see it, and so will all your friends, so have a good laugh." I finally went on the fifth show and swished my twenty-five foot pipe to the tune of "Autumn Leaves." The audience was yelling for the panel to gong me out, but panelists Mort Sahl and Jaye P. Morgan, who recognized me, wouldn't let Jamie Farr (who didn't know me), gong me. Mort and Jaye P. gave me 10 points each, and Jamie Farr said I belonged on the Alaskan pipeline with that pipe, and gave me three points. So I almost won, and all I wanted was to be gonged and get out of there. Ma and Pa got a great laugh out of it, as did some of my friends who saw the show. I still have the videotape, and pull it out once in a while for a good laugh.

CHAPTER SEVEN:
THE 1980∫

rom the time I arrived in LA in 1959 through the 1960s, the bulk of my musical life was spent on record sessions, averaging fifteen record dates a week. In the 1970s it meant mostly filmed TV programs, though of course there were some movies, jingles, and concert tours in there as well.

Starting in the 1980s, and for most of the time since, it has been mostly movies. The studios began using electronic instruments in earnest, and most musicians were afraid they would be replaced by an electronic keyboard or machine. But, for me, nothing was further from the truth. Composers were asking for my ethnic instruments on their sessions more than ever, because it became apparent that electric sounds made my ethnic percussion instruments sound even more organic and real. We became a complement to each other.

Some composers, like Lalo Schifrin, Jerry Goldsmith, and Dave Grusin, began to see the value in mixing a lot of the percussion instruments together. Schifrin used some new techniques in film scoring that had never been tried before, as in *The Hellstrom Chronicle*, when he used the percussion section as a string section. He had us bowing on the vibraphone, tuned glasses, water phones, saws, cymbals, and gongs. He told me to bring thirty pairs of brushes, as he had the string players playing like the percussion section. They swished the brushes on the bellies of their violins and violas, and the cellos and basses played on the strings with the eraser part of pencils. I called all the string players I could, to tell them not to bring their expensive instruments to the sessions on those days. There were sounds we got with percussion and with the orchestra that no amount of electronic instruments could ever duplicate.

We started a percussion ensemble with many of the players I had gathered for Harry Partch's ensemble, and we played new pieces at our gatherings. We would meet at the warehouse, where all my instruments were stored in the early 1980s, to write and play new percussion music at least once a week.

After buying a condo in Honolulu, we performed a series of clinics on our childrens' books and at a big drum shop there, then played a series of concerts while collecting more Pacific Rim instruments like tuetti, lava rocks, and conch horns. (Tuetti are slit logs, either small or quite large, hollowed out and beat upon with sticks to create a loud percussive rhythm; lava rocks are two pieces of stone struck together to create a high pitched knocking sound, creating a rhythm pulse to go along with song or dance. A conch horn is a large sea shell that has a hole drilled or hollowed at the top in which one can blow, creating a sound like a bugle or trumpet.)

I took this opportunity away from the studios to transcribe Frederick Delius' *On Hearing the First Cuckoo in Spring* for six marimbas and bass marimba. My theory teacher from high school days, Asher Zlotnik, had introduced me to Delius' music, and I fell in love with his compositions and orchestrations. I also re-orchestrated it for solo vibraphone, and as a solo vibraphone piece with bass accompaniment.

When we got back to LA, it was right back into heavy studio work. Picking a day at random from my 1980 date book, here's an example of a typical day: 9 a.m.-noon, working on jingles for McDonalds and Taco Bell; 1 p.m.-7 p.m, work on a television movie called *Masada*; and 8 p.m.-11 p.m., work on a recording session with John Denver.

That year I recall Ernest Gold's *Used Cars*, Nelson Riddle's *Rough Cut*, James Horner's *The Hand*, Bill Conti's *Gloria*, Lalo Schifrin's *Brubaker*, Basil Poledouris' *Blue Lagoon*, John Barry's *Raise the Titanic*, and *Galactica* by Stu Phillips, my 1950s Army band buddy.

I worked a lot with John Rubinstein, son of the famous concert pianist Arthur Rubinstein, and we became good friends. Aside from his great acting career he is a brilliant composer, and he wrote music for a film called *The Curse of K*. I asked him, "John, what was it like growing up with a famous father?" He said, "I didn't get to see my father very much growing up, as he was always on the road playing concerts. When I was nine years old I entered a Beethoven piano competition, and I hadn't seen my father for over a year, and he walked in as I was about to play. He was the judge for the competition, and I got so nervous that I just couldn't play."

Another time we were working on a film score, and he told me that he was going to Paris to visit his father, who was celebrating his 91st birthday. When he got back, I asked him, "John, how was the visit with your father in Paris?" He said, "I didn't get to spend too much time with him because his eyesight is getting very bad, and he can't see to read the music very well, so he's practicing eight to ten hours a day to memorize as much music as he can before he loses his sight." I said, "Wow, at 91, he's practicing that much? John, can I please tell that to students who ask me if they still need to practice? What an inspiration!"

The year 1981 meant work on many movies with Bill Conti, Jerry Goldsmith, Henry Mancini and Buddy Baker. I also recorded the music for the African and Japanese Pavilions at Disney's Epcot Center in Orlando, Florida, using many of my ethnic instruments.

With Sinatra there was a TV special and an album arranged by Gordon Jenkins, and I was fortunate to meet and work with Luciano Pavarotti on his movie, *Yes, Georgio.*

Once when Sinatra and Pavarotti were together Frank asked him, "Luciano, when you're singing loud and you want to quickly soften your voice, how do you handle that?" Pavarotti answered, "You just shut-a your mouth." Sinatra fell on the floor laughing at that one!

The TV show *Dynasty* began its nine-season run, and there was also work on *Falcon Crest* and *Fantasy Island.* From the day Camille was out of school until the day before she went back in September, Celeste and I took her to Hawaii. This time we went to Maui, where I played concerts with Bud Shank, Joe Burnett, and Buddy Collette. We loved Maui so much that we made arrangements to sell our condo in Honolulu and buy one in Maui. Whenever I returned home, composers would call to ask what was new in the way of my instruments. It got to the point where they didn't care what country the instrument came from–as long as it was a new or different sound, they wanted to be first to use it on their project.

I'll never forget the last time Pa came to visit, especially to see his namesake, Camille. He used to love to go to the track to bet on the horses and wished he could take Camille with us, but she was only about eight years old. I took him to Santa Anita, and he would sit in the clubhouse with his head buried in the racing papers, giving me orders to bet $50 to win on number 4, $50 to place on number 6 and $50 to show on number 2, and $50 dollars across the board on number 3. That's a total of $300 on a race, but he seemed to hit every one. I said, "Pa, at least come down to cash in and collect your winnings in the $50 window, so I can have time to stand in the $2 window for my own bets." He would say, "No, you go for me, I'm busy figuring out the next race."

This went on for several races and he continued to win in just about every one. I decided to look over his shoulder and see what he was looking at so intently in the racing form, and was startled by what I saw. I said, "Pa, we are at Santa Anita racetrack in California and you're looking at a racetrack schedule for Suffolk Downs back East. What are you doing?" He said, "But I'm winning, so be quiet and go place my bets!" I couldn't believe it, for he came home with a pocketful of winnings!

Pa passed away on Christmas Eve 1980 and, for me, it represented the end of an era. Although he never played music, he knew the names of most of the Italian operas and who composed each one. He had made me practice when I was a kid and I believe, since we came from such a rough neighborhood, that his saying that I had to practice for many hours every day of my young life if I expected to be a good musician was his way of keeping me at home. I thank both my parents for this and I often think of them, their humble beginnings in this country, what they both made of their lives, and how they helped inspire the lives of my brother and me.

Over 700 movies are in my listing for the 1980s, and yet there were a lot of TV shows as well like *Dynasty*, *Moonlighting*, and *Knots Landing*, to name just a few. Film composers often received assignments to do a TV series, but because of their heavy movie writing schedule they would write the main theme for the beginning and end of each week's show and then assign the writing of each weekly episode's music to one of the orchestrators who helped them with their film assignments.

The real money is in composing, and I try to encourage musicians to think seriously about writing. I'm not sorry I remained a player all these years, as I've had a full and rewarding musical career, but writing is where you make the most money. For example: when we record the music we get paid once for that recording, period. But the person who writes the music gets paid a negotiated fee over and above mere union scale, and every time that music is played he is paid a healthy royalty. If a show plays for twelve weeks during a season and you only wrote the main theme for that show, you are paid a fee every time it's played on the air. If you wrote all the music for that show, you are paid a royalty for each time each of those musical cues are played. It may then go into reruns for the summer, and it most likely may be shown in different countries around the world and go into reruns there as well.

The musicians went on strike in the early 1980s to share in that reuse royalty, and felt strongly enough about it to go out for 147 days. Yet we lost, and still do not receive any compensation after the initial payment for our TV film services, though we do receive a small reuse payment when we work on a film used in another market. If you work on a film, for instance, which is shown a few years later on TV or made into a video, you can receive a very small annual payment. (Your ASCAP or BMI royalties are paid four times a year.) If you work on a large number of films, that payment can be substantial, but it is still nowhere near the amount received by the composer.

The TV show *China Beach* can act as a good illustration of this. Composer Paul Chihara, who has a career as a serious composer and conductor, did most of the writing when he realized how lucrative it is to compose—and, in his case, also conduct—for TV shows like this one.

One of the composers who I had listened to when I was in music school was Alex North, and I was thrilled to be playing his music for films. In the main title of a movie called *Under the Rainbow*, North had me playing on a half-full whiskey bottle. I hit the bottle with a soft xylophone beater, while moving the bottle to let the liquid slosh around. It got a great sound, and I was so surprised that a fairly elderly composer would use such an innovative sound in his score. I added some thick oil in the bottle, which made the sloshing slower and gave it more of a bending sound. Alex loved it, and I loved him for using it and giving me the freedom to add to the sound's uniqueness.

John Williams gave up playing piano in the studios and concentrated more on composing his early scores like *Airplane, Beyond the Poseidon Adventure, Jaws, Close Encounters of the Third Kind,* and *Raiders of the Lost Ark.* Sometimes a composer and a director will hit it off, and that composer will work nearly exclusively for that director. If they are in synch with each other's thinking, it becomes a rewarding relationship because they both know what the other's concepts are for the film. This was the case with John Williams and Steven Spielberg. Spielberg comes to every recording session and walks around the orchestra, talking to all the players.

Spielberg did *The Color Purple* around this time, and this was an interesting project. Although Quincy Jones was the composer on this film, we played cues by as many as twelve different composers. Quincy wanted to get a lot of different types of feelings for the film and asked many people to write the music. I'm proud to say I was on every session for every composer for that movie.

At rehearsals, John Williams does something unique among composer-conductors. Most will say, for instance, "In bar 14, strings, give me a *crescendo,* and brass, in bar 16, put in your mutes. Now let's take it from bar 14, and try it." John Williams will say, strings, in bar 14 give me a *crescendo,* and brass in bar 16, put in your mutes. Now let's go from bar 17." He gives you the courtesy of knowing you marked your music and understand what he wants you to do, so you don't have to try it, just move on to the next section. I think this is the mark of a great and thoughtful conductor, but also one who is efficient, saving time while getting things done thoroughly.

Some new composers came onto the scene in the 1980s. Bill Conti recommended me to Basil Poledouris, and I was his principal percussionist from the beginning of his writing career on films like *The Blue Lagoon* and *Amerika.* The first film took place on a deserted island, so I was able to lay down an assortment of jungle-type sounds with a lot of my primitive instruments. The second film was about a Russian ship that got grounded off the coast of a New England town, full of funny dialogue. We used some odd sounds, including an instrument I invented called the Water Chimes, a series of four brass discs that dropped into a trough of water. With a pedal you can lower the discs into the water and bend the sounds downward microtonally in pitch and this instrument has been used for comedies like this one, but also for scary scenes.

When I got to the studio, the water chimes had been filled with water, and Shelly Manne had put live goldfish in the trough. When I hit the discs and dropped them into the water, the goldfish would stop moving as if they were dead—or, at least, deaf.

Shelly was famous for funny stunts, including one he pulled just before lunchtime. We were working with Jerry Goldsmith, who said, "Sit tight, folks, for just two minutes. Shelly, we need a two-minute drum roll for this scene. When the red light came on, Shelly started playing the drum roll and pulled his stomach way in, so his pants fell down while he kept playing his drum roll. The whole band tried desperately not to laugh out loud so they wouldn't ruin the recording.

One morning, I got a call from Los Angeles' Mayor Tom Bradley. He told me Lionel Hampton was in town, and he wanted to see if I could get some vibraphone players to come down to City Hall and play a surprise concert for Hamp. I gathered twenty-five vibe players representing fifty hands, plus a rhythm section, to play "Flying Home" for Hampton. We had to set up outside City Hall, as twenty-five vibraphones just couldn't fit in the Mayor's office. Hampton showed up in a limo, and got out as we began playing our piece for him. He was so excited that he naturally grabbed a pair of mallets, and started to play with us. The Mayor presented him with the keys to the city, and declared it Lionel Hampton Day.

With Bill Conti during these years, we worked on *Boulevard Nights*, *The Right Stuff* and the TV mini-series *North and South*. I had been collecting Taiko drums from Japan, and when Bill began the *Karate Kid* movies I got to use a lot of these Japanese instruments from my collection. Bill has a great sense of melody in his writing; many composers use orchestral dissonance to play drama in their scenes, but Bill has a way of using very lyrical melodic content in every dramatic sequence. There was a small drum I called a Monkey Drum, which showed up on screen in the *Karate Kid* movies, and I was able to duplicate this sound later. It's always a joy to be able to come up with just the right instrument required for a project.

John Barry, who had come over from London, called to talk about instruments for *Out of Africa*, which he was scoring at Paramount. When we got onto the scoring stage, John said, "Emil, I want you to stay at the end of the day with your percussion section and look at a scene that needs some African instruments." So after the orchestra was excused, director Sydney Pollack told me to watch the film and see what I thought would work with the action on the screen.

After viewing the picture, I told John Barry I knew just what African instruments I had that would work with this sequence. He said, "Do it, and you pick the players you want and the rhythms you want them to play." This happens on occasion, and it's always gratifying to be able to get off the written page and be somewhat creative in the studios.

This happened with Michael Kamen as well, who called me the first time he came to LA from London, though he originally was an oboe player from New York. He said that George Harrison suggested calling me as he was working on a picture called *Lethal Weapon* at Warners, and he asked me to bring a lot of strange-sounding instruments. There was a fight sequence between Mel Gibson and the "heavy" bad guy, and he wanted me to watch the screen and catch every kick and punch that I saw on the screen with a weird percussion instrument. The scene lasted for about six minutes, so I had a ball hitting opera gongs from China, angklungs from Bali, slit logs from Africa, and Taiko drums from Japan, plus even more. Michael went home with what we recorded, and scored what I laid down for a ninety-eight-piece orchestra; he even gave me the ASCAP royalties for that cue in the movie. We became great friends, and I worked on all the *Lethal Weapon* and *Die Hard* movies with him.

Jerry Goldsmith was one of the composers who would come to my warehouse for every new project. We worked together on many films, including *The Exorcist*, the first *Star Trek*, *Gremlins*, and *Poltergeist*. Jerry's movies all required a lot of strange sounds and he had every new electronic instrument that came out, yet he always used a lot of percussion in his writing. He knew how much my organic ethnic instruments enhanced the electronic sounds he bought to the studio, and how well they worked for each film that he scored, in addition to the 100-piece orchestra he also used for most projects.

A friend who worked at NASA gave me a series of aluminum tubes. I suspended them horizontally and played them by wearing gloves with powdered resin that produced very high violin-type harmonics. Jerry loved this instrument, which I call the rub rods, and we used it a lot in *Poltergeist*.

Camille was in her teens and didn't think much about the fact that her father was a musician until she went to a concert by Oingo Boingo, which is what she was listening to in those days. At the end of the concert she went backstage to meet Danny Elfman, the lead singer and guitar player with the band. Somehow my name came up and Danny said, "You're Emil Richards' daughter? Hey, guys, this is Emil Richards' daughter! We all know your dad, he's cool." Well, Camille came home and I was suddenly her hero. The guys in Oingo Boingo knew me, and to her, I was somebody! Well, from that day on I have been a somebody to Camille, and I guess I have Elfman to thank.

Elfman used my percussion work on *Beetlejuice*, *Ghostbusters 2*, all the Pee-Wee Herman movies, and *Howard the Duck*. Danny is a very creative writer, very knowledgeable about percussion, and he has quite a collection of Balinese, Oriental and African instruments of his own.

One very unique thing Danny does is to insist on having many gongs and cymbals on each session. He says, "If you play a cymbal, I don't want to hear that cymbal again in the same cue. I want to hear different colors and sounds of cymbals and gongs every time." Being a percussionist, I'm aware of the sameness of sound when hitting the same cymbal or gong, but was surprised that there were any composers who understood this. He keeps you on your toes, and wants to hear different sounds for every percussion instrument he asks for. This is great for me, because I can bring new sounds to the studio for Danny and I know he's going to really appreciate them.

In the middle of all this were some recordings for Celine Dion, Juice Newton, Toni Basil, Wayne Newton, and Letta Umbulu. I also did sessions with Barry Manilow, who has hundreds of songs and knows just the right time to record and release them, a knack more artists should have.

In 1988, Joe Porcaro, Dave Mackay, and I, who had all played together as kids in Connecticut and then in LA when we had first moved there, formed another jazz quartet called Calamari. We played in many of the area's jazz clubs and gained quite a following. If you get hung up in the studios you don't really get that much of a chance to keep the creative juices flowing, so going out and improvising helps keep you from feeling stagnant while just reading music "by the pound" every day.

Every November, at the Percussive Arts Society convention, we get to hear new music and new players and see new percussion instruments that have been invented. I went to these conventions every year and started to do clinics and performances there as well. As a result I started to get invited to come and lecture at different colleges as well as invitations to play concerts with my rhythm section and to give summer percussion camps teaching mallet and rhythm techniques.

In the summer of 1983 we headed for Sardinia, where at the Tropicana Gelateria I was to play with some of the jazz musicians from Maui. We were amazed to find that this place, where people came to eat ice cream and listen to jazz, held over three thousand people. Antonio Pirluzu, whom we had met in Maui, owned the place and rented a villa right on the Mediterranean for the band and their families. We were supposed to play from 10 p.m. to midnight, but at ten minutes after ten each night, Antonio would say, "The pasta is getting cold, you have to take a break and eat now!" So, we only played less than an hour each night and ate plenty of pasta and other great foods. We've made such lasting friendships, and the island is so peaceful and beautiful, that we have gone there every September since.

One of the things that make ethnic music so exciting is that it is performed with large numbers of people. In Bali, for instance, a whole village of people will participate in the playing of instruments or be among the dancers or singers involved in the performance. This is what makes the music so overpowering to see and to hear. At the end of this decade, we took a trip to New Mexico to see a gathering of all of the Western tribes of American Indians perform their music and dances. Although their music is not very sophisticated, it is most impressive because of the large amounts of people involved in the performances. Of course, the trip also meant returning with many great drums and rattles.

CHAPTER EIGHT:
THE 1990/

Throughout this decade, I averaged between 35 and 40 films a year. There were many more dates in clubs with my quartet, Calamari, and trips to colleges and concert halls for clinics and performances.

Around 1990, about 15 to 25 percussionists began getting together and experimenting with large percussion ensembles. We were all writing music and meeting at the warehouse where I stored my collection of instruments. To counter the new electronic sounds that were beginning to dominate the recording industry, we tried mixing all these colors to discover new and interesting combinations of sounds.

I began teaching at the Dick Grove School of Music in the evenings, and had as many as 40 percussionists in my classes. Each year, I was surprised to see how many students were interested in a percussion career. This interest spurred me to encourage students toward forming percussion ensembles or groups to play as much diverse music, and as many different ethnic rhythms, as they could.

This came at a time where more and more musicians were afraid of losing work due to electronic instruments, which were in full use in the studios. It was especially true in television work, as more composers or, actually, musicians who bought all the latest electronic gear, were able to record the shows on their new equipment at home.

Recording studios cropped up in garages and back rooms all over Los Angeles. As I mentioned before, it didn't seem to hurt my work, because ethnic and organic percussion instruments complemented electronic sounds.

The electronic players began a new scale category. If a musician recorded alone, he could charge a multi-track scale, which was greater than double the regular musician rate. This much-higher scale compensated for the time involved in dubbing on top of his own playing. I began getting calls for my percussion instruments with this new multi-track scale, allowing me to work less and make more so I could be free to teach out of town. It also meant I could perform away from LA, since I had spent two decades in the studios and could fulfill my desire for more jazz playing, teaching, and traveling.

Rocky 5 (I had also done the original) was another film with Bill Conti, and on another, Necessary Roughness, his orchestrator Jack Askew and I did a rhythm session before the recording. We came up with some great rhythmic phrases—for instance, instead of just writing in 3/4 time, I suggested a bar of 5/4 and one of 7/4, equaling 12, or four bars of 3/4.

Some of my metal sounds, like brake drums, steel beams, and muffled fight bells were used by Danny Elfman on *Dick Tracy* and *Edward Scissorhands*, and I did all the xylophone playing on Danny's main title for *The Simpsons*, though I no longer do the weekly episodes.

For the wolf sounds in John Barry's *Dances with Wolves* I rubbed a Super Ball on gongs, and Michael Kamen used my tuned gongs from Java and Bali and my rub rods in his *Die Hard* films. I played on *Godfather III*, one of the last film scores that Carmine Coppola wrote for his son, Francis Ford Coppola.

With John Williams you could always expect to play great music and we recorded *Home Alone*, which became one of the year's most popular films. The next year he wrote a good score for *Hook*, but the movie bombed. Soon we were up to *Star Trek V*, and I think I played on every one, as well as on *The Next Generation* TV series.

By this time, Clint Eastwood and I were on a first name basis; he started calling me Amyl Nitrate whenever he saw me. Unlike many directors, he shows up to all the sessions for movies he produces or acts in, all scored by Lennie Niehaus. For a while he became mayor of Carmel, and during a session for The Rookie, I said, "Hey, Clint, do we now have to call you 'Your Honor?'" and he said, "No, call me "Your Decadence!"

From 1992 on, I was taking at least two trips a year to Maui and playing at a club there called Blackie's Boat Yard. It was enjoyable to get away to our condo after a hectic studio schedule and to play jazz at the club four evenings a week. There was also a clinic in Spokane, Washington, and one in San Francisco, where I picked up some more Chinese instruments I needed for a *Tom and Jerry* feature cartoon film I was working on with Henry Mancini.

We also visited Ma in Connecticut, and Celeste found out something I had never known. Ma had sent Celeste all her recipes of Sicilian things she had cooked for me as a kid and that she knew I liked. Celeste is a great cook, but though the dishes tasted good, they were somehow different. When we arrived, Celeste suggested that Ma make some of those dishes and she watched without saying anything and wrote everything down. When we got home, Celeste found that, in almost every case, Ma had left out one or more important ingredients in the recipes she had sent Celeste. All we could figure is that Ma just wanted me to miss her cooking.

I loved working with Elmer Bernstein, because he knew his craft better than anyone else. If a producer or director tried to change what Elmer has written, Elmer would remind them that they had agreed to let him write the music, with no interruptions or changes until after he had finished recording. We did two together in 1992, *Babe* and *Oscar*. For Basil Poledouris' *Return to the Blue Lagoon*, I used a lot of the logs and African drums from the original, and that year finished up with Michael Kamen's score to *Robin Hood, Prince of Thieves*. Michael makes sure there are never less than six percussionists on every one of his scores.

Before that, though, we traveled to Boston at the invitation of Vic Firth, who was the timpanist with the Boston Symphony. Vic also has a $3 million-a-year drum and timpani stick business, and he asked me to come up with some unusual sticks for his line. I suggested a pair of timpani sticks with small BBs inside the heads. In *West Side Story*, Leonard Bernstein scored for maracas to be struck on timpani, but the sound is not so great. With our mallets, the drum still sounds pure with the addition of the maracas' rattle as well. Celeste came up with the same thing for marimba sticks, and Vic loved them both.

We also thought of an improvement variation of the old slap mallets that Red Norvo used on the vibraphone, Puelli sticks made of reed instead of bamboo (which easily crack in cold climates). Vic loved all these ideas, and we also presented him with a jingle stick, a clapper, a popgun, and a wind chime made out of drumsticks. They are big sellers for Vic, and Celeste and I get monthly royalty checks from these products.

While in New England, we visited with Jerry James who was helping us put a book together called *The Essence of Sight Reading*. You cannot really teach someone to sight read well, but there are many devices that can help a person read easier, and this book applies many of the principles that I have learned through the years.

After clinics at Fresno State in California and Arizona State University, I came to a major realization that teaching and passing along everything I had learned was what I really wanted to do at this stage of my career.

After a month in Sardinia, we traveled to Vienna for a visit with Veronica Haslinger, who had been an exchange student during Camille's high school years. Veronica and her parents took us to Salzburg, where every summer we heard Mozart's great brass and choral music played in the churches and cathedrals of the town. We also drove with them to Belluno, in the Italian Alps, where I played a concert with some jazz players from that region. The drive through the Alps from Austria into Italy was very impressive, with meadows of wildflowers everywhere.

But, our idyllic journey was short-lived. The morning after the concert in the Alps, we got a call from LA informing us telling us that my godson, Jeff Porcaro, had died of a heart attack. We immediately caught a plane and came right home in time for the funeral. Jeff had played with so many great artists, and his dad

Joe and I had even worked on a film he scored called *Dune*. Jeff was a great musician and a great person, and I still miss him very much.

The year 1992 seemed to be the year of sequels, including *Robocop 3* with Basil Poledouris, *Batman Returns* with Danny Elfman, and *Lethal Weapon 3* with Michael Kamen. With Bill Conti, there was the 64th Oscar show and a big prison movie called *Blood In, Blood Out*, on which I played cimbalom.

There have been many great composers in the Newman family, and I worked with just about all of them. First there was Alfred Newman, the head of the music department at 20th Century-Fox when I first came to town, and his brother Emil Newman. When Alfred passed away another brother, Lionel Newman, took over at Fox, and I played on many of his scores as well.

Before Randy Newman began writing films, we had worked together on many recording sessions. In 1992 I first played for David Newman, one of Alfred's sons who was a studio violinist before his composing days, on *Hoffa* and *The Mighty Ducks*. I would work with another of Alfred's sons, Thomas Newman, in years to come.

That was the year I feel James Newton Howard really broke out and was recognized for his brilliant score to *Alive*. James' writing was fresh and mature, as if he had been writing for films all his life.

In 1992, the Percussive Arts Society convention was held in New Orleans, and as usual we were able to hear new percussion music, see new products, attend seminars, and hear performances of drummers and percussionists from all over the world.

On another trip that year, we visited an antique shop in New York's Greenwich Village that calls us when they receive some unusual instruments. In a corner, Celeste noticed some Tibetan cymbals that she knew I just had to have. Celeste taught me not to act excited when I see something I desperately have to have, so the dealer will not jack the price up. As a collector I have a tendency to get overanxious, and Celeste cools me out.

I finished that year with an album project for Aretha Franklin, the *First Lady of Soul*.

At the start of 1993, the PAS called to say that they wanted to open a percussion museum. They had found a donor in Lawton, Oklahoma who would donate as much land as necessary, and they had the support of the Oklahoma Chamber of Commerce. In addition, the donor would also match whatever funds we could raise to start this museum. The only thing missing were instruments, so my commitment to donating a good portion of my collection began the fund drive. We soon raised $365,000, which became $730,000 with the Oklahoma foundation match, and the museum was built. In that first year I donated my marimba grande from Guatemala, marimbas from Africa, Bali, and

Mexico, my entire gamelan collection from Thailand, some from South America, and two or three rare marimbas made in the United States. In addition, there were drums, cymbals, and various percussion effects from India, the Middle East, Asia, and Europe, totaling $57,000 worth of instruments donated to the museum.

In those days, I was playing evenings with my quartet, Calamari, and traveling to do clinics in New York and San Antonio, Texas. I recall a one-day trip to Sausalito for work on a Linda Ronstadt album called *Winter Light*. The studio had all-glass walls which looked into the redwoods, providing a beautiful setting in which to work, and even had a full-time cook on duty.

Camille was a sophomore at USC, and she signed up for a Semester At Sea. This program allowed ship travel around the world for a whole college semester, and because she had traveled so much with us, this clinched her desire to remain a traveler for the rest of her life. Celeste and I met her in Nassau in the Bahamas, where we used the opportunity to buy some steel drums and other Caribbean percussion instruments. The trip then took her to South America, Africa, India, Malaysia, China, and Japan, and we didn't meet her until months later in Seattle. She had made friends in India and China, and she returned to Bali for almost a year since that experience. Having been conceived in Bali, she was curious to visit, and she fell in love with it as we had years before.

Whenever I saw Sinatra in those years, he usually greeted me with "Hey Daig (short for Dago), how are you? Everything okay?" But at Capitol Records in 1993, while working on the first *Duets* album, he didn't know who I was, or who anyone was. It was terribly sad. He tried to sing three nights in a row, but just couldn't see the words or remember the songs at all. I said to the producer, Phil Ramone, "Frank does not sound all that great, why are you putting him through this? He's already recorded all these songs already, why not just use those songs?" Phil replied, "We can't use the original recordings, because they belong to his kids. Don't worry, wherever Frank goofs up the words or the singing, I'll put in the other duet voice."

On the fourth night, Frank said "Hey, Daig" to me. It was very surprising, and I knew he was having a good day and remembering a lot more. He recorded nine of the twelve songs that night, and he sounded surprisingly good. It was the last album I played for him, because I was in Europe when he did the second *Duets* album. It was the end of a great singing career, and I don't believe there will ever be another singer or man like him. He was always great to me, and I will always cherish the years I spent playing behind him on tours, in intimate clubs or concert halls, recording studios, and on movie soundtracks.

The duet singers on that project never actually came to Capitol Records. Instead, they literally phoned in their parts from different parts of the world through a high-speed ISDN line. There were some technical challenges and some huge phone bills, but this was a new way to allow someone to record from anywhere.

About that time, just after the Oscars, Bill Conti's *Rookie of the Year* plus Jerry Goldsmith's *The Vanishing* and *Dennis the Menace* were happening. There were also a couple of albums with Ry Cooder, and another with Roger Kellaway's new Cello Sextet. Since Roger added two more percussionists to the

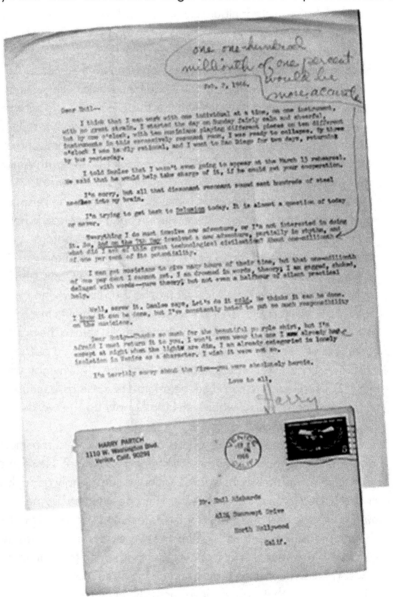

Harry Partch letter, 1966

band, I was freed up to concentrate on the great marimba parts he had written for me.

The year of turning even more old TV shows into movies continued, with Lalo Schifrin writing the score to *The Beverly Hillbillies*. Some of the other important movies I played on that year were *Jurassic Park* with John Williams, *Nightmare on Elm Street* (Danny Elfman), *The Three Musketeers* (Michael Kamen), and *Son of the Pink Panther* (Henry Mancini).

In 1994, I donated my entire library of percussion books to the Percussive Arts Society, along with autographed scores from Harry Partch and Frank Zappa. I also donated my personal letters from Partch, spanning the last twelve years of his life, as well as many additional instruments. Though I had owned

Some of Emil's 750 percussion instruments

over 750 percussion instruments, I still had over six hundred of them in my personal collection.

I also completed my solo album of original compositions, *Wonderful World of Percussion*, with some tracks overdubbed as many as thirty times with many instruments from my collection. The intention was to demonstrate how the marrying of different percussion instruments can create the most interesting colors, and also proved that percussion alone can make a full, great-sounding ensemble which could be utilized in an album or a movie score. This CD is out under the Emil Richards Music label, has sold nicely through the years, and seemed to represent the perfect title for this book.

Summertime meant a return to Maui to relax and play at Blackie's jazz bar. Then the Paiste company invited us to their cymbal factory in Lucerne, Switzerland, putting us up in a beautiful $600-a-night castle overlooking the lake. We visited the factory every day, evaluating their new line of cymbals and gongs, and they spoke at length of the healing properties made by the sounds of the Paiste  gongs. I have been most impressed of the awareness this family has with gong therapy, and if the day ever comes that there are too many percussionists and not enough jobs, their mission can shift to healing people through the vibrations of gongs, cymbals and other percussion instruments.

Celeste, Camille and I headed back to Sardinia, where we played again at the Tropicana with some of the same musicians, and then visited some of Pa's family now living in Rome. Some of their children are Camille's age, and they have continued their friendship and correspondence through the years.

Upon our return, Lalo Schifrin called and asked if I would play percussion for the Glendale Symphony, for which he was conducting. I made all but two concerts, because things became busy very quickly. There were clinics at the University of Hawaii in Honolulu and the Lewis and Clark College in Portland, Oregon.

In November, 1994 the whole family came to the PAS convention in Atlanta, where I was inducted into the Percussive Arts Society Hall of Fame, an honor previously bestowed on such notables as Harry Partch, Lionel Hampton, Gene Krupa, and Red Norvo. I am now listed in the Hall of Fame roster between Buddy Rich and Max Roach, not bad company to be in. That year I was also voted onto the PAS Museum's—and the Society's—Board of Directors.

Besides four movies and the Oscars in 1995 with Bill Conti, I also began working with Randy Newman, who wrote *The Paper* and *Maverick*. Randy is probably the funniest of all the Newmans, and keeps the orchestra laughing constantly. Once he was talking about his deceased uncle Lionel, famous for swearing on an exalted level, and finished by saying, "Well, I know Uncle Lionel is looking up at us right now from somewhere!"

With Jerry Goldsmith there was *Angie and The Shadow*, and Basil Poledouris had a big movie called *Wind*. James Newton Howard had become the hot composer through films like *Junior* and *Wyatt Earp*, and scored many films for Kevin Costner, who came to all the recording sessions. James usually called me in to pre-record some of the more exotic percussion sounds, so that during the large sessions—between 85 and 100 players—we could concentrate on the orchestral percussion.

By now there were usually one or two electronic keyboardists, who had become just another section of the orchestra, and there were at least four to six percussionists on most big movie sessions.

The last record I worked on in 1994 was with Tony Bennett. I got to know him through the bass player John Giufridda, who had played in my quartet back in Connecticut in the late 1940s and early 1950s. Johnny Mandel, who is one of my all-time favorite writers, did the arrangements for Tony Bennett. If you ever want to learn a song from the published music, you usually have to change some of the chords. With Johnny Mandel's songs, all you have to do is play what's on the paper and it's always so great and so right.

We closed the year with a score by Elmer Bernstein called *I Love Trouble*. Elmer's son Peter was writing some cues with him then and his daughter, Emily, was doing all his orchestrating.

At the beginning of 1995, I became the head of the percussion department of the Los Angeles Music Academy (LAMA) in Pasadena, and Joe Porcaro became head of drum studies. The school attracted serious students from Germany, Austria, Japan, China, Korea, Italy, and South America, as well as a large number of students from the States. Students could attend either before or after attending college, and we really whipped them into shape for their musical careers. Besides percussion studies I taught studio techniques, and each week I would take two or three students with me to the studios to see firsthand what it was like to get into recording sound tracks for movies.

That summer, on our way to Europe, Celeste and I stopped in New York to do a clinic at West Point and afterwards played with their 17-piece jazz orchestra, the Jazz Knights. It gave me the big band bug again, and I began thinking about writing some new music and returning to record with this band.

In Germany, we visited the Sonor drum factory in Bad Berleburg, which was building mallet instruments. Oliver Link, the third-generation owner of the company, asked me to come and evaluate the vibraphones, marimbas, xylophones, and orchestra bells they were making. I think I discouraged them with so much constructive criticism, because shortly after this trip they sold the company to Honor, who eventually sold it to a Chinese company. They now only make drums, and have discontinued production of mallet instruments.

From Germany, Oliver Link took us to Vienna to meet his stepfather, who at the age of 86 was studying musicology. Oliver also took us to an old museum where Herr Link was studying all of the early books on musicians during Mozart's time. In all his studies he only found two female musicians. All the musicians who worked at the palaces and courts in those days were fed and clothed very well, but their families went hungry.

Herr Link had come across letters from musician's wives, asking for the money their husbands never received for their services. While they were in the employ of the kings and queens and barons they were treated very well, but were never paid in money for their families. He even had the books retained by the governments in those days, and showed us that on any given day, Antonio Salieri was paid more than Mozart for his composing services.

From Vienna, Oliver took us on a trip to Prague. It was fascinating to see so many musicians playing on the streets with a tin cup or a hat to receive tips from onlookers and passers-by. There were no places for these musicians to work, and the streets were full of some of the greatest artists you could ever hope to hear, just playing solo–or in chamber groups–for pennies on the streets.

We stopped again in New York on this trip and met Charles Ranada and Will Friedwald, who interviewed me for books each of them were writing on Sinatra. On returning to the West Coast, we went up to San Francisco for a jazz festival organized as a tribute to Conga drummer Armando Peraza, a fellow player with the George Shearing Quintet, and to vibist Cal Tjader, who had recently passed away. Armando was told to wait until after intermission to be introduced before coming out to play, but when he heard the first beat of the concert's very first song, he ran out and started playing until the end. Latin music inspired me to return home and begin writing songs for a Latin album.

After another Oscar show with Bill Conti, there were lots more scores with James Newton Howard, including *The Juror*, *Outbreak*, and *Waterworld*. Costner was at all the sessions for that last film. Steven Seagal is another actor-producer who shows up on all the scoring sessions for his films. I recall working on the first *Toy Story* with Randy Newman that year, as well as on a CD with Bette Midler.

FLAPAMBA
Marimba-like instrument made by M. Brent Seawell. Its suspension differs from the standard marimba as it is suspended at its ends, with much tension applied. It has resinators enclosed in a wood box frame. The range is two octaves, the same as the lowest two octaves of the standard American marimba (commencing at one octave below middle C). It is played with the fingers or with very soft yarn mallets. Its lower octave produces fairly long liquid sustaining tones. Its upper octave somewhat produces the sound of the slap-tongue bass clarinet or the boo bams (tuned bongoes). It has a diatonic range.

Flapamba

Some new composers were coming up on sessions as well, like Robert Folk (*Ace Ventura 2*), Hans Zimmer (*Broken Arrow*), David Katay (*Clueless*), Bill Ross (*Little Panda*), David Franks (*Mia, Child of Hollywood*), Lee Holdridge (*Pinocchio*), Anthony Marinelli (*T. Rex*) and David Benoit (*Stars Fell on Henrietta*).

In early 1996 my Latin plan worked out through an Afro-Cuban CD called *Luntana* on my own label, Emil Richards Music. Both Al McKibbon and Chuck Domanico played bass on the album, Dave Mackay and Mike Lang were the pianists, Francisco Aquabella played congas and bata drums, Louis Conte played timbales and congas, Efrain Toro played congas, Joe Porcaro was on set drums, and I played vibes, marimba, flapamba, and octa marimba, as well as writing a lot of the songs on the CD.

Joe Porcaro and I took our wives to the Musikmesse international musical instrument trade fair in Frankfurt, Germany, where we found a piano and bassist and played at the music festival. It was a completely different show than the NAMM in America, since there were instrument makers from parts of the world that never displayed in the US, and I was able to buy some African and Asian instruments never shown before here at home.

Upon our return, I got a call to go to up to George Lucas' Skywalker Ranch in Marin County to work on a movie called *Mars Attacks*. Danny Elfman had written the score and insisted on my playing along with musicians from the San Francisco Symphony. It's a great environment to record in, but the attitude there is to do as much non-union work as possible. That didn't apply to me as I usually get more than union scale, especially when recording out of town.

On a trip to the museum in Oklahoma, I was officially installed in the Board of Directors of the Percussive Arts Society. Celeste hadn't realized how many

84

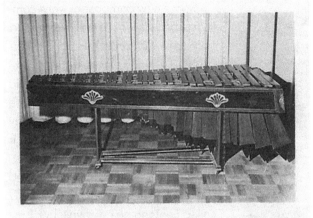

MARIMBA GRANDE (Buzz Marimba - Guatemala)
The larger of the two "Marimba Doble" has six octaves plus four semi-tones. A buzzing sound is produced by a membrane that covers an aperture close to the base of the resonators. Four men play at this marimba (piccolo - tiple - centro - bajo). The piccolo and tiple players double the melody (two mallets each) while the centro and bajo players carry the harmonic, chordal and bass parts (with three mallets - two in the right hand). The tones of this instrument "buzz" from its lowest note, G, through C, 3-1/2 octaves above. The higher tones (non-buzz tones) sound like the upper range of a standard xylophone.

Marimba grande

instruments I had donated to the museum, and when we went through the museum she said, "My God, this looks like our living room!"

That summer we traveled to Costa Rica, visiting our friends who had owned the place in Sardinia. They had decided to move to Tamarindo and build a hotel and twelve homes to rent out to tourists. Antonio took us around to two old marimba makers, and in one shop I just grabbed some mallets and started playing on the newly built marimba. The builders stopped their work, picked up mallets, and began playing with me on the same instrument. It was a great experience, and of course I bought one of their marimbas to take back to California.

Joe and I, again with our wives, returned to do a summer camp in the mountains of upper Austria in a town called Bad Goisern. We agreed that Austria is one of the most beautiful countries in the world. Students and teachers from all over northern Europe attended, and after this camp many came back to Pasadena to study with us for a year. Before coming home Celeste and I went to Switzerland, where I bought some of the largest cowbells in the world. We spent countless hours watching the bell maker work on these bells, which have an indescribable sound. They are so large and heavy, yet they hang them around all the cows' necks.

Some other films from 1996 were *Primal Fear* and *Space Jam* by James Newton Howard, *City Hall*, which was one of four with Jerry Goldsmith, and *Inde-*

At 20th Century-Fox, 1996

pendence Day with a British composer, David Arnold. We finished Michael Kamen's *101 Dalmatians* and *Mulholland Drive* with one of my favorite composers, Dave Grusin.

One night my quartet, Calamari, was playing a jazz gig at a club called Chadney's in Burbank, and I was surprised to see Robby Krieger from the Doors in the club. We hadn't seen each other since the 60s, and he had come to tell me that Doors drummer John Densmore had written a book and mentioned me in it. This was a surprise, and I now became a hero to my young nieces and nephews who were still into the Doors' music.

In early January, as I was walking along on the beach in Maui, I heard Ma call me. I turned around to find the beach deserted, but I was certain I had heard her voice. When I returned to the condo, there was a call from my brother telling me the time was near for Ma to leave this earth, so Celeste and I left for Connecticut to spend the last few weeks with her. She passed away at the age of 93 toward the end of January, 1997.

After Pa's death I had taken Ma with us to Hawaii and to Los Angeles at least once a year until she was in her late 80s, and she simply didn't want to travel anymore. Both my parents came to America at young ages and made something of their lives, and made it much easier for me and my brother to make something of ourselves as well. I will be forever grateful and indebted to my Ma and Pa, and thankful for all they were able to do for me in my life.

In March of that year we were elated to be invited by my brother Domenico and his wife to visit Aruba and spend some time together. It was great to remember our parents and the time we spent while growing up in Hartford.

I missed the Academy Awards in 1997, but I worked on the first annual Screen Actors Guild show and albums with Mickey Hart from the Grateful Dead, Richard Carpenter's tribute to Karen Carpenter, and Liza Minnelli.

Celeste and I went back to Maui twice more that year, as well as taking a trip to do clinics at the University of North Texas in Denton. The rest of that year was spent working on three new study books: *Essential Sight Reading, Mallet Chord Studies,* and an updated edition of my *Range Finder for the Percussion Seeker,* which now listed over 700 of the percussion instruments in my collection and is added to this book as Appendix 5.

I returned to the 69th Academy Awards with Bill Conti in 1997, and worked on *Air Force One, The Edge,* and three more with my old standby, Jerry Goldsmith. Clint Eastwood made two films that year with Lennie Niehaus' music, *Absolute Power* and *Midnight in the Garden of Good And Evil.* He still calls me Amyl Nitrate, and inspired me this time to write a jazz tune called "Emil's Night Rate!" There was a big Steven Spielberg film with John Williams, *Amistad,* that used many of my African instruments, and there were Danny Elfman sessions with *Flubber* and *Men In Black.* James Newton Howard was getting better and better with each film, and greatly in demand. That year we worked together on *My Best Friend's Wedding* and *The Postman.*

Every year, new film composers were arriving. Joe Porcaro's youngest son Steve left the group Toto and had written songs for Michael Jackson and Prince. He was a close friend of James Newton Howard, and James started to send Steve some film projects. Joe and I worked on his first major project, an Eddie Murphy film called *Metro,* and were delighted that Steve P (as we called him) was now a film writer.

Some other new composers on the scene were John Frissel, who we worked with on *Alien Resurrection* and *Dante's Peak,* and Mark Mancina, who wrote *Speed 2.*

As I look back over the years, the old, well-known film scorers were writing less and less, with more new composers on the scene. I believe it's due to the advent of electronic instruments. In earlier days, a composer would play the main themes for the producers and director on a piano, and he'd say, "Now, here's where the strings will come in" or "This is the part the French horns will play."

In today's world, a composer must play the whole score on his or her synthesizers, as if auditioning, to get all the cues approved before it can actually be put on paper for the orchestra to record. Most of the older composers began to say, "I'm not auditioning for this job. You either take what I write or I will not do the project." That's why, in most cases, those composers are no longer the mainstream of today's scoring.

The year 1998 marked sixty years that I had spent time behind bars—that is, vibraphone, marimba, xylophone, and orchestra bell bars. That February, Joe and I did clinics and a concert at Grinnell College in Iowa. It was cold, but the reception was warm and I became convinced that I wanted to do more and more clinics and concerts at colleges around the world. The next month I returned to West Point, playing with the Jazz Knights band. I became even more determined to write all-original music and record a big band album on my next trip. We did a marimba recital with 50 players, which hadn't been done since Claire Omar Musser had done this in the 1950s. In the future we plan to do this type of performance again, with as many as 100 marimba players.

The four of us hit the road again to go to Sardinia, and to visit Joe's mother's birthplace in Naples. There was also a visit to the Isle of Capri. We met many musicians in Naples and Rome who knew who we were, and we made some great connections for returning to do concerts in different parts of Italy.

But every time I came home, I went right back into the studios to work. This time it was a call from Ry Cooder to put some marimba on an album he had just recorded in Cuba, and I'm proud and thankful that he called me for this project. He also put out a great film about the event, called *Buena Vista Social Club*.

In April I made my first visit to San Juan, Puerto Rico for a spring rhythm symposium, though Celeste had been there many times. I always thought that Cuba was the only country with great Latin players, but I found that Puerto Rico also had some of the best I have ever heard. We heard a guiro player who used masterful rhythms, and met a man that had recorded all the Beatles' songs in 6/8 Nanigo rhythms. My purpose was to explore East Indian rhythms as they apply to Latin and jazz playing, which was very interesting to all the Puerto Rican musicians, but what they showed me was enlightening as well.

Stockholm, Sweden was a midsummer destination for a percussion camp. The students at this percussion and rhythm-section college had come from Finland, Norway, Sweden, Denmark, and Holland. Since I love teaching, especially students so eager and advanced, it was a great summer for me. In fact, it was so stimulating that upon arriving home I wrote a book with 108 pages of great mallet exercises called *Music and Rhythm Permutations*. Using a computer, I found that I could turn an exercise upside down and inside out, thereby developing a multitude of variations on each exercise.

I had often heard Diane Schurr sing, but wasn't aware of what a great pianist she was until we worked on an album together. Camille came with me on this project, as she was beginning to produce a few new groups and wanted to see first-hand how a producer worked with an artist. Since the producer was the renowned Ahmet Ertegun, she received a great lesson.

After the 70th Awards show with Conti, we did *Wrongfully Accused*, and I did the first of four Jerry Goldsmith movies in 1998—*Star Trek 9, Mulan, Small Soldiers*, and *U.S. Marshals*. David Arnold retuned from England to do *Godzilla*. He was very young, yet he loved percussion, and used six to eight musicians playing on all my large Japanese Taiko drums and Chinese gongs. We worked

With Joe Pantoliano (Joe Pants) at Sony Studios, 1999

on his scores longer than any others; they usually take three to five days to record, Jerry Goldsmith averages six to eight days and Danny Elfman ten to twelve, but Arnold was averaging fourteen to sixteen days to complete his scores.

It's always fun to play Lalo Schifrin's music, like on *Rush Hour* that year, and with Michael Kamen who came over from England for *Lethal Weapon 4*. Michael writes a huge, symphonic-style score on every soundtrack on which he works. I worked with Randy Newman on *Pleasantville* and finally with Thomas Newman on *Meet Joe Black*.

Of all the younger Newmans, I think Tom is the most talented and gifted writer. Like a lot of the young composers, Tom felt more comfortable with players close to his own age and, for this reason, I started to work less for the younger writers. This was rightly so, for it's a natural progression for them to feel more comfortable with their own peers that they'd gone to school with. The year finished out with Hans Zimmer's score for *The Thin Red Line*.

Through Paul Marchetti, a drummer I played with whenever I was in Maui, I got to know the actor Joe Pantoliano. Joe, who everyone calls "Joe Pants," was in *La Bamba*, *The Fugitive*, *The Matrix*, and the TV show *The Sopranos*. Whenever he knew I was on the lot, he always came over to say hello.

Calamari was now playing at a new club called Rocco's near Mulholland Drive, and in late 1998 we recorded an evening at the club. Early the next year we released the CD, *Emil Richards and Calamari, Live at Rocco's*, the first straight-ahead jazz record under my own name. The album got a lot of airplay in the Los Angeles area, as did *Luntana*, which had also been heard as much in Miami and San Francisco as well.

On February 10, 1999, the musicians roasted Jerry Goldsmith and they asked me to get up and say a few words:

"Among all the composers I have ever met, Jerry Goldsmith is definitely one of them. I first met Jerry in the early 1960s. He had white hair even back then, which leads me to believe that he very well may be older than dirt, rope, or mustard. He's always used the top-of-the-line percussion instruments such as lion's roars, slide whistles, and tuned temple blocks.

He was the first composer to use the Vietnamese and Cambodian bamboo instrument called angklungs, and the very American kitchen utensils known as stainless steel mixing bowls, as musical instruments.

Shelly Manne worked with Jerry most of the time. Jerry would often address the strings as "Celli," and Shelly would yell, "What?" Jerry would get annoyed and say, "Not you, Shelly—Celli!"

When Jerry first started to use odd time rhythms in his writing, his conducting was a bit erratic—or was that erotic? He loved to rehearse the odd time-pieces without a click-track, and we would yell,

"Uh, Jerry, can we use the click-track, we can stay together better." Of course, the truth was that with a click-track, we wouldn't have to look up from the music. But after Jerry had been coached, he became proficient in conducting all the odd-time rhythms. He wrote so many that Shelly once said, *"I wonder if Jerry would let me borrow some of these odd time cues for a spastic dance I have to play tonight."*

The recordist at M-G-M, the studio now known as SONY, is named Sue, and whenever she marks a take I will occasionally yell, "YO SUE." Actually, no matter what guy at what studio marks the take, I will still yell "YO SUE." Jerry always looked at me with this bewildered look on his face as if to say, "What the hell is he talking about?" The trumpet section gets a kick out of that look, because he never figured out who the hell Sue is, or what am I yelling about.

I've worked with Popi (Alfred Newman), Bernard Hermann, and Alex North, among some of the older more respected composers in LA, and Jerry definitely fell in this category--respected and older. Besides being one of the greatest musicians I have ever had the pleasure to know, I considered Jerry a great friend. Besides the music, the greatest thing I've learned from Jerry is how to treat my wife. When Carol came into a session, Jerry stopped everything and embraced her. The respect he showed her is an inspiration I try to emulate. I always appreciated Jerry for this.

I did clinics that year in Portland, Oregon, Santa Barbara and Ventura in California, Chicago, Kentucky, and Ohio. It reinforced my need to teach, and I really enjoyed teaching at the college level.

Once, in the early 1980s, my early timpani teacher Al Lepak came out to LA on a sabbatical. I had commissioned him to write a piece for mallet instruments and symphony orchestra, but unfortunately, I never took the time to learn that piece and perform it. When Al arrived from Hartford, he said, "I know you're busy, but are you doing any teaching?" I said, "No, I just don't have enough time." He slapped my face, just hard enough for me to take notice, and said, "It's your duty." Those words struck a chord. He also said, "You are carrying on a tradition in percussion, and especially out here in the studios, where many percussionists just don't know what you do, or what is expected of them as players. You must give back." Now here I was, doing many more clinics and master classes on percussion and really enjoying it.

May of 1999 marked forty years since I had moved out to LA from New York and had gone right to work on a record session and a jazz club on my first day in town. It was amazing that after forty years of doing records, jingles, live TV, film TV, and movie soundtracks, my phone was still ringing and that I was still being called for the top sessions in town.

Once again I did the Awards with Bill Conti, and we also worked together on *The Thomas Crown Affair*. It still astonishes me that I worked on the original soundtrack with Michel Legrand in 1968.

In addition, I worked on the Grammy Award show that year with Jack Elliott. I knew Jack back in Hartford when his name was Erwin Zucker, but he changed it while we were still living back East. I had done all his *Charlie's Angels* TV shows, as well as many others, through the years.

Clint Eastwood came to Warner Bros. as usual that year, during our recording of Lennie Niehaus' score to *True Crime*. With Jerry Goldsmith, I played on *13th Warrior* and *Haunting of Hill House* and with Elmer Bernstein on *Wild, Wild West*. It was one more remake and didn't seem to go over too well, but how could any score miss with Elmer doing the writing?

Animators used a completely new technique of computer-animated imagery for *Dinosaur*. Disney loves James Newton Howard, and continues to call him for their projects, but during that busy year he also composed *Mumford*, *Runaway Bride*, *The Sixth Sense*, and *Snow Falling On Cedars*.

That year we played with the Hawaii Jazz All-Stars at the Jazz Festival in Maui, and we also took our annual trip to Sardinia. We also visited the Tuscany region with our friend Oliver Link, the former head of the Sonor drum company. It wrapped up an incredible decade, full of old and new challenges, music, and friends.

CHAPTER NINE:
THE 2000*J*

n the year 2000, I did more teaching and fewer studio calls. Early in the year we went up to Seattle to do clinics at the University of Washington, where Tom Collier, a great vibe player, is the head of percussion. After my clinics we played a concert together—Tom on vibes and me playing marimba—recalling the times we played together in the early 1980s in LA, so we had a blast. I also went to Nashville to do some teaching with Joe Porcaro and to play a concert.

Burt Bacharach led the 72nd annual Academy Awards show that year. I hadn't worked with Burt since the early 70s when I was on a lot of his hit recordings like "Raindrops Keep Falling on My Head," and Dionne Warwick's "I'll Never Fall in Love Again," as well as working on a couple of movies with him at Fox.

I'll never forget something he did when we were doing record sessions together at Herb Alpert's studios, A & M. Herb had bought the old Charlie Chaplin film studios on La Brea Avenue in Hollywood and turned them into a state-of-the-art recording facility. One day we were listening to the playback with Bacharach through the most huge and expensive speakers you could buy at that time when Burt said, "Hold it, I'll be right back." He ran out to his car and brought in these tiny speakers he had taken out of his car doors, and said, "Now let's hear the playback through these. Everything sounds great on the big ones, but I want to hear it through these cheap car radio speakers, because I know if I hear it all in these, than it will surely be in the big expensive ones as well." I thought that was great. Whenever he did television shows, films, or record sessions he would carry those cheap little speakers into the studio and want to hear all the playbacks through those first.

Before going back to Maui in April, Celeste and I went to West Virginia to do some clinics and some concerts. I was surprised to find over fifty percussion majors, though most of them were not very good. I asked the head of the percussion department: why so many students, and why were most of them not up to the standards of say, North Texas State, where there are over 150 great percussion majors? I was told that these students all loved percussion, and in spite of their lack of talent they all wanted to be involved somehow with percussion as a vocation. So he was stressing their studies in the "business" of music. By this he meant that some would work for, or run, music stores. Others might want to join a drum manufacturing company and work as sales reps, or go into artist relations.

He thought that because the field of percussion has become so specialized and, because being the best in their field does not guarantee employment, he was preparing them for another aspect of the music business where they might at least have a chance to get work. Since there are so many more percussionists than there are jobs these days, I would encourage students to form large percussion ensembles where many players can play together. Also, because the field of percussion is so vast, one must be like a doctor: know a lot about the general field but be sure to specialize, and to be the best at one area of your field.

In spring we went back to West Point and played a concert with the Jazz Knights, West Point's elite big band. I brought all-original compositions, and it was recorded at the end of 2000 and issued as *Emil Richards with the Jazz Knights*. It was released on my own label, with my daughter Camille's artwork. I'm as proud of her covers on the last four of my CDs as I am of the music on them. I also played on a CD for the group Manhattan Transfer around this time.

In July we went to Taiwan to teach at the National Institute of the Arts University. Steve Houghton came also to teach drums to the students. The head of the camp is Tzong-Ching Ju, who has 26 percussion schools in Taiwan with over 25,000 students and who, since this tour, has been appointed head of cultural affairs for the entire country. The name of his University is now called National Taipei University of the Arts.

He asked me to return in June of 2002 to teach and perform once again. We taught an eight-hour day, six days a week, to elementary school, junior high, high school, and college-level students. This was very gratifying, since the students at every level were all great players and eager to learn. My job was primarily to teach improvisation, and the students just loved it and caught on quickly. Although I had an interpreter there with me all the time, I found that the language of music is enough to communicate with. Celeste was there to remind me when I pushed the students too hard, or to remind me when I should perform more to show the examples clearer. Steve Houghton and I did a concert at the Chiang Kai-Shek Hall, a huge auditorium, which we filled to capacity. It's amazing how much they love American jazz there.

In September we took our annual trip to Sardinia, and went up to Abruzzo to visit my father's relatives once again, unaware that my cousin Claudio Di Vincentis was visiting there also from Venezuela. He was there to visit his twin brother, Fiore, and to celebrate their 70th birthday. There was another birthday, of a cousin who was about five when I made my first visit after the Second World War at age fourteen.

Little did they know that I was also having a birthday, and none of us knew that the four of us had been born on the very same day, September 2nd. This was cause for a huge party, with the whole town invited, and I met a few people that were still alive that remembered my father and my grandfather. As we were in the car leaving around eight that evening, Celeste remarked, "This party started at eleven this morning, it's still going strong, and they're still bringing out dishes we haven't even tried yet!" That's the way it is in Italy and, I'm sure, in a lot of countries when families get together after a long time apart.

From the time I started recording with Jerry Goldsmith, this was the first year that we had worked together on fewer than two films a year. He wasn't slowing down, but he and his wife Carol loved to travel and he was scoring films in England and elsewhere. It has become cheaper for the studios, so they're going to Canada, Europe, and Asia to do the film music.

Scoring a movie is like building a house. You take out a loan and you spend to get things built. When you are almost finished you are low on cash, so you scrimp and sacrifice on your sprinklers and landscaping. Music for film is like the landscaping. When you have spent millions on actors and exotic locations, you now look for the music as cheaply as possible, because you are almost out of money. This seems to be happening more and more in the whole Hollywood film business, with more independent producers and major studios looking to other places to make their films.

I worked with Jerry with *Along Came a Spider*, then *Unconditional Love* and *Vertical Limit* with James Newton Howard, with a lot of great percussion for me to play in the latter film. With Danny Elfman I did *Proof of Life* and *Family Man*, and *Frequency* and *X-Men* with Michael Kamen. Once or twice throughout the year I played on a series of new Mickey Mouse, Donald Duck, and Pluto cartoons. Donald Rubenstein wrote a score to *Pollock*, and the actor Ed Harris came to the sessions every day. I also played on Rubenstein's first vocal album and his voice reminded me of Tom Waits, on whose albums I had also worked. There was also an album with Shirley Horn with arrangements by one of my favorites, Johnny Mandel. I ended the year with Clint Eastwood's *Space Cowboys*, scored as always by Lennie Niehaus.

In 2001 I was voted to another term on the PAS board of directors, running until the end of 2003. Bill Conti again did the 73rd Academy Award show that year, and we worked together on a film called *Tortilla Soup*. He used a lot of the musicians on my Latin jazz album, *Luntana*, after he heard the album.

We did a clinic as well as a concert in Tucson, Arizona, which now houses the complete library of Nelson Riddle and Artie Shaw's music. At the opening of the Nelson Riddle library, they asked me, Linda Ronstadt, and Paul Horn to perform and to talk about our experiences with Riddle. Here are my comments:

I first met and played with Nelson in 1959 on a Dean Martin Live TV Special. As a result of that show he recommended me for a tour with Frank Sinatra which also included Paul Horn, leading to TV variety specials with Nelson for Dean Martin, Frank Sinatra, and Sammy Davis, Jr. In 1960 we recorded the song "High Hopes" with Nelson and Frank Sinatra, but with the words changed for a commercial helping John F. Kennedy's bid for the White House.

In 1962, after Kennedy became president, he asked Sinatra to do a world tour for underprivileged children of the world. Both Nelson and Billy May condensed all the large orchestra arrangements down for a six-man combo, and we played a 10-week tour of the world which established hospitals for children in every country we visited. Those great arrangements that Nelson created sound as full as the full 60-piece orchestras they were originally written for.

When Sinatra started Reprise Records, Nelson Riddle became the lead arranger for most of the artists recording on that label. With Nelson, I got to record with Bing Crosby, Rosemary Clooney, Nat King Cole, Ella Fitzgerald, Dean Martin, Sammy Davis, Jr., and Frank, just to name a few. Sinatra then became a partner in Warner Bros. Pictures, and I got to play on the scores that Nelson composed for some of the films they made like "Oceans 11" and "Robin and the Seven Hoods."

One of Nelson's trademarks, musically speaking, was to utilize the augmented 11th in much of his writing. In simpler terms, it's like playing in the key of (F) Major over a (G) Major triad. I was fortunate enough to perform with Nelson in every aspect of his musical career. His high musical standards and complete awareness of every musical situation gained my highest respect for him as a musician, and as a man.

Two new composers appeared in 2001. A guitar player named Waddy Wachtel scored *Joe Dirt*, and Argentinian Ruy Folguera wrote the TV adaptation of the *Magnificent Ambersons*. Ruy wanted to use the glass harmonium for this score; this instrument is a series of glasses filled with water for tuning, played by rubbing your fingers over the rims of the glasses. The range of my tuned glasses is only two and a half octaves chromatic, and the range Folguera needed was much larger, so I suggested he let me bow the ends of the vibraphone bars to get somewhat the same sound.

Ruy is a friend of fellow Argentinian Lalo Schifrin, and he did some orchestrating for Lalo on *Rush Hour 2*, on which we also worked that year. Lalo's writing is better than ever. He writes so rhythmically, and he loves to use a lot of my strange instruments like water chimes, dharma bells (which I used to use on all the *Kung Fu* shows), the flapamba, bass marimba, and a series of pitched Chinese drums. My daughter Camille introduced Lalo to a new agent, and he is considering scoring more films again.

For Hans Zimmer's *Pearl Harbor* I played all the Japanese drums, and we worked with the group Hiroshima. The sessions for Danny Elfman's *Planet of the Apes* took twelve days, and there were only two of us who had worked on

Part of Emil's collection

the Jerry Goldsmith original in 1964. We did Disney's animated *Atlantis, Big Trouble*, and *America's Sweethearts* with James Newton Howard in 2001.

Celeste and I went back to West Point to play another concert with The Jazz Knights big band. This time I brought some new charts with me, beginning to build up my library of big band charts as I was often asked to perform with a 17-piece jazz band.

After playing vibes with a quartet on weekends and marimba with a Latin band during the week, we returned from Maui to work on Jerry Goldsmith's *The Last Castle* before leaving for a month in Sardinia and Italy. It would be the last score I would play for Jerry, as I will explain later.

Our usual Sardinia trip to visit friends and play music was graced by a surprise visit from Camille, who had flown over from Spain to spend some of her vacation with us. She was about to fly home on September 11 when we saw the news on CNN about the terrorist attack on America. Camille decided to stay until the end of the month and fly home when we left. I cannot tell you how wonderfully the Italian people treated us, sympathetic to our country and to us as Americans. All the Italian flags were flying at half-mast, and American flags cropped up everywhere. Our hotel gave us free meals, and upon hearing that we missed our ride to small villages, people offered to drive us back to our hotel in their personal cars.

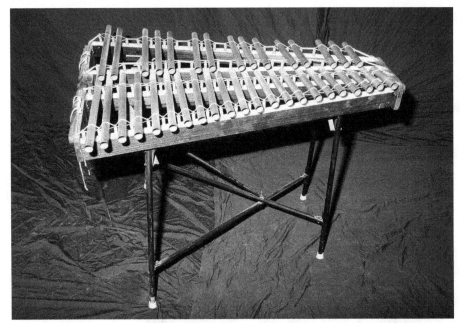

Brass Tube Pipe Gamelan

We met a sculptor named Penuccio while in Sardinia, who lived in a small village where young artists from all over Europe came to study with him. He works with large stones, which he cuts into many sliced pieces. When rubbed with another stone, these rocks produce many different musical pitches, and the larger ones produce deeper resonant tones. Of course, I bought two of these beautiful pieces to add to my percussion collection. I'm trying to arrange a show where Penuccio can exhibit his work in the U.S., and the Percussion Museum, then in Oklahoma, was interested in buying one of his larger pieces for the museum entrance.

In the last week of September, we got an e-mail from George and Olivia Harrison to come and spend some time with them in Lugano, Switzerland. We flew to Milan, and George had a car waiting to pick us. When we first got to his house he looked a bit tired, but he soon perked up and was his old self, laughing, singing, and playing some of his new songs for us with his guitar. It seemed strange that he forgot some of the words to his songs. This was not like him, and we left since it seemed he was getting tired. He called us to come back the next day, and we had a great time with him and Olivia watching videos of his homes in England and in Maui. We left for America, and it was a bit strange to be flying for the first time since the attacks on the World Trade Center.

We left for Maui in early October, as I had some concerts to play. The airports were empty, but security was time-consuming. After Maui, Celeste and I took our nephew and Celeste's mom to Chicago and then to the USC-Notre Dame

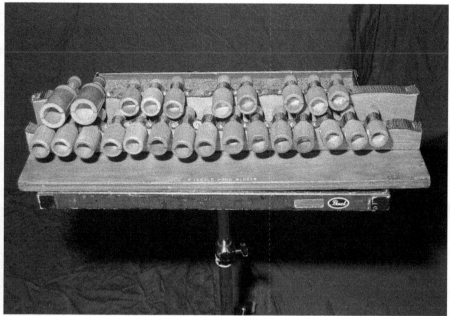

Piccolo wood blocks

football game in Indiana. We had planned to take our nephew to the Sears Tower, as we had taken him to the World Trade Center the year before, but it was closed for security reasons. Instead, we took him to Big John, the John Hancock building with 100 stories.

We then left for Germany to surprise Oliver Link, whose father used to own Sonor, the percussion instrument factory. Oliver had given me many instruments when his family owned the business, and Celeste and I surprised him by showing up for his wedding ceremony. I played in the church for the wedding, and the reception was a fifteen-hour affair.

Upon our return we flew to Hartford for my 50th high school reunion. I had never been to a reunion before, and I didn't think I would recognize very many people, but it was amazing that everyone looked pretty much the same, except grayer, fatter, and shorter. There were 150 former students who attended, and about 180 who had died. I had written the class song back in 1951, and they passed out copies for everyone. They had arranged a vibraphone there for me to play on, and they all sang while I played the class song. It was a beautiful moment for me.

We heard from Olivia Harrison, who was in Connecticut. She and George were in Staten Island, New York, as George was seeing a doctor there for some treatments. We asked if we should drive down, but George was a bit weak and they said they might come to see a doctor at UCLA soon, so we flew back to Los Angeles.

Contrabass marimba

Though we flew back to Maui for some more concerts, we stayed in touch with George and Olivia. While in Maui, I got a call from a percussionist from LA who informed me that Jerry Goldsmith was replacing me as his first percussionist for the last day of *The Last Castle*–and for all his future recordings. I was told that Jerry's timpani player, lead trombone player, and his concertmaster were also let go, and no reason was given. After working for the man for over thirty-five years, it was hard to have to hear this news from another player. We are all near, or over, 70 years old, but Jerry is older than we are. Age may have had something to do with it, but since I think musicians get better with age, it is hard to fathom why Jerry made this decision, and it hurt.

We heard from the Harrisons again the night before we returned from Maui. They called and asked if we would come over to visit with George as some of his friends, including Ravi Shankar, were coming over to visit. We said we would call as soon as we arrived. The next day George rested all day, and we did not get to see him. On the following evening, Thursday, November 29th, we got a call that George Harrison had passed away, and would we please come by to spend a few quiet minutes before the press was notified. One of the dearest men I had known was gone and it was sad, yet peaceful and joyous all at the same time. Besides being a great musician and human being, George was truly a spokesman for the Lord. I will miss his physical body for the rest of my life, yet I feel his presence still.

Celeste and I flew over 90,000 miles that year and spent the rest of the year at our home in LA I had one more picture to finish in 2001 for Richard

Gibbs, the former pianist with Oingo Boingo, called *Queen of the Damned*. Richard is a composer who uses mostly electronic instruments in his scores, and decided to use all organic percussion on this one. Some of the instruments from my collection that we utilized on this project were water chimes, flapamba, tubolo, aluminia-phone, 31-tone bells, rub rods, taiko drums, metal angklungs, and the guts of an old piano.

In January of 2002, Celeste and I flew for some jazz gigs and a visit with Olivia, George Harrison's wife. She was spending a few months at their home in the islands to reflect and to mourn in silence. Sandra, composer Michael Kamen's wife, was there keeping her company, and it was great just to be there and to spend a little time with them. Olivia's son Dhani had gone back to England to finish work on three albums George had been working on; they were pretty much complete, but needed just a little more work in editing. Back in Lugano, Jim Keltner and I had offered George our services if there were any drums or percussion to add, and George told me and Dhani that there would be little, if anything to add. "I want to keep it simple," George had said.

Back in LA, it was back to work with Danny Elfman on *Spider-Man* and the animated *Treasure Planet* with James Newton Howard. Celeste happened to meet Gail Zappa, Frank's wife, and they spoke about George Harrison. Celeste is trying to hook Olivia and Gail up, since both wives lost their famous guitar-playing husbands to the dreaded big C.

In the middle of February, we went to Heidelberg, Germany to do some concerts at a US army base. The troops, as well as the German people, were very receptive to jazz. Drummer Steve Houghton and I played with a quartet, a 17-piece jazz band and a 60-piece army concert band. After another March visit to Maui, I was called back in April for Danny Elfman's *Men in Black 2*.

Right after these sessions I left for the International Percussion Festival, held once every three years in Taipei, Taiwan. Steve Houghton and I were asked to bring a jazz quartet to do three concerts in three different cities in Taiwan. All three concerts were sold out before we arrived, as American jazz is hot in Asia. We had a wonderful reception and were invited back for the next International Percussion Festival in 2005.

Signs, with a score by James Newton Howard, took up the final days of May. As section leader, I used standard instruments plus some unusual ones: Japanese Taiko drums, rhythm logs, bowed gongs, rubrods, and brake drums.

We left for Maui in June, thinking I had the whole month to work on some of my own music and to play weekends in a Lahaina club. I ended up playing vibes and bells for a Hawaiian artist's Christmas album, and soon was asked to come back to work on Clint Eastwood's *Blood Work*, again with Niehaus. The stage at Warners has been renamed the "Clint Eastwood Recording Sound

Stage," as the studio was ready to close the stage down. It wasn't cost-effective for the studio to bring the recording board up to state-of-the-art qualifications, but Clint insisted he wanted to continue recording. With financial help (probably a lot from Clint), it was refurbished.

Every time I say I'm about to retire from the studios, another interesting project comes along. I don't think I could ever retire from playing music, but I now have forty-three years as a Hollywood studio percussionist and I do want to get out and play more jazz and give back in the form of teaching through seminars at music schools around the world.

The fifth annual Maui Film Festival was held in mid-June, and Clint Eastwood was honored there. A private party in his honor was held at the house of Shep Gordon, a friend who manages Alice Cooper, and many of the major chefs of the world were invited. Shep usually has Mark Elman, another famous chef, come in to cook for these affairs. Since Clint was being honored, I decided to bring a small jazz group and surprise him by playing. The party was attended by Jerry Moss (of A & M Records), Mo Austin and his wife, Alice Cooper and Don Ho.

Our old friend Rosanna Arquette was there doing a film about women in the cinema, as was Bo Derek. I reminded her of the *Tarzan* movie I had worked on with her late husband, John Derek, and she remembered all the African percussion instruments I used on those sessions. I also met Michael Laemmle, who was showing a documentary film he did on spiritual leader Ram Dass. I was surprised to find out that he was an heir to the Laemmle film family, the original creators of Universal Pictures.

In July we went back to Maui to play some more gigs with a jazz quartet. We are making a CD with this group, calling it the MJQ: the Maui Jazz Quartet. Composer James Newton Howard was there visiting with his family, and Celeste and I got to play some golf with him. He told me about a composer-conductor named Robert Pollack, who is working with the Maui Symphony and Maui Chamber Orchestra; since then, he has contacted me to play some of his contemporary pieces for small jazz ensemble, percussion, and orchestra. We performed this free-form concert, with dancers, along with the showing of some Kandinsky paintings on stage. At the end of the concert we showed four of the paintings to the dancers and to the audience and surprisingly, most of them guessed which of Kandinsky's paintings we had played to.

In August of 2002, I was called back to LA to work again with Danny Elfman on an Anthony Hopkins film called *Red Dragon*. The picture needed a lot of my weird and mysterious sounding instruments, so I came into LA to work on it. In August of 2002 I was called back to LA again to work with Danny Elfman.

I celebrated my 70th birthday on September 2nd with a group of friends on the island of Sardinia and received news that Lionel Hampton had passed away at the age of 94. Hamp was the grampa of the vibraphone and aside from Red Norvo, Hampton was my only influence growing up. When any one would ask me what instrument I played, I would say, "the vibraphone." They would usually say, "what's that?" And I would answer, "you know, that instrument that Lionel Hampton plays." They would then immediately know what I was talking about.

The vibraphone is not a very old instrument and Lionel Hampton, Red Norvo and Adrian Rollini were the first and only influences that were around when I was growing up.

By September 7th, Joe Porcaro and Fred Mace, two guys I have known for over 60 years, joined us with their wives in Rome and we all went to Sicily and Calabria to seek out our families' early roots. It was a great experience for all of us to reconnect with our families once again.

While in Palermo, we stopped at a club where Joe Porcaro and I were recognized by a Sicilian drummer and vibes player. They brought instruments to the club the following night and we played a jazz gig with them for the price of a 12-course, all-Sicilian meal. The music was great and the food was better.

Emil, Celeste and Fred Mace, 2007

In Rome, my cousin Giuseppe Delli Castelli set us up with a bunch of studio drummers and percussionists and it was surprising to realize how much they all knew about us and all our method books, the records we played on, and the movies we had worked on. We have set up some great friendships, and connections for returning next year to perform and to do clinics.

There was also a call for a Michael Kamen score for *On the Ropes* with Meg Ryan, and music by Lalo Schifrin for *Bringing Down the House* with Steve Martin. Lalo is great to work for, and his music is always interesting–and hard. I even got to play some timpani on that score, as well as vibraphone, marimba, and xylophone. Lalo says he is staying in the US, as he wants to score more films in LA

I received a call from Olivia about a big concert at Albert Hall in London on November 29th, to commemorate the first anniversary of George's passing. Ravi Shankar asked me to come over to perform on vibraphone and marimba with him. I was also asked to play percussion with Michael Kamen's large orchestra, which will play behind Paul McCartney, Eric Clapton, and others. We left for London a week before the concert, and there were 25 musicians from India. Ravi Shankar wrote all-original music for the concert, and his daughter Anoushka played sitar and conducted the Indian music for the concert. The music was quite complicated and hard, and one piece was written in nine-and-one-half time, but we had a week to rehearse before the concert.

We worked in one studio while Eric Clapton, Paul McCartney, Jeff Lynne, Tom Petty, Billy Preston, and Ringo Starr rehearsed in the studio next to us, and I kept going into their rehearsal to speak with percussionist Ray Cooper and drummers Jim Keltner and Steve Ferrone. I spoke each day a little with Eric Clapton, and toward the end of the week Jim Keltner called me by name and Eric said, "Jim, I didn't know that was Emil Richards I had been talking to him all week! You must formally introduce us." This made me feel especially warm.

Ravi Shankar asked me to get a cymbal at rehearsal to play at the end of one of the compositions, so I went next door where the rock band was playing and asked one of the roadies to loan me a cymbal and a stand for the concert. At the end of the concert the roadie came up to me and said, "You know, that was Ringo's cymbal you used for the concert and he would really like you to autograph it for him." I must say, this too was a wonderful moment.

We played the concert at Royal Albert Hall in London, and I was reminded that the last time I had been there was with Frank Sinatra. I played with the Ravi Shankar group during the first half of the concert and then went to sit with Celeste and Camille during the second half. When McCartney, Ringo, and Eric Clapton all played together on "My Sweet Lord," I jumped up on stage and played percussion with Ray Cooper until the end of the concert.

All proceeds for this concert went to Harrison's favorite charities, including funds from the movie, documentary film, CD, and DVD of the evening. I received a Grammy in 2004 for this concert, which was an enormous outpouring of love for George's memory.

James Newton Howard, who was in London to do a concert with Elton John, was in the audience and asked me at intermission to keep the second week of January 2003 open for the film *Dreamcatcher*. Michael Kamen also asked me to hold some time open in early January for a film that would be a prelude to *The Exorcist*.

In March of 2003, I started to do TV film shows again. I hadn't done very many in the last 20 years, but was now getting called to do jazz vibe or heavy xylophone parts. Some of the shows were with new composers like *Jag* with Steve Bramson, *Enterprise* with Bryan Tyler, and *King of the Hill* with Roger Neil. Bill Conti did the Academy Awards at the new Kodak theatre in Hollywood, and then Hans Zimmer called me to play some very fast xylophone parts in *Stickman*.

April was a busy month, with a jazz festival with drummer Steve Houghton and some clinics in Wichita, Kansas, and a concert in Honolulu at the University of Hawaii with a quartet and their seventeen-piece jazz band.

May was busy in the studios, with *The Incredible Hulk* for Danny Elfman and both *Hidalgo* and *Dreamcatcher* for James Newton Howard. Just before leaving for Italy, I went to perform for Hans Zimmer on *Matchstick Men* and *Pirates of the Caribbean*. I used a lot of xylophone, vibes, and marimba on the first score, and plenty of deep drums and timpani on the second.

Oliver Link met us in Sardinia that year, along with our Maui friends Mark and Judy Elman. Mark is one of the famous original Pacific Rim chefs, but we turned him on to some great native Sardinian dishes.

Also joining us was Paul Marchetti and his family; Paul had played drums there with me a decade before. We all traveled to Rome together and ended up in Milan, where, at the Blue Note jazz club, we ran into Jean (Toots) Thielemans, the guitar and harmonica player from back in our George Shearing Quintet days in the 1950s. We had a lot of catching up to do after nearly 50 years of not having seen each other, with the only exception having been a Quincy Jones movie session in the early 1970s.

When we got home in early July, I got called in by Hans Zimmer to work on *The Last Samurai* movie, where I got to use and play all of my Japanese drums and instruments. I also played a large concert with Gunther Schuller, and did some teaching for the Henry Mancini Institute summer program. If that wasn't busy enough, I took my jazz quartet in a club to perform and we recorded and filmed the group digitally. That gives the viewer the option to be able to watch any player you choose when listening to the group perform. This is surely the future of recording, and you can now rent movies with that option of watching many different angles not on the director's final cut.

In July I also took an 18-piece jazz band into a new venue called The Canyon Club, where a different band performs every Wednesday night. So far they have booked the Count Basie Orchestra, along with Louis Bellson's, Frank Capp's and Jack Sheldon's orchestras. I now have accumulated 26 big-band charts from albums I have done with Quincy Jones, Allyn Ferguson, Sam Nestico, Nelson Riddle, and the Jazz Knights West Point band from my latest CD.

I have gathered the cream of the Hollywood jazz players for this band, and we are billed as Emil Richards and the All Star Big Band, which I hope we can keep together and working.

Some of the best musicians anywhere played some of these charts on an Aix DVD entitled "Emil Richards/JoePorcaro Allstar Big Band," a joyful treat for all of us.

By the end of 2007, the Percussive Arts Society Museum will have completed its move to Indianapolis, Indiana. The Museum houses a large portion of my donated percussion instruments.

Besides all the teaching at colleges, my work for movies and TV shows is still thriving as I play scores by some old friends and three new composers: Michael Giacchino, Walter Murphy and Ron Jones.

From 2004 until halfway through 2007, I worked on three more Academy Award shows and the films *Mean Girls, The Incredibles, Spider-Man 2, Rush Hour 3, King Kong, Mr. And Mrs. Smith, The Weather Man, Charlotte's Web, Flags of our Fathers, Mission Impossible 3, Nacho Libre, Unaccompanied Minors and Ratatouille.* Television shows included *LOST* with Michael Giacchino, *Family Guy* and *American Dad.*

A new crop of work has begun with video games, which surprisingly require large orchestras, and I am now getting calls for this type of work as well.

To see a complete list of all the movies, TV shows, and artists I've been fortunate enough to work with, plus lots of other insights and information, readers can check out my new website, www.emilrichards.com, as well as the Appendices in this book.

Emil and Joe Porcaro, 2005

Emil and Celeste at Golden Gate Park, 2013

CHAPTER TEN:
SUMMING UP

f I can paraphrase my career into the four phases of Hollywood's tough music business, it would sound like this:
-Who is Emil Richards?
-Get me Emil Richards!
-Get me a young Emil Richards!
-Who is Emil Richards?

Luckily that final rimshot isn't really true yet, but it gives a sense of how cold things can be in this business. As I've said before, advice to young musicians about finding work here must be different now than it was 20 years ago.

Though things are always changing, and not always in the best interests of musicians, I'm glad to have had an effect on the pay scales and the rights we all fought for. I'm also proud to have raised the awareness of many composers of the musical possibilities inherent in the infinite world of percussion.

It's still a kick to get calls from some of the best composers around, though clinics have become an enormously rewarding aspect of my life. To give back some of my good fortune and to affect the lives of young players is a special satisfaction, and I'm willing to do every clinic I can. I've played with some of the great musicians in more countries than I could list, and each one has given me something to learn.

These years have been filled with great friends, fascinating experiences, and the thrill of collaboration with some of the world's greatest musicians. I have experienced the joy of doing what I love, performing on the highest level, and reaching as many people as possible, with my soul-mate Celeste always by my side and our beloved Camille, Claudio, and Emilio Jr. with us at the most important moments. And, of course, with the invaluable and constant support of Celeste and Camille as collaborators in making this book a reality.

My book's coda returns to the beginning, as I echo the words of my teacher Asher Zlotnik so many years ago: I'll be a musician until I die.

APPENDIX 1: ARTISTS I HAVE WORKED WITH

Alex Acuna
John Addison
Toshiko Akiyoshi
Alessi Brothers
David Allen
Debbie Allen
Peter Allen
Steve Allen
Laurindo Almeida
Herb Alpert
Bob Alzavar
Ed Ames
Nancy Ames
Animals
Paul Anka
Apollos
Francisco Aquabella
David Arnold
Leo Arno
Association
Attitudes
Frankie Avalon
Hoyt Axton
Mitchell Ayres
Ayres Rock
Burt Bacharach
Joan Baez
Tom Bahler
Bob Bain
Baja Marimba Band
Buddy Baker
Lucille Ball
H. B. Barnum
Ron Barrett
John Barry
Steve Bartek
Count Basie

Toni Basil
Les Baxter
Beach Boys
John Beal
Johnny Beecher
Louis Bellson
Tony Bennett
Richard Rodney Bennett
David Benoit
Bobbie Bensen
Elmer Bernstein
Peter Bernstein
Dick Berris
Ken Berry
Joey Bishop
Bjork
Blondie
Sunny Blueskys
Bobby Sox and the
   Bluejeans
Willie Bobo
Jimmy Bond
Pat Boone
Mike Botiker
Jim Bowen
Euel Box
Jimmy Boyd
Terence Boylan
Brazil 66
Brazil 88
Walter Brennan
Alan Broadbent
Donnie Brooks
Bruce Broughton
Les Brown
Lou Brown
Ray Brown

Lenny Bruce
Bob Brunner
Buffalo Springfield
Jim Buffington
Sonny Burke
Ralph Burns
Sam Butera & The
   Witnesses
Artie Butler
Dr. Buzzard
Anita Bryant
Billy Byers
Byrds
Bobby Caldwell
Tutti Camarata
Glen Campbell
Larry Cansler
Al Capp
Captain and Tennille
Pete Carpenter
Richard Carpenter
Carpenters
Vikki Carr
Keith Carradine
Johnny Carson
Benny Carter
Dick Cary
David Cassidy
Joe Castro
Ray Charles
Checkmates Ltd.
Don Cherry
Chicago
Paul Chihara
Cheech & Chong
Christy Minstrels
Petula Clark

Roy Clark
Stanley Clarke
Alf Clausen
Dick Clemmens
Rosemary Clooney
Leonard Cohen
Roy Colcord
Nat King Cole
Natalie Cole
Judy Collins
Michel Columbier
Perry Como
Chris Connor
Ray Conniff
Louis Conte
Bill Conti
Ry Cooder
Sam Cooke
Al Cooper
Carmine Coppola
Don Costa
Alexander Courage
Michael Cradon
Michael Crawford
Bing Crosby
Gary Crosby
Billy Crystal
Crystals
Hoyt Curtin
Vic Damone
Bill Dana
Vic Dana
James Darren
Bobby Darin
Robert Davi
Don Davis
Hod Davis
Mac Davis
Sammy Davis, Jr.
John Davison

Doris Day
Dick DeBenedictus
Nick De Caro
Buddy De Franco
Milton DeLugg
Jim De Pasqual
Rick De Silva
Frank DeVol
Blossom Dearie
John Debney
George Delerue
Al De Lory
Martin Denny
John Denver
Neil Diamond
Celene Dion
Eric Dolphy
Joao Donato
Donovan
Steve Dorff
Bob Drasdun
Skip Drinkwater
Buzzy Drootin
George Duke
Patty Duke
George Duning
Jimmy Durante
Clint Eastwood
Duane Eddy
Harry (Sweets) Edison
Randy Edelman
Cliff Eidleman
Scott Elder
Danny Elfman
Jonathan Elias
Bill Elliott
Jack Elliott
Mama Cass Elliott
Dean Elliott
Don Ellis

Herb Ellis
Bob Emenaker
Ashly Erwin
Jack Esque
Everly Brothers
Percy Faith
Fantasia
Leonard Feather
Jose Feliciano
Allyn Ferguson
Jerry Fielding
Jack Fields
Sally Field
Fifth Dimension
Findley Brothers Inc
   (F B I)
Eddie Fisher
Ella Fitzgerald
Fleetwoods
Myron Floren
Bob Florence
Robert Folk
Tennessee Ernie Ford
David Foster
Four Freshmen
Four Preps
Charles Fox
Sergio Franchi
David Michael Frank
Ian Freebairn Smith
Ernie Freeman
Gerald Fried
Hugo Friedhofer
Friends of Distinction
Dominic Frontiere
Annette Funicello
James Galway
Marvin Gaye
Russ Garcia
Dave Garfield

Art Garfunkel
Judy Garland
Erroll Garner
Snuff Garrett
Mort Garson
Gary LeMel
Gary Lewis and
   the Playboys
Lowell George
Bobbie Gentry
Joseph Gershenson
Michael Giacchino
Richard Gibbs
Terry Gibbs
Bob Gibson
Hershel Gilbert
Johnny Giuffrida
Jack Goga
Ernest Gold
Billy Goldenberg
Elliot Goldenthal
Goldiggers
Jerry Goldsmith
William Goldstein
Benny Golson
Good News
Miles Goodman
Robert Goulet
Buddy Greco
Kathy Green
Larry Green
Richard Green
Urbie Green
Lorne Greene
Glen Gray
Merv Griffin
James Griffith
Charles Gross
Dave Gruson
Arlo Guthrie

Earl Hagen
Merle Haggard
Corky Hall
Lani Hall
Dorothy Hamill
Lionel Hampton
Hari Har Rao
Joe Harnell
Richard Harris
George Harrison
Mickey Hart
Jim Haskell
Goldie Hawn
Jack Hayes
Lee Haywood
Dick Hazzard
George Heck
Neal Hefti
Hugh Heller
Jim Helms
Rick Henn
Bernard Herrmann
Ken Hersch
Hi Lo's
Hindustani Jazz Sextet
James Hines
Al Hirt
Don Ho
Johnny Hodges
Lee Holdridge
Hollyridge Strings
Bill Holman
Bob Hope
Lightnin' Hopkins
Scott Hopper
Paul Horn
Shirley Horn
James Horner
Steve Houghton
Thelma Houston

James Newton Howard
Bones Howe
Jerry Immell
Germaine Jackson
Michael Jackson
Jackson 5
Joni James
Jan and Dean
Maurice Jarre
Jazz Knights
Gordon Jenkins
Dr. John
J. J. Johnson
Plas Johnson
Pete Jolly
Jack Jones
Quincy Jones
Bill Justice
Aashish Kahn
Michael Kamen
Artie Kane
Saul Kaplan
Dana Kaproff
Eddie Karam
Fred Karlin
David Katay
Del Katcher
Danny Kaye
Lainie Kazan
Shane Keister
Roger Kellaway
Gene Kelly
Jim Keltner
Stan Kenton
Anita Kerr
Barney Kessel
Morgana King
King Family
King Pleasure
Kingston Trio

Kirby Stone Four
Michael Kitakis
Eartha Kitt
John Klemmer
Gladys Knight and
    the Pips
Buddy Knox
Irwin Kostal
Andre Kostelanetz
William Kraft
Robert Kraft
Irene Kral
Diana Krall
Bob Krasnow
Jim Kremens
David Kurtz
Tom La Puma
Don Lamond
Cleo Laine
Frankie Laine
Ben Lanzarone
Steve Lawrence
Vicki Lawrence
Henri Lazarof
Peggy Lee
Michel Legrand
Al Lepak
Lettermen
Gus Levine
Jerry Lewis
John Lewis
Liberace
Gorden Lightfoot
Limeliters
Mort Lindsey
Little Feat
Nils Lofgren
Jackie Lomax
Julie London
Claudine Longet

Bill Loose
Trini Lopez
Lord Buckley
Louis Prima
Carmen McRae
Yo-Yo Ma
Mamas and the Papas
Mark Mancina
Henry Mancini
Johnny Mandel
Harvey Mandel
Manhattan Transfer
Barry Manilow
Hummie Mann
Johnny Mann Singers
Shelly Manne
Ann-Margret
Anthony Marinelli
Dick Markowitz
Dick Marks
Angela Marley
Joe Marsala
Dean Martin
Tony Martin
Cu Cu Martinez
Hugh Masekela
Dave Mason
Johnny Mathis
Peter Matz
Peter Max
Paul Mazursky
Billy May
Dennis McCarthy
Murray McCloud
Gene McDaniels
McGuire Sisters
Scott McKenzie
Al McKibbon
Rod McKuen

Barbara McNair
Joel McNeely
Greg McRitchie
Zubin Mehta
Gill Melle
Allen Menken
Pat Metheny
Pete Meyers
Microtonal Blues
    Band
Harry Middlebrooks
Bette Midler
Jody Miller
Charles Mingus
Liza Minnelli
Louis Miranda
Red Mitchell
Joni Mitchell
Vic Mizzy
Monkees
Lou Monte
Hugh Montenegro
Guy Moon
Hal Mooney
Melba Moore
Airto Moreira
Jaye P. Morgan
Angela Morley
Ennio Morricone
Chris Morris
Zero Mostel
Mother Hen
Alphonse Mouzon
Larry Muhoberac
Maria Muldaur
Gerry Mulligan
Murph The Surf
Spud Murphy
Walter Murphy
Anne Murray

Lyn Murray
Jim Nabors
Oliver Nelson
Ricky Nelson
Sammy Nestico
Ira Newborne
Anthony Newley
Alfred Newman
David Newman
Lionel Newman
Randy Newman
Thomas Newman
Andy Newmark
Juice Newton
Wayne Newton
Lennie Niehaus
Harry Nilsson
Jack Nitzsche
Alex North
Odetta
Ohta-san
Jeffrey Osborne
Osmond Brothers
Johnny Otis
Jim Owens
Patti Page
Marty Paich
Basil Palidouris
Mosha Paranov
Van Dyke Parks
Harry Partch
Partridge Family
Pastels
John Pattituci
Luciano Pavarotti
Don Peake
Dave Pell
Armando Peraza
Richard Perry
Oscar Pettiford

Flip Phillips
Stu Phillips
Don Piestrup
Nicholas Pike
Lily Pons
Joe Porcaro
Jeff Porcaro
Steve Porcaro
Mike Post
Hari Prasad
Elvis Presley
Billy Preston
Don Preston
Andre Previn
Bob Prince
Juliet Prowse
Richard Pryor
Flora Purim
Queen Latifah
Jack Quigley
Ron Ramin
Sid Ramin
Chuck Rainey
Alla Rakha
David Raksin
Don Ralke
Don Randi
Sue Raney
Kenny Rankin
Lou Rawls
Don Ray
Johnnie Ray
Ray Charles Singers
Helen Reddy
J.A.C. Redford
Joe Renzetti
Debbie Reynolds
George Rhodes
Jerome Richardson
Kim Richmond

Nelson Riddle
Righteous Brothers
Johnny Rivers
Mavis Rivers
Howard Roberts
Pete Robinson
Jimmie Rodgers
Shorty Rogers
Kenny Rogers and
    the First Edition
George Romanis
Linda Ronstadt
Ronettes
David Rose
Leonard Rosenman
Larry Rosenthal
Bill Ross
Bob Ross
Diana Ross
Nino Rota
James Rowe
Don Rubinstein
John Rubinstein
Pete Rugolo
Leon Russell
Bobby Rydell
Craig Safon
Eddie Safranski
Daniel Saidenburg
Buffy Saint Marie
Soupy Sales
Joe Sample
Sandpipers
Tommy Sands
Mongo Santamaria
Hal Schaefer
Lalo Schifrin
Al Schmidt
Eric Schmidt
Tom Scott

Don Sebesky
Shadowfax
Marc Shaiman
Lakshmi Shankar
Ravi Shankar
Walter Scharf
Dianne Schurr
George Shearing
Roberta Sherwood
Raymond Shiner
David Shire
Leo Shuken
Judee Sill
Alan Silvestri
Carly Simon
Paul Simon
Frank Sinatra
Nancy Sinatra
Singers Unlimited
Frank Skinner
Felix Slatkin
Michael Small
Bruce Smeaton
Keely Smith
Paul Smith
Smothers Brothers
Mark Snow
Richie Snyder
Terry Snyder
Joanie Sommers
Sonny And Cher
Phil Specter
Dusty Springfield
Dick Stabile
Jo Stafford
Dakota Staton
Kay Starr
Fred Steiner
Max Steiner
Charles Stern

April Stevens
Connie Stevens
Morty Stevens
Risë Stevens
Rod Stewart
Georgie Stoll
Morris Stoloff
Richard Stone
Billy Strange
Igor Stravinsky
Barbra Streisand
L Subramaniam
Supremes
Ralph Sutton
T-Bone Walker
TakShindo
John Tartaglia
Grady Tate
Duane Tatro
Steven Taylor
Nino Tempo
Tom Tedesco
Toni Tennille
Mike Theodore
Jean ("Toots") Thielmans
Ed Thigpen
Danny Thomas
Ken Thorne
Michael Tilson Thomas
Tiny Tim
George Tipton
Cal Tjader
Curry Tjader
Mel Torme
Toto
John Tropea
Tanya Tucker
Johnny Ukulele
Richie Valens
Art Van Damme

Dick Van Dyke
Dante Varela
Billy Vaughn
Sarah Vaughn
Bobby Vee
Ventures
Carlos Vidal
Johnny Vines
Vinx
Al Viola
Vogues
Wally Waddell
Tom Waits
Randy Waldman
Wendy Waldman
Shirley Walker
Benny Wallace
Rick Warren
Dionne Warwick
Sadeo Watanabe
Dennis Weaver
Jimmy Webb
Lawrence Welk
Fred Werner
Paul Weston
Bob Wilbur
Will Mastin Trio
Andy Williams
John Williams
Larry Williams
Pat Williams
Paul Williams
Roger Williams
Flip Wilson
Jackie Wilson
Nancy Wilson
Jimmy Witherspoon
Scott Wojahn
Arthur Wright
Gary Wright

Glen Yarbrough
Lee Young
Frank Zappa
Si Zentner
Hans Zimmer
Harry Zuckerman

There isn't something special to say about every one of the 700-plus artists with whom I've played with in the last 52 years, but as I go over this list I would like to mention a few who I found exceptional as musicians and as important people in my musical life, who left a lasting impression on me and/or my musicianship and who have become lasting friends to me and my family.

Alex Acuna is a great drummer and percussionist from Peru. We have worked together for many years on movies with Michael Giacchino and with other leading composers and musicians. In 2010 and again in 2011, we worked together on *John Carter of Mars*, *Super Eight*, *Cars 2*, *UP*, *Star Trek: the Prelude*, and *Land of the Lost*. Whenever we can both work together on a project, it is a joy for each of us.

Airto Moreira is another great Brazilian musician that I worked alongside on live concerts and recording sessions back in the 1970s.

I first met Toshiko Akiyoshi in 1955, when I was stationed in a U.S. Army Band in Sendai, Japan and she was playing with her quartet in a club in Tokyo. There was a vibraphone belonging to a player from the other band playing opposite her group, so I got up and started playing with her in the middle of her set. We became fast friends and I played with her whenever I could get a break from my army duties during the year and a half that I was stationed in the First Cavalry Band.

David Allen was one of the first singers I got to work with when I moved to LA in 1959. He was from Connecticut, as I was, and we became fast friends. You could not help but love his great voice.

The marvelous dancer and choreographer Debbie Allen provided plenty of glamour when she came to the rehearsals for some Academy Award Shows.

Laurendo Almeida was one of the first guitar players I got to work with in the Hollywood recording studios in the 1960s and 1970s. He was a member of Shelly Manne's "LA 4," and we played together on a lot of South American projects.

I got to work with Herb Alpert on a lot of his early projects in the LA area, including working with Herb and Tom Tedesco in the Baja Marimba Band concerts at many LA venues. When the band began selling a lot of the early records we played on, Herb asked if we would go on the road with the band, but we were quite busy in the recording studios and we suggested some other musicians for the tour.

In the 1970s I recorded a lot with Ed Ames, one of the Ames Brothers, playing on all their records and Ed's solo works. He was busy as an actor, and his brothers all became famous as singers as well.

Francisco Aquabella was one of the greatest conga players in the world. He and I both had our sons born around the same time in 1958. We played together a lot during that time, so I became godfather for his son Mario, and he became godfather for my son Emilio at the same time. We remained friends and played together many times through the years until his death in 2010. He was also one of Cuba's most influential Bata drum players.

Leo Arno was the orchestrator for all of Maurice Jarre's scores, especially the score to *Doctor Zhivago*. Leo wrote a section in that movie for 25 of us playing snare drums in one scene, and Leo played snares right along with us. He was a great writer, and a great player as well.

Mitchell Ayres and I first met and worked together in New York in 1956, where I did many record dates that he wrote for, especially with Perry Como and the Ray Charles Singers.

In his early years, Burt Bacharach recorded at A&M Records and I played on many of his big hits, often with Dionne Warwick. Burt used to bring his own little, inexpensive speakers into the sessions. He said, "If it sounds good on my little, inexpensive speakers, then I know it will sound good on the better speakers in people's homes"–a lesson well learned.

Buddy Baker was the head of music at Disney Studios in the 1960s, and I was able to work on many of the Disney cartoons that he wrote for in those days. I also played and used many of my ethnic collected instruments on all the music that he wrote for the Disneyland ride *It's A Small World*. Buddy was a special person and a very musical talent.

H. B. Barnum was one of the most talented musicians that I have ever come across. He could play every instrument in the orchestra, and on many record sessions would pick up many different instruments and play along with us on any number of tunes. He loved music and had a grasp for any and every instrument in the orchestra. Since I play vibraphone, which isn't all that common of an orchestral instrument, I asked him to play my part on a recording we were doing, and to my surprise he picked up my mallets and played it flawlessly. What a remarkable talent!

John Barry was a talented English composer, and I must have played on every score that he ever wrote. He would play a two, four, eight, or sixteen-bar musical phrase and then repeat it right after playing it. This was his unique style, and I don't know of any other composer that I ever worked with that used that technique.

Working with Count Basie was just marvelous, and I got to work with him on two albums that we did with Frank Sinatra, one we called "Frank and Splank." I also accompanied Frank Sinatra performing live with Basie's band in Las Vegas on three occasions. Frank loved singing with the Basie band, and it made him want to sing and swing every single night.

The Beach Boys, in the early days, never played instruments behind their vocals. A group of recording musicians became nicknamed "The Wrecking Crew," and we did all the early recordings of the Beach Boys and lots of other groups I'll get to. I played tambourine and timpani on all the early records of the Beach Boys, and I would like to think that because of our playing, that we contributed to their having so many "hit" records.

Johnny Beecher was a pseudonym for Plas Johnson. Plas was under contract with another label and wanted to put a couple of albums out that his company was not ready to commit to, so we went in and recorded some great music with Plas using the name Johnny Beecher. Plas Johnson, in my opinion, is one of the best tenor sax players in the world.

Louis Bellson was a dear friend and one of the greatest drummers in the world. I met Louie when I first got to LA in 1959, and indirectly he was the first one responsible for my beginning to collect musical instruments. Louie had a set of Boo Bams, and he said he had used them only once and someone gave them to him, and that he wanted me to have them. A few months later we were doing a record session together, and I said, "Louie, that cymbal sounds great." He unscrewed it from his cymbal stand and handed it to me. He was the most generous, giving person I have ever met. We worked on an album together in 1959, and he said, "Emil do you have a song we can play on this album?" He gave me the composer's rights on that song, the first royalty payment that I had ever received. There have rarely been any human beings as kind or generous than Louie Bellson.

Elmer Bernstein was one of Hollywood's prime composers, and I was fortunate to play on many of his scores. Elmer did not like the "powers that be" to come on the stage when we were recording and bother him with musical changes. On many occasions the director or producer would stop the recording, as they do on most composers' scoring, and want to make immediate changes right on the spot. Elmer would say, "Gentlemen, you hired me to write the score, and I have written a score. Please allow me the opportunity to record the score you hired me to write, and if you don't like the finished product, you can pay me for my efforts and *then* I will listen to your new, or changed opinions." It was an approach I never saw any other composer take.

Near the beginning of Blondie's recording career, Debbie Harry called me in and told me she really liked marimba and wanted to use it on a lot of her recordings. We then recorded one of her hits, "The Tide is High." She was great to work with and a very musical artist.

I worked very often with Willie Bobo, one of the finest Latin timbale players, recording many times with him along with Mongo Santamaria and Armando Peraza. We also played live very often when I was on the road with the George Shearing Quintet in the 1950s, and I learned many of the Afro-Cuban beats and phrases from him.

Jimmy Bond and I first met in 1957 when he replaced Al McKibbon on bass with the George Shearing Quintet. I learned the business side of being a musician from Jimmy. When we moved to LA, he got heavily into producing and also the real estate market, and became very successful.

I did all of Pat Boone's recordings in the 1960s. He had a great natural singing voice, and he never looked like he aged. He seemed like a very religious person, and always respected everyone he came in contact with.

Jim Bowen became the A and R man for Frank Sinatra's record company, Reprise Records. I think he came from Nashville and we all thought he wouldn't know how to lead a record company, but he proved to be very talented and chalked up gold records for many of the artists on Sinatra's label.

I was fortunate to record many of the records with Sergio Mendez and Brazil 66, all the way up to Brazil 88. He is a fine musician and a great person, and I learned a lot about his country's music from playing with him.

The great Western actor Walter Brennan came to the record studios quite often in the 1960s to narrate stories on record while we played behind his speaking voice. It was a thrill to be around such a great actor, and we all marveled at the timing and concept he had for the written voice in a musical setting.

Allen Broadbent is a great pianist from Down Under, and I had a chance to work together with him quite often in the recording studios. Besides being a great jazz pianist, Allen went on to accompany some of the finest singers in the business and conducted for them as well. His jazz concepts and feeling were always impressive to hear.

When I first met Bruce Broughton at CBS Studio Center, he was a copyist working on many TV shows. He later became a composer of many great scores to films and TV shows that came out of the Hollywood studios, and is still active and teaches at the film school at USC.

I first met the legendary bassist Ray Brown when he first moved to LA in the early 1960s and came into the recording studios. Ray had a nickname for everyone, and I became the "dipper" since he said I was always dipping into other percussionists' cases to see what they had, and what I needed to acquire.

We worked together on many TV shows and all the movies that Quincy Jones had written for, as well as most of the movies and TV shows that came out of Universal Studios through the 1970s and 1980s.

I first met and worked behind Lenny Bruce when I first moved to LA in 1959. We worked at a club on the Sunset strip called the Renaissance Club. Lenny would get arrested almost every weekend for his risqué language, but he loved musicians and he always wanted a jazz group playing behind his act.

Billy Byers was a major trombone player in the studios when I first got to LA in 1959. He was also one of the best big band jazz arrangers out there, and was also busy playing and writing. He loved vibes and wrote parts for me on many of the TV shows that came out of Universal Studios in the 1960s and 1970s. I would count him as one of the most gifted big band jazz writers to come out of Los Angeles.

Glen Campbell first came to LA as a guitar player, though he didn't read music very well back in the days when there were five to eight guitar players at every session. At the first run-through, Glen would sit quietly and listen to the song being rehearsed. On the second run-through, he would strap on the guitar and play the arrangement from memory. He memorized every song after the first time he heard it, which we found amazing. He played in the studios for only a few years before he branched out to become a great big singing star. He not only had a great voice, but he is a great instrumentalist as well and I'm proud to say remained friends for many years.

I was in on many of the Carpenters', and also the Captain and Tennille's, early hits. In those days we just recorded maybe three to four record sessions a day, and never stopped to consider that we were making such hit records. Both these groups became quite popular, and as a member of the Wrecking Crew I was in on all of them, averaging 15 to 19 record sessions a week.

I was also called for many of the Vikki Carr recordings. She took her singing very seriously, and on many occasions during the session you could look over and see her crying. If it was a sad song, the lyric would get to her and as she was singing, tears would be streaming down her face. It was inspiring to see someone take her work so seriously.

One of the first alto sax players I got to work with in LA was Benny Carter. He also was serious about his music, and his sound was legendary. He was a gentleman in every sense of the word. Everyone at Capitol Records loved him for his playing and for his writing. We became quite close and I remember saying, when he was in his mid-90s, that he had continued to sound better and better as he got older.

Although I got to record on some of Ray Charles' more famous latter recordings, I played much more with the other Ray Charles, the singer/composer/choral leader, recording a lot with his Ray Charles Singers while in New York City in 1959. He was very busy in those days with that singing group, and I got to play on a lot of the TV specials he did with Perry Como and Mitch Ayres.

I first met Don Cherry when he and Ornette Coleman formed their first quartet in LA in 1959. My old army buddy Don Payne was playing bass with them on their very first rehearsals, and I used to go and hang at their house during the beginning of that famous group's early formation. Don and Ornette were revelatory musicians and started a new movement of semi-free playing, along with some very difficult written music. It was a great learning experience for me to sit in on the group's early formation.

I recorded many of the Nat King Cole Trio recordings he made at Capitol Records in the 1970s along with a large orchestra. Nat was a great musician as well as a great singer, and I never heard him make a mistake while recording. He may have forgotten a lyric on a song, but never messed up musically in all the years that I recorded with him. Once Nat was doing a show that was going to Broadway with Barbara McNair, and during the rehearsals in LA Nat asked me to open the show in San Francisco with him. All went well, and the show left for a cross-country series of dates before opening on Broadway. I came back to LA after San Francisco since I was getting very busy in the studios. Sadly, the show never made it to Broadway and closed in Milwaukee, but it wasn't because of Nat, a truly great singer and pianist, that the show didn't make it.

I was in on most of the early recordings for Natalie Cole. She has a great talent like her father, inheriting some of his musical abilities like the same easy-going style and great musical pitch. I played on the duets recordings she made with tapes of her dad, with "Unforgettable" being the most famous.

Michel Colombier was a young French composer who had perfect pitch. He used to come by my house to get the range of all of my unusual percussion instruments to catalog for his writing needs. He had me play the whole range of each instrument and he would write down their ranges. This was way before I had a catalog listing all my instruments with their ranges. It was because of him that I started to put the Rangefinder catalog of all my instruments together (which is included in this book).

When I first got out of the Army in 1955, I moved to New York City and met Chris Connor, working for her around New York and the Jersey shore. She loved vibes, and had me play and do her recordings during that period until I left to go on the road with the George Shearing band.

I first worked with Bill Conti on the very first *Rocky* film and have since played on every film Conti has scored. He has great musical taste and his writing is more in the classical style of the early opera composers, with melody lines always singable. Bill always surrounded himself with the best musicians in Hollywood, and his writing for them was always top-notch. I also played on twelve or so Academy Award shows that Bill Conti composed for and conducted.

I also played on every one of the major scores that Don Costa wrote when he moved to LA from New York City; he soon became the musical director and head writer for Frank Sinatra and Reprise Records. He had a great musical sense and a very melodious concept in his writing.

I first met Michael Craden when I first moved to LA in the spring of 1959. Michael had just gotten out of art school and he wanted to play music, so he gave me art lessons and I gave him vibraphone lessons. We put together a free-form musical group called A. H. A. (the Aesthetic Harmony Assemblage), playing weekends over two years at the Cosmic Star Auditorium on Santa Monica Boulevard. People either loved or hated our free-form playing and abstract painting, and I acquired many of Michael's paintings through the years. Michael moved to Toronto and became a member of the now-famed NEXUS musical ensemble, collecting strange and microtonal instruments to use in their performances.

I played on most of the Academy Award shows that Billy Crystal emceed, as well as some of his records and his TV specials. He is always funny and fun to work with; he loves musicians and likes to be treated as if he were one of us.

Hoyt Curtin (the uncle of *Saturday Night Live* comedian Jane Curtin) wrote all the cartoon music for Hanna-Barbera, including *Yogi Bear*, *Huckleberry Hound*, and all those other popular shows. Millions of people know his music though few know his name, and I was fortunate to play on most of those shows for many years. Aside from being a great writer for cartoons, which takes a special skill, Hoyt loved to play jazz; before every session he would sit at the piano and have us join him in a 10- to 15-minute jam session prior to recording, and then again after the session was over. This made those sessions memorable and great fun.

Robert Davi is an actor typecast in gangster roles, yet he is the closest singer to Sinatra that I have ever worked with. Since 2011, Robert has asked me to play with him whenever he goes out around LA and to Las Vegas to sing. He is now famous and popular as an actor, and determined to do the same in his singing career. His first movie, when he was 20 years old, was with Sinatra, and he now wants to carry on the Sinatra banner. I feel he has what it takes to come as close as anyone to fill Sinatra's huge shoes.

I played on many of the recordings that Sammy Davis, Jr., one of the greatest entertainers I ever worked with, made in the 1960s and 1970s. He could sing, dance, and act with the same ease in each area, always entertaining and a pleasure to be around. He used to also pick up different musical instruments and play them as if that was the only thing he did his whole life. I once walked into the famous Sy Devore clothing store to buy a tuxedo, and they sold me a tux that Sammy had ordered but never picked up. At that time his tux fit me perfectly, and I wore it for many years.

One tour that's hard to forget came with the George Shearing Quintet and Miles Davis, John Coltrane, Cannonball Adderley, Wynton Kelly, Paul Chambers, and Philly Joe Jones, as well as the Gerry Mulligan Quartet with Chet Baker, Donald Bailey, and Whitey Mitchell. It was the dead of winter in 1958, doing one-nighters on a bus. Most musicians got sick on that tour, so there were nights when we pooled all the healthy guys in the three groups and played with just one larger group for the whole evening. This was a highlight of my "road" days, and something I will remember for the rest of my life.

French composer Georges Delerue loved percussion, and when we did a film with him you could be sure there would be lots of unusual percussion sounds written into the scores. He often came to the warehouse where I kept all my exotic percussion instruments and we'd play on them for hours, getting the sounds he liked to inject into his writing for films.

Martin Denny had a group of musicians that played music from the South Sea Islands, and when he came to Los Angeles he'd call me to record on his albums because he loved all the exotic percussion I had in my collection. He would send me his tapes and asked me to select some of the exotic instruments I had in my collection to use on his albums. It was great to receive that kind of freedom to add interesting sounds to his ensemble.

John Denver would fly his private plane to record with some of us in the LA area, and I worked on most of his albums. He had a genuine folk quality which made it fun to work with him, and it was a tragedy when he lost his life flying in that plane.

George Harrison called me one day and said his close friend Donovan would be calling me to record on his new album. He had asked George for the names of musicians in the LA area he should call to record with, and George gave him my name. We had a lot of memorable times recording and spending time with him when he would visit LA

I first met George Duke, a highly talented musician and composer, through working with Frank Zappa. When George asked me to play mallets on some of his albums I was thrilled, as he usually used Ruth Underwood, who was Frank Zappa's star mallet player and a superb musician, and it was gratifying that he called me to record on some of his albums as well.

George Duning was one of the first film composers I had a chance to work with when I first got to LA I had been doing records and TV shows, and when I got a call to play on some of his film scores I felt that I had really made it in this town.

I started working on more film scores back when Jerry Fielding was writing films that Clint Eastwood starred in. I'm proud to say that I have worked on most of Clint's scores since the 1970s. He works very fast, and he knows what he likes and what he wants in the music department. It is now 2012, and in the last four or five years Clint has been playing piano and composing most of the music on his films. His son Kyle is also a very talented musician, and aside from his playing string bass on all of Clint's film scores, his dad has been letting him compose some of the music for his films. The Warner Bros. recording sound stage was about to close down until Clint insisted that he wanted to record his scores only on the Warner Bros. recording stage, so they put in a brand new recording board and brought it up to very modern standards. It has now been renamed the Clint Eastwood Recording Sound Stage.

I can honestly say that I have recorded on every score that Danny Elfman ever worked on in America. He led the group Oingo Boingo, breaking up that band to concentrate solely on film scoring. He has consistently gotten better and better as a composer, and I can say that he is one of my all-time favorite composers of film scoring. His collection of ethnic percussion instruments is now much larger than mine. He has one of the best grasps of film score writing than anyone else in this town or anywhere else in the world, and seems to get better with every project he takes on.

Jack Elliott was a pianist from my hometown back in Hartford, Connecticut, and we worked together on many projects here in LA He and Allyn Ferguson were composing partners for many TV shows, including *"Charlie's Angels,"* and I played for them for all the years that show—and many others—and also worked with them on a concert series that lasted for a few years here in LA called The New American Orchestra. This was a series held at the Dorothy Chandler Hall and featured the new symphonic works of some of America's leading film and jazz composers.

Don Ellis and I were both studying East Indian music and formed a group called the Hindustani Jazz Sextet, at a time when it was quite difficult to find musicians interested in playing jazz in odd time rhythms. We found a few players who became dedicated to playing this type of music, and were the first ones to implement odd rhythms into our playing. It was a time of exploring music and rhythms for both of us, and it really enhanced our continued musicianship through the years.

Jerry Fielding wrote great music for films, and it was extremely hard to play. Most composers realize that there is just so much time allotted for recording the score for a film and therefore don't write music so difficult that it would take longer than the time allotted to record. Jerry Fielding didn't care; his music was hard, and he expected you to play it. For this reason, Jerry insisted on the best musicians available on all his sessions, and I am proud to say that I was one of the musicians that played on most of his scores.

I loved Ella Fitzgerald's singing, and feel fortunate to have been able to play on most of the recordings she made with Nelson Riddle arranging and conducting in LA It was a thrill to go to Las Vegas several times with a band that played with her and Frank Sinatra at Caesar's Palace.

Ernie Freeman was already a famous piano player doing record dates by the time I first moved to LA in 1959. By 1960 he was writing the arrangements we recorded behind Jan and Dean, the Everly Brothers, the Mamas and the Papas, the Jackson Five, the Fifth Dimension, Petula Clark, and Marvin Gaye, to name just a few. I worked with Ernie on record dates for more than ten years, and I considered him a great musician.

Hugo Friedhofer was one of the older composers in Hollywood when I arrived; perhaps not a great conductor, but a superb musician. One technique I learned from him was that, on a chase scene, if the orchestra was playing very fast and the action on the screen came to an abrupt stop, he would put a triplet on the note when you wanted the orchestra to slow down, and this would stop your orchestras fast pace right away. We first met when he was working with composer Earle Hagen in music for the Mod Squad and I Spy TV series.

Everyone loved Judy Garland, who was one of the great legends in Hollywood. I worked on all of her TV specials and never tired of hearing her sing with that strong, always in-tune voice, belting out a song more powerfully than anyone else could. After many songs you could see tears streaming down her face, and I honestly believe she took her craft more seriously than almost any performer I have ever worked with.

Jerry Goldsmith was one of the most prolific composers to come out of Hollywood, and we worked together on almost every one of his films. Jerry loved coming to my warehouse and picking out percussion instruments that most composers had ever heard of, and then using them in his scores. He was the first composer to ever use metal salad bowls as a musical instrument—a sound that became famous when the apes entered in the original Planet of the Apes.

When Merv Griffin first moved to LA from New York around 1970, he brought his whole variety show out with him and formed his own orchestra. I was asked to be the percussionist on his show, and I did the show five times a week. We would record three shows one day and two the next, so it didn't interfere with most of the other work I was doing at that time. I soon got so busy doing movies that I stayed on that show less than a year; after that, it was mostly film work for me.

What a great musician and wonderful person George Harrison was! I met and started playing with George around 1970, and found he loved Indian music.

In fact, he loved all music. He was one of the most serious musicians I've ever met and yet also had a very comical streak that most people did not know about him. We became close from the time we first met until he died. George always had an instrument in his hands, and music was an essential part of his life. We also both practiced Transcendental Meditation, and this brought us closer. It was a joy to play with him and to spend time with him in LA, England, and on our Dark Horse tour through America in 1974 with Ravi Shankar, Tom Scott, Jim Keltner, Willie Weeks, and Billy Preston. His wife Olivia and my wife Celeste also became good friends, so it was a joy whenever the four of us could spend time together.

Jack Hayes was half of the team of Leo Shuken and Jack Hayes, two of the best orchestrators to come out of the LA talent pool. I played their arrangements from the early 1960s and many of Jack's right up to the end of 2011 when Jack, who outlived Leo, passed away while still orchestrating for Michael Giacchino. They orchestrated for all the best composers who came out of Hollywood, from Jerry Goldsmith to Lalo Schifrin.

I got to record for Michael Jackson from the time he was a small boy with the Jackson 5 up until, as a grown man, he was recording all his own hits. During those times, we would have to sign a contract that we would not disclose anything that went on in the recording studio during his recording sessions. It was a pleasure to play on his recordings because he was a joy to play for, and he greatly appreciated everything the musicians added to his famous hits.

J. J. Johnson, one of the most celebrated jazz trombone players, decided to make LA his home sometime in the 1970s and along with Earle Hagen, began to compose for TV assignments. He stayed out here for about ten years, writing for many TV shows, and it was a pleasure to be called to play on most of his very well-written scores; he brought some spice and some very hip writing to the Hollywood television scene. He eventually moved back to New York and I missed him, and his writing, greatly.

Everyone in the LA recording studios liked the mega-talented Quincy Jones. I first met Quincy in the mid to late 1950s when I was on the road with the George Shearing Quintet, and we have been friends for all these years; I've played on just about every film score Quincy ever wrote, and a lot of record sessions that he wrote and or conducted on. I would say that everyone who has ever met Quincy has been, and remained, his friend. He saw an early draft of this book and said, "There are a lot of similarities between us, and mentions of so many musicians we have known and worked with."

George Harrison also told composer Michael Kamen to look me up when he came to LA, and I believe I played on every one of his scores from that time on until his death in 2003. Michael was also an accomplished oboe player and he and loved to go into the double-reed section and play with all the great musicians of the orchestra. I miss him as much as any of the musicians and friends that I have known and played with in my musical life.

Canadian composer Eddie Karam and I met in the early 1960s, and he wrote the charts for some of my own records. He has a great understanding of the odd time rhythms that I utilized in my albums. He is now orchestrating for John Williams' films and has written and contributed some terrific big band charts for my 17-piece jazz orchestra.

Drummer Jim Keltner and I first worked together in the early 1970s when we did recordings with George Harrison, then on the 1974 Dark Horse tour. Jim's concept comes from a solid jazz background, and he is known as one of the oldest rock-and-roll drummers still on the scene today. We, and our wives, have remained very close and see each other often. Although Jim does not like to travel much anymore, he is one of the most sought-after drummers still on the scene in 2012.

Robert Kraft has become the head of the music department at 20th Century-Fox Studios. We share a love for Thelonius Monk and his music, and each of us tries to find stories about Monk that the other may not have heard. He is a unique musician, and he has a great knowledge of everybody you can imagine in the music business. Every time I am at Fox I make it a point to stop in on Robert Kraft to find out something about music that I may not know, because he is always full of great stories about so many of music's diverse personalities.

Michel Legrand is one of the finest musicians I know, an incredibly dedicated musician and simply tops in his craft. He has such a great way of presenting his ideas and comments to an orchestra, and he'll often sing your part as a way of explaining what he is trying to get across. I love to hear him rehearse an orchestra, as it's a joy to hear him sing all the different parts as he goes around the orchestra demonstrating, in song, how he would like each part interpreted.

Henry Mancini was surely one of the most likeable composers to work with, and he had a genuine, wonderful sense of humor. He loved jazz and always tried to incorporate it in his music. He was one of the first film composers to incorporate songs into his scores and many of them are still standards, perhaps the most famous of them being "Moon River." Henry set a high standard that is still recognized after all these years.

Johnny Mandel is universally regarded as the musician's musician. In most popular song writing, it's very common to rewrite and re-harmonize some of the chords that the original composer used in his score. If you play the melody and the chords that Johnny Mandel wrote, you can never get any better than that. His harmonic writing was the best of any composer that I ever worked with, with the finest innate sense of melody and harmony. It was often said that if you played what Johnny had written, it would be better than anything else anyone else could come up with. The proof is in the many beautiful songs he has left the world.

Shelly Manne was one of the most accomplished drummers to play on film scores, since every composer in town would ask for Shelly to play on their score. He was the most giving and receptive drummer for everyone's writing. He was even given his own series that ran for about six years that I played on, and used, a lot of my collection of African instruments. Shelly not only wrote all the music for that show and conducted it, but also played percussion with us in that section as well. He had such a great sense of timing that it is understandable why drummers and percussionists make great composers.

I am proud to say that I played on most of Dean Martin's recording sessions and most of his TV specials; he was always a delight to work with, as he made everything fun and enjoyable. There were times when you were sure Dean had forgotten the lyrics to a song or a line in his dialogue, but he always came through. It constantly made me believe that Sinatra was right when he said, "Dino doesn't drink all that much, he just makes you think that he does. In fact, I spill more than Dean drinks." Those were Sinatra's words!

I worked on all the first recordings that Hugh Masekela sang when he first came to LA from Africa. He had a fresh and pleasing voice, played little African riffs on trumpet, and was liked by all the musicians from the very beginning of his coming to America.

I worked on most of the early hits that Johnny Mathis had as a singer with Allyn Ferguson writing most of those charts, and on a lot of TV specials that he did during that period. He may have missed a lyric on occasion, but his intonation and singing was right on the money every time.

Billy May was another musician's musician. He could write music for full orchestra faster than anyone that I had ever seen before or since. Billy had the biggest musical ears in the business, and he would write away from the piano as if it all came completely naturally to him. He would have a project assignment a week or two before a session, but he would choose to wait until the last minute to write the score and parts. He seemed to know that it would come out better if he waited until the last minute under pressure to motivate him to write a score for a recording session. He also loved to play trumpet and would often sit in and play along with the trumpet section on recording sessions. He loved to laugh and have a good time on sessions, and he made everyone comfortable and relaxed on every thing we did with him.

The Microtonal Blues Band was a group I started in the late 1960s. It was after meeting the iconic composer Harry Partch, who invented a scale with 43 tones to the octave in all his instruments, and he inspired me to form a jazz group with Dave Mackay on piano, Joe Porcaro on drums, Chuck Domanico on Bass, Don Ellis on quarter-tone trumpet, and me on quarter-tone xylophone and various microtonal instruments. We used to play at a club called Donte's, and recorded an album under that title. Those experimental days with microtonal instruments and scales, along with Indian rhythms, were great learning days for us all.

One of the funniest people I have ever known was Vic Mizzy, who wrote for *The Addams Family* and *Green Acres*, to mention just a few. His music was always enjoyable to play because he always came up with unusual sounds using the conventional orchestral instruments. I used to play vibes with a fuzz tone and a wah-wah pedal to create some comical underscoring for his shows. He was always open to trying new sounds for his scores, and I got to create some interesting instruments for his shows. One instrument that I invented for *The Addams Family* was the Water Chimes. These were 4 metal discs which, when struck, could be dipped into a trough of water which microtonally lowered their pitch.

The Italian composer Ennio Morricone became famous on this side of the Atlantic for all the spaghetti westerns that were filmed and recorded in Italy. Whenever he had an American film project, I was on his list to be called to work on his scores. I used to call him "the composer of many colors," as he would come up with the marrying of certain instruments that I had never before heard played together in that fashion. It is so gratifying to experience composers who go out of their way to come up with colors of sound that they can put their label on and call their own.

Sam Nestico is one of the most talented big band jazz writers in the world. I have played on the last three or four of his big band albums, and it's always a swinging pleasure to play those wonderful charts that Sammy writes. He likes adding vibes to his big band, so I am fortunate that he calls me to come to play on his albums. He can make any band swing hard by the great figures he writes for each section. I would go anywhere, or do anything, to play on a Sammy Nestico chart, especially with him up front conducting his own arrangement or composition.

The three Newman brothers that I had worked with were Alfred Newman, who was the legendary head of 20th Century-Fox Pictures; Emil Newman, his younger brother, who also wrote scores for films; and Lionel Newman, who became the head of music at Fox when Alfred passed away. All three brothers were great film composers, and I got to work with all three of them. The first film I worked on when I arrived in LA in 1959 was at 20th Century-Fox, on Alfred Newman's *The Diary of Anne Frank*, with much more of his work to come. Lionel also conducted for most of the films that Jerry Goldsmith scored for Fox. These three highly-musical brothers also had great singing voices, and would correct their music by singing some of the parts to the members of the orchestra as they directed and interpreted each section' parts. More recently, I've worked on scores written and conducted by Alfred's two sons and daughter, David, Thomas, and Maria Newman, who are also highly accomplished film scorers. Their nephew Randy Newman is another major film composer, best known for his Toy Story scores and a long list of other accomplishments. It was a unique experience to have been associated with this gifted family.

I worked on most of James Newton Howard's many scores in the 1980s and 1990s. What I loved about working with James was that he had someone else, like Artie Kane, conduct, so that he could sit in the booth with the score, listen to the music being recorded, and make corrections and additions from the booth. He gets a great deal accomplished with this method, which gives him complete control of the entire orchestra from the booth. He is one of the most prolific of today's Hollywood film composers, and every score of his has always been a gem. Of all the composers in Hollywood, I miss recording on his scores the most.

Marty Paich was one of the first composers that I worked for when I moved to Hollywood. He was writing for Shorty Rogers' big band, which I became a member of when I first moved to LA in 1959. I also played extensively for Marty on his many TV projects and recordings. Marty wrote most of the orchestrations for Sarah Vaughan, and he used me on vibes for most of those sessions. He was one of the true big band jazz writers to come out of the West Coast.

I learned the most after music school when I met the composer Harry Partch. His unique instruments were all microtonal and self-built, and he had many of us learn to play them. His system was based on 43 tones to the octave, and his harmonies and rhythms were quite different than any that I had ever heard before in my life. I quickly became a disciple of his music and instruments and sponsored his move from Petaluma to Los Angeles and did all I could to present him and his music to the film composers of Hollywood. Three prominent composers that were interested in his theories were David Raksin, Lalo Schifrin, and Frank Zappa. I introduced many percussionists to Partch and his music, and we rehearsed at his studio in Venice, California, and performed concerts of his works at UCLA and at the Whitney Museum of Art in New York. I remained close to Partch and his music until his death on September 3, 1974. Harry had willed half of his instruments to me, but at the time, I had a large collection of my own ethnic instruments and felt they would be better served to remain together rather than to be split up between Danlee Mitchell and me.

I played for Luciano Pavarotti on his movie *Yes, Georgio*, and found him to be one of the most impressive artists that I ever had the pleasure to work with. On several days during work on the movie, he felt a cold coming on and insisted on staying in a separate studio at 20th Century-Fox where we were recording the music. He was very cautious not to abuse his famous throat in any way, referring to it as his instrument. After he was sure the cold symptoms had passed, he came into the recording studio with the rest of the musicians and finished recording his part of the score. I found him to be a dear, friendly man and a tremendous talent.

When I was first discharged from the Army in 1956, I moved to New York City and did a lot of casuals with Flip Phillips, working out on Long Island with Charles Mingus and Ed Shaughnessy. Flip was one of the people to encourage me to move to LA and to get into the Hollywood film studios. He said that playing jazz was great, but the big bucks in the 1950s was in becoming a studio musician and doing all sorts of recording sessions. It took a few years of playing on the road and doing gigs in New York before I eventually decided to move to LA and get into the film studios.

I have known Joe Porcaro since I was in first grade around 1938. We played in a band during grammar school and faked our age, playing in clubs during junior high school. We both joined the Hartford Symphony when I was in 10th grade. Our quartet played around Hartford from the time I was 16 until I got drafted when I turned 22. A few years after I moved to LA, I convinced Joe to move out to California with his family. I was the godfather of his first son, Jeff, and still see Joe and all his family socially at least once a week. We have been playing in the studios, and with our jazz group, in clubs around LA throughout all these years, and we are still doing so in 2012. Joe has been my longest and closest friend these last 75 years.

I worked for and with Shorty Rogers from the time I first moved to LA in 1959, playing on all his recordings and with his big band. Shorty was a very spiritual man and a great composer and trumpet player, and I learned humility from him. He was kind and respectful to every human being. He became a close friend and I looked up to him for his humbleness as well as his great musical abilities. We spent many hours talking about music on the phone and whenever we got together, which was often.

I worked on most of Leonard Rosenman's film scores, finding him to be a master writer and conductor. His scores were always very interesting to play, because he had a great knack for writing for percussion and always wrote interesting parts for me and the members of the percussion section.

When the famous Italian classical composer Nino Rota, who also wrote the scores to all the Federico Fellini films, *Romeo and Juliet*, and *The Godfather* epic came to LA, I was fortunate to be asked to play on his scores. He was such a great conductor, and so easy to follow, that we usually followed his baton and didn't use the click-tracks through headphones as we did with most conductors.

Pete Rugolo was an excellent composer who loved brass, and most of his writing was with a lot of loud brass. Shelly Manne was his favorite drummer and he took a liking to me on percussion, so I got to work on almost everything that he ever wrote on the LA scene. He was not only a talented composer, but one of the sharpest dressers on the scene.

Alla Rakha was Ravi Shankar's tabla player, and I had the opportunity to play on many concerts with him and Ravi. I learned so much about Indian music and rhythms from hanging out with him whenever I could on the tours we made together. I would try to sit next to him on many airplane flights, and keep pencil and paper handy, because Alla would get up in the middle of the night and start reciting great rhythm cycles, and I was always ready to write them down. If you asked him to repeat what he sang, he would always give you a different one, so you had to be ready to get it right the first time!

Lalo Schifrin is another composer who loves percussion and often uses strange and exotic percussion sounds on all his scores. He also likes to use the string section as a percussion group, with the percussion section bowing on percussion instruments essentially becoming the string section. Lalo is one of the most inventive composers that I have ever performed for, always looking for new and unusual sounds and unique sounding instruments in everything that he composes. I love his music and his keen awareness of the different sounds that can be gotten out of an orchestra. I have performed on virtually every score that Lalo has written.

After the Army I moved to New York to work in the studios and got a call to go on the road with the famous George Shearing jazz quintet. The blind, British-born George had moved to the U.S. and formed one of the only groups that used a vibraphone. I was fortunate to get the call to join his quintet, traveling for three years to what seemed like every jazz club, college, and concert hall across the U.S. It was a great experience to begin a career playing with such a well-recognized jazz group from mid-1956 to the spring of 1959.

Frank Sinatra was certainly the greatest singer and performer that I have ever worked for, and I travelled with him on and off from 1959 to 1972. He was easy to work for and we traveled the entire world on many occasions with a six-piece combo, as well as performing with the Count Basie Orchestra on many occasions. Aside from playing in a small band and a large jazz band with Sinatra, I also worked on all his movies, his TV shows, and for his record company, Reprise, in all their artists' recording sessions.

One of the legendary Golden Age film composers that I had heard about when growing up in Hartford was the great Max Steiner, so it was something special to actually work with him on one of his last scores, *Two on a Guillotine*, in 1965. He was as impressive as I had imagined and found, through him, that the bigger the name, the nicer the person. What a thrill it was to work with one of the most accomplished of all the film composers.

Cal Tjader and I both played the same instrument, so it was not too likely that we could get to work together. But after he left George Shearing's Group and I took over, he decided to form his own Latin jazz band with different composers writing pieces for him to record. He asked me to come into the studio to play and record all the written charts, and he would improvise on the chord changes on top of the written-out parts that I had played. I had been in an army band with Cal's brother Curry in Japan in the early 1950s, and that's how I came to know Cal. We became good friends, and after I came to LA, after leaving the Shearing group, we recorded his first albums together.

When I first met John Williams, he was a pianist in the Hollywood film studios. I had worked with his dad, John Sr., who was a percussionist at Columbia Pictures. When John T. started to write scores for films, I got to play on most of his sound tracks. John is one of the most brilliant composers in the history of film music and I worked with him on most of his scores. He has two younger brothers, Don and Jerry, who are both outstanding timpanists and who naturally are first to be called for his sessions. John is one of our most beloved American composers, who has developed and honed his craft more brilliantly than any living musician on the scene today.

APPENDIX 2: DRUMMERS I HAVE WORKED WITH

I am going to begin way back in 1938 (so some of my dates from memory might be slightly inaccurate), and I hope I don't offend any drummer-friends that I have overlooked. My intention is to name as many drummers as I can with whom I have come in contact in my musical career.

I was six years old when I met my oldest and dearest friend, Joe Porcaro, in September of 1938. I ran into Joe on the first day of school, playing his drumsticks on the sidewalk of the grammar school playground. Pushing through the crowd of kids he attracted, I introduced myself, told him that I played xylophone, and that we should get together and play. Well, we've been getting together to play ever since.

One of my earliest teachers at this period was Adolf Cardello, a drum and mallet teacher in my hometown of Hartford, Connecticut. Whenever the big band drummers came through town they would come to visit my teacher at his studio, so in the late Thirties I got to meet and hear Gene Krupa, Cozy Cole, Gus Johnson, Don Lamond, and Lionel Hampton, who was as fine a drummer as he was a great vibe player. I grew up on "Hamp" and his vibe playing, and would play on marimba along with his vibe solos on records. My neighborhood was like a little Harlem, and we had a big stage theater just like the famous Apollo. Whenever Hamp's band came to town, my mom would pack me a lunch and I would go to the theater at 11 in the morning, catching four or five stage shows of Lionel Hampton and his band. I knew the guys in his band would hang out and eat in my neighborhood, so I would put on Hamp's records really loud, open the window, and play marimba along with his albums, hoping he would hear me play.

When Joe and I were between 8 and 10 years old, our local priest started a band at our church. We got to read stock arrangements for big band, with Joe on drums, me on xylophone, and some brass- and reed-playing kids who have gone on to become professional musicians. One of our young friends in those kid bands was trombonist Wayne Andre.

While still too young to play in clubs, I would lie about my age to get to play with drummer Johnny Vines, who used to perform with all the Dixieland players. I got to play with guest artists who came through town to play with our group on weekends, and had the chance to play with musicians like Bobby Hackett, Jack Teagarten, Ralph Sutton, Joe Marsala, Wild Bill Davison, and Vic Dickerson, and sometimes Buzzy Drootin (who was born in Kiev, Ukraine) would come in from New York to play drums with us.

When I was in tenth grade, Alexander Lepak recommended me for the Hartford Symphony Orchestra. Arthur Fiedler from the Boston Pops was our guest conductor for that first season. Our section consisted of Joe Porcaro, Tele Lesbines (who has completed many seasons as timpanist with the Milwaukee Symphony), Al Lepak as principal timpanist, and me as mallet player with the orchestra. I stayed with the orchestra until completing two years of college, working under Maestros Moshe Paranov, George Heck, and Fritz Mahler.

In 1953, after my second year of college, I got drafted. I spent my two year army hitch in the First Cavalry army band, stationed in Japan. Curry Tjader, brother of Cal Tjader, was the drummer in our band. Curry practiced longer and harder than any drummer I've ever known. He also studied mallets with me in that band, and a few years later he joined the Baja Marimba Band as their bass marimba player. I met and played with Toshiko Akiyoshi, and one of Japan's leading sax players, Sadao Watanabe. When ever I had extra time in Tokyo, I met and played with drummer J. C. Heard, who was living in Japan at that time.

In 1955, as soon as I got out of the army, I moved to New York and met Ed Shaughnessy. We both studied with the same theory teacher, and he decided to study mallets with me. He had a gig on weekends out on Long Island and asked me to join his quartet, with Flip Phillips on tenor and Charlie Mingus on bass. I used to try to play so many notes on vibes, when taking my solos with Ed on drums, that Mingus used to yell out "Breathe! Breathe!" during my solos. He taught me a valuable lesson in those days, to use space in my playing.

I also met a studio drummer in NY by the name of Terry Snider, who liked my playing a lot and helped me to get studio recordings on mallets with Perry Como, Mitchell Ayres, and the Ray Charles Singers. In the evenings I would go out to New Jersey to play for Chris Connor. I know the bass player was Oscar Pettiford on some of those gigs, but I can't remember the drummer.

I also met Ed Thigpen in New York at this time. He was just getting off the road and decided to stay in town to be with his family and to study some vibes with me. Just at that time, I got a call from George Shearing to join his quintet. Ed Thigpen called as I was getting my things ready to leave for the road. He said, "I just turned the drum chair down with Shearing so I could stay close to my family, and to study vibes with you." I said, "Gee, Ed, I just accepted the vibe chair with Shearing, and I'm leaving on the road." To this day Ed tells me he wishes we both could have been together on that gig. I know he would be playing vibes as well as he plays drums, and that would be awesome.

As it turned out, Percy Brice was the drummer who joined Shearing's quintet at the same time I did. Armando Peraza was playing congas, and Al McKibbon was the bass player with the band. Al knew a lot about Afro-Cuban music and played good congas too, as he had been on the road with the first master of

Afro Cuban Conga players to come to America, Chano Pozo. They were both with Dizzy Gilespie's Orchestra. This was to become the greatest learning experience of Afro-Cuban music I would have for the rest of my life.

The Shearing band got to play together with many other bands on US tours, and one I'll never forget took place in the dead of winter. Our Shearing group played along with Miles Davis' band, which had John Coltrane, Cannonball Adderley, Paul Chambers, Wynton Kelly, and Philly Joe Jones on drums. The other groups were drummer Chico Hamilton and his group and Gerry Mulligan's group with Donald Bailey on drums. There was a bad flu epidemic, and our drummer Percy Brice was the first one to get sick. Chico Hamilton played with us for one night, then he got sick and drummer Donald Bailey from Mulligan's band got the bug. Philly Joe played drums in all the groups for a couple of nights. We ended up doing a few nights with a few players from each band making up just one band. It was a killer flu that year but I was thrilled to get to play with some of the best jazz players on the scene at that time.

After a couple of years with Shearing, Ray Mosca joined the band on drums and Jimmy Bond joined on bass. I stayed with the band for another year and a half and Armando Peraza introduced me to Mongo Santamaria and Willie Bobo, who were playing with Cal Tjader's Band. I got to record a couple of albums with them.

When I first moved to LA in 1959 the first musician I ran into was Jerry Steinholtz, who introduced me to Francisco Aquabella, Carlos Vidal Bolado, and Louis Miranda, all great Afro-Cuban musicians. Jerry and I have remained the best of friends. I had met Paul Horn on the road; he had been with Chico Hamilton, and was now also settled in LA I joined his band the first night I moved to town, and the drummer in that band was Billy Higgins. Another drummer I had met on the road was Larry Bunker, who was playing drums with Maynard Ferguson's band. We met again in LA in 1959, and he was the drummer when I first joined Shorty Rogers' big band. Some of the other drummers who played with that band at that time were Shelly Manne, Stan Levy, Gary Forman, and Mel Lewis. I played a lot with Paul Horn at the Renaissance Club on Sunset Strip, which also featured blues singer Jimmy Witherspoon, Lenny Bruce, Lord Buckley, and Paul Mazursky, who became a great producer-director on the Hollywood scene. Some of the fans that would come to hear our band were aspiring stars Dennis Hopper, Kim Novak, and James Coburn. Besides Billy Higgins, drummers Maurice Miller and Milt Turner played with us at that club and for even more years at Shelly's Manne Hole.

I started doing more and more studio work, and Milt Holland and Sammy Weiss were the first drummers I worked with. Milt had studied tabla and Indian rhythms with master tabla player Chatur Lal, who was playing with Ravi Shankar at the time. Milt was the first one to turn me on to the Indian rhythm cycles. On my first studio call I played vibes and marimba, and Milt had to loan me a tambourine, triangle, and cabasa. Milt said "Emil, there's a drum shop across the street from the musician's union where you have to go to pick up your checks. Why don't you go to the drum shop when you get paid and buy the percussion instruments you get asked to play on a studio call?" I said "Man, are you kidding? I came to town with a vibe and marimba; that's all I'm going to play." Many years later Milt was on a session with me where there were 12 percussionists playing on about 40 of my 650 instruments. He reminded me of what I had said years earlier. Well, I have to admit my collecting did get a little out of hand!

At the beginning of my studio days, each studio had a staff drummer. I worked with drummer John Williams, the father of composer John Williams, at Columbia Studios. John Sr. had come to town with Jerry Colonna, who was a trombone player before he got into comedy with Bob Hope. John Sr. had two more sons who are great percussionists in the studios: Jerry Williams, who played drums on a lot of the live TV shows, and Don Williams, who plays drums on all the stage shows that come to town and is also one of the finest timpanists in the film studios. There was also Frank Carlson at M-G-M, who was Woody Herman's first "Herd" drummer; I averaged about 3 days a week at M-G-M with Frank for years. There were Bernie Mattinson at Paramount, Richie Cornell at Fox, Milt Holland at Universal and Irv Cottler at Disney Studios, with Nick Fatool doing a lot of the record dates at Capitol Records. I believe the only studio that didn't have a steady drummer was Warner Bros., where Shelly Manne, Alvin Stoller, and Larry Bunker would play when needed.

I worked with Alvin Stoller a lot on TV film from the early 1960s. We worked on shows like *McHale's Navy, The Andy Griffith Show, I Love Lucy, Gomer Pyle, The Flintstones, Yogi Bear, Huckleberry Hound, I Spy,* and *Mod Squad.* Alvin could really play mallets but would tell me not to let the leaders know, because he wanted to only play drums.

The first live TV show drummer I worked with in LA was Bill Richmond, when we were doing Dean Martin and Frank Sinatra specials with Nelson Riddle as leader. Bill went on to become the screenwriter and later on, producer, of all the Jerry Lewis movies. When Bill left, Irv Cottler (known as Mr. Time) did all the shows. No matter what the tempo was, Irv would lay it down the same every time. I used to check his tempo with a metronome, and it was uncanny how he could nail it the same way every single time.

The first road tour I did with Sinatra was in 1960 with Sol Gubin, a great time-keeper, on drums. Not only is he a great show drummer, but he plays great piano and mallets as well. Through Irv Cottler I met Remo Belli, Buddy Rich, and Louie Bellson. Though some are gone, those of us left remain close friends.

In 1962 I traveled around the world with Sinatra and a sextet with Irv Cottler on drums. This was when I began collecting exotic percussion instruments. Irv remained Sinatra's drummer to the end of the singer's life.

One of the great percussion writers in films is Jerry Goldsmith, who used me and Shelly Manne on all his calls. Once we were working on a picture called Poltergeist. Shelly loved to play on my Paiste cymbals with mallets, and just before our lunch break Jerry said, "Everyone sit tight for just a couple of minutes, I need Shelly to give me two minutes of a long cymbal roll to a loud crescendo. Emil, hit a tam-tam at the end of the crescendo, on cue." Well, the red light went on and all eyes were on Shelly as he started the roll. All of a sudden he let his pants fall down, and the whole orchestra was trying to suppress their laughs while the tape was rolling! Shelly showed me the sound of rice on a suspended bass drum. He was also the first one to bring the water phone to the studios. Joe Porcaro, Shelly, and I were working with Jerry Goldsmith at Disney Studios on a film project the day Shelly passed away.

The first drummer to turn me on to the record date scene was Earl Palmer, who was the top drummer doing record dates at the time. I started to average about 18 record dates a week with Earl, playing some vibes and a lot of timps, cymbals, and tambourine. We played for Nat Cole, Rosie Clooney, Bing Crosby, and Ray Charles, to name a few.

A short time after I started doing records, drummer Hal Blaine came on the scene; he was the first one to introduce multi tom-toms with the drum set on records. We did all the recordings for the Beach Boys, the Monkees, The Everly Brothers, and Jan and Dean, to name just a few. I also worked with drummers Frank Capp, Frank DeVito, Norm Jeffries, Nick Ceroli, and Chiz Harris on sessions. A little later Paul Humphrey and Harvey Mason were as big as Earl and Hal on the record date scene.

In-between the record dates, I was still doing a lot of live TV jobs like *The Judy Garland Show*, with Shelly Manne and Larry Bunker on drums; *The Danny Kaye Show*, with Irv Cottler on drums; and *The Red Skelton Show* with Frank Capp on drums. With Capp, we also played on *Bonanza* and *Little House on the Prairie*. I even got to be a contestant on the Gong show as a gag to make drummer Mark Stevens, and the rest of the guys in the band, crack up.

Some of the first TV film shows I worked on only had a budget for one percussion player. I never really played set drums, but there were more mallet parts than drum parts on some, so I got to play drums on all the *Mr. Ed* TV shows and a few of the *Addams Family* and *Munsters* shows.

The mid-1960s saw a lot happening in LA I was studying tabla and Indian rhythms with Harihar Rao, and so was Don Ellis. Don and I formed the Hindustani Jazz Sextet, with drummer Steve Bohannon and his buddy Tom Scott on sax. After a time Joe Porcaro became drummer with us in that band, and we played at Shelly's Manne Hole with that group for years.

Through the Don Ellis days, Tom Scott brought John Guerin on the scene to play jazz drums in the clubs and in the studios. Dante's became the hot jazz club, and John became the hot drummer there and on film calls. Steve Ettleson also worked Dante's at this time, and probably subbed for more drummers in more groups than any other living drummer.

Larry Bunker needed a break from the studio scene, so he took a year off to go play with the Bill Evans trio. He later became the drummer with us when Stan Kenton formed his Neophonic Orchestra in LA

Around this same time, Nat Cole decided to get a musical show ready for Broadway, with him and Barbara McNair as the principal stars. I went with the show from the beginning and we had Lee Young, brother of Lester Young, on drums. I left the show after a few months, but Lee Young and I remained dear friends.

In the summer of 1964, I took a month off to go to Lake Tahoe to a meditation retreat, renting a house with Paul Horn along with guitar player Robby Krieger and drummer John Densmore from The Doors. We used to have jam sessions after our meditations in the evenings, and John played great drums.

I met Frank Zappa early on in his recording career and played on one of his first hit albums, *Lumpy Gravy*, as well as some of his other albums, like *200 Motels*, and was a member of his Electric Symphony. I participated in Zappa projects when drummers Terry Bozzio, Vinnie Colaiuta, and Chad Wackerman were with him. I got to work with Ralph Humphrey, another Zappa alumnus, on a lot of East Indian projects with L. Subramaniam's Group.

Once, while working on a movie project with Vinnie Colaiuta and Steve Schaeffer on drums, Vinnie would not stop noodling, and he was playing such great stuff that he had Joe Porcaro, Larry Bunker, Jerry Williams, and me flipping out over his chops. He was driving the leader crazy, as he was trying to correct some notes in the orchestra. The conductor said, "Who keeps playing all the drums when I'm trying to talk?" Larry Bunker was so in awe of Vinnie's chops that he didn't mind taking the blame (or really the credit), so Larry raised his hands and said, "It was me!"

In 1974 I did the ten-week Dark Horse tour with George Harrison and Ravi Shankar. We had two great drummers with that band, Andy Newmark and Jim Keltner, plus the great Alla Rakha on tablas. I used to sleep next to Alla Rakha on the plane, and he would get up in the middle of the night and start reciting some complex rhythm cycles, and te-his, and I would write them all down on pieces of scrap paper. Between him and Ravi Shankar, I learned some great rhythm permutations. You don't usually think of violin players as rhythm players, but L. Subramaniam, from Madras, India, who played violin with us on that tour, taught me more about rhythm than anyone else in life.

Jim Keltner and I have done other projects with George Harrison, and also with Ry Cooder. We remain close friends, as I do with every one mentioned in this remembrance.

Through an album I did with Louie Bellson, I met and played with Alex Acuna, Manolo Badrena, and both Walfredo Reyes, Sr. and Jr. Through the years Alex and I have done movie projects together with other great Latin drummers including Paulinho Da Costa, Francisco Aquabella, Louis Conte, Carlos Vega, and Efrain Toro.

When the electronic drums came on the scene, they were first used extensively on jingles. Some of the first drummers I worked with on these projects were Steve Schaeffer, Denny Siewell, and Harvey Mason.

Being that I grew up with Joe Porcaro, it was obvious that I would be godfather to his first born, Jeff Porcaro. Now Jeff was doing record and movie projects with Miles Davis, and he composed all the music for the movie, Dune, which his dad Joe and I worked on with him. All three of us also worked together on some of James Newton Howard's movie projects.

There are many wonderful drummers, and wonderful people that I have mentioned, that have left this planet for the next dimension. There must be one heck of a drum circle going on somewhere out there....

In the 1990s I played with many drummers who were still here on the West Coast, all great friends and musical brothers. Joe Porcaro and I are still co–leaders

Emil, Jeff and Joe Porcaro, and Jim Keltner, early '90s

of a jazz group we call Calamari, and we are both sponsored and supported by the Paiste cymbal and gong company. I am also sponsored by Yamaha and Mike Balter Mallets. We are grateful to another fine drummer, Rich Mangicaro (who now also plays percussion with the Eagles and Glenn Frey), the Paiste family, Jerry Steinholtz, the Toca family, Vic Firth and his family, and Remo Belli and his family for their encouragement and support through the years.

After George Harrison's untimely passing in 2001, there was a one-year remembrance called "A Concert for George," held in November of 2002 at Albert Hall in London. I got to play with the Ravi Shankar Indian Ensemble and on the second half of the program with drummers Ringo Starr, Jim Keltner, Steve Ferrone, and percussionist Ray Cooper.

Up until 2006 I had done many Disney and 20th Century-Fox cartoon sessions with drummers Peter Erskine, Ralph Humphrey, Vinnie Colaiuta, and Bernie Dresel. I am still doing clinics with drummers Steve Houghton, Don Williams, and Joe Porcaro.

I have done at least 25 Academy Awards shows with Harvey Mason playing drums. There is little drum set playing in the film industry these days, but when drums are called for, it's usually Steve Schaeffer or Harvey Mason who do the drumming.

I am thankful and most grateful to all the drummers I have been blessed to work with in my career, and apologize to the many fine drummers I didn't remember to mention.

To all drummers, I'd say it's a joy to have "Rhythm Be Our Business!!"

APPENDIH 3: EMIL ON TEACHING

go to colleges throughout the country, and occasionally in Europe on, teaching seminars on Music. The topics I teach are: "Percussion in the Recording Studios," "Odd Time Rhythms and their Application in the Modern Orchestra," and "Making Percussion Sounds on Found Objects."

On the first day, I sometimes ask students whether they think they're very good. Usually someone will say, "Well, some people think I am." So I say, "Well, if you were going in for brain surgery and you asked the doctor if he was good, would you like him to say, "Well, some people think I am?"

PERCUSSION IN THE RECORDING STUDIO

There are some composers who write for television or for films who really know the percussion language and instruments, but on the average most composers are not that aware of the capabilities of the percussion family of instruments. What I try to impart in this clinic is the range of percussion instruments which could be used and their use within the context of the orchestra.

Here are the standard percussion instruments that each and every percussionist in the LA area has in his or her arsenal of instruments usually required by a composer:

Chimes, Marimba, Orchestra Bells, Standard Drum Set, Timpani, Vibraphone, Xylophone.

Other percussion instruments that are considered "standard" are:

Anvil, Bamboo Wind Chimes, Bell Plate, Bird Whistles, Boat Whistles, Brass Wind Chimes, Bulb Horn, Concert Bass Drum (Gran Cassa), Concert Snare Drum, Cow Bell, Cricket Clicker, Cymbal(s), Duck Call, Field Drum, Fire Bell, Fight Bell, Glass Wind Chimes, Jingle Sticks, Piatti, Piccolo Snare Drum, Pop Gun, Ratchet, Ship's Bell, Siren Whistle, Slap Stick, Sleigh Bells, Tom Toms, Triangle, Washboard and, Wood Block.

The percussion instruments that are considered Latin are:

Au Go Go Bells, Bongoes, Cabas, Castanets, Cencerro (Latin Cow Bell), Chocalho, (Shaker), Claves, Conga Drums, Cuica, Giro (Scracher), Jawbone (Quijada), Maracas, Maraca Sticks, Pandero (Braziilian Tambourine), Puelli Sticks, Reco Reco (Scratcher), Sand Blocks, Timbales, Vibraslap.

My clinic demonstrates how they are played and how they are used within the context of the orchestra. It is surprising how many composers are unaware of this complete list of standard percussion instruments, their range, and their context within an orchestral application. A clinic is usually one to two hours at the most, so that it is not usually possible to demonstrate accurately all of the standard instruments in one clinic session alone.

ODD TIME RHYTHMS AND THEIR APPLICATION
IN THE MODERN ORCHESTRA

Having studied rhythm through performing with Ravi Shankar and some of India's master musicians, I have devised a technique of sub-dividing rhythms. In this way, I can show all the possibilities of adapting these subdivisions into a rhythmic language rarely used in Western music. With this system, there will never be a rhythm that will confuse a player. It opens up the endless possibilities of the rhythmic techniques that we have at our disposal. I tell musicians attending this clinic to be sure to have pencil and paper to write down some of the permutations of these rhythms, as they will eventually have a bible of numbers to call upon to write out rhythms for composition, for improvisation, and for discovering how these rhythms can fit in the framework of any musical or rhythmic context. There is enough material here to last the composer, or serious musician, a lifetime.

This is not a clinic that I have put on paper, for its practical use requires living with musicians who can permute these numbers and clap out their various possibilities.

Let's start with the simple number of 8. How many 3s are there in the number 8? There are two 3s and a 2.

What the Indian musician will do is to find how many combinations there are with two 3s and a 2:

332
323
233

Now, breaking the 3s into 2s and 1s, we can get smaller numbers and many more rhythms.

21212
12122
21221
12212
21212
22121

By beating your foot and clapping out these rhythms, you can see how they can apply to counterpoint when two or more people clap out the various rhythms, or how they can be incorporated in the permutations of rhythms. This is using the simple number of 8. Now, if you double your number to 16, you can find how many 3s in 16:

3 3 3 3 3 1
3 3 3 3 1 3
3 3 3 1 3 3
3 3 1 3 3 3
3 1 3 3 3 3
1 3 3 3 3 3

And after beating out these rhythms, you can then break the 3s down to 2s and 1s. You now get:

21 21 21 21 21 1
12 12 12 12 12 1
21 21 21 21 1 21
12 12 12 12 1 12
21 21 21 1 21 21
12 12 12 1 12 12
21 21 1 21 21 21
12 12 12 1 12 12
21 1 21 21 21 21
12 1 12 12 12 12
1 21 21 21 21 21
1 12 12 12 12 12

How many 5s in 16?

5 5 5 1
5 5 1 5
5 1 5 5
1 5 5 5

Break down the 5s into 2s and 3s:

23 23 23 1
32 32 32 1
23 23 1 23
32 32 1 32
23 1 23 23
32 1 32 32
1 23 23 23
1 32 32 32

Now break the 3s down to 2's and 1's

2 21 2 21 2 21 1

2 12 2 12 2 12 1

1 2 21 2 21 2 21

2 21 2 21 1 2 21 (etc)

How many 7s in 16?

223 223 2

223 2 223

2 223 223

Now break the 3s down to 2s and 1s.

Now double your number to 32.

How many 3s in 32, and what's left over?

How many 5s in 32, and what's left over?

How many 7s in 32, and what's left over?

How many 9s in 32, and what's left over?

How many 11s in 32, and what's left over?

Break every thing down into 2s and 1s, and you have a lifetime of work here.

You can see where you move the smallest number over each time:

3 3 3 3 3 3 3 3 3 (2) (Now move the 2 over to the left one place.)

3 3 3 3 3 3 3 3 (2) 3

3 3 3 3 3 3 3 (2) 3 3

3 3 3 3 3 3 (2) 3 3 3

3 3 3 3 3 (2) 3 3 3 3

3 3 3 3 (2) 3 3 3 3 3

3 3 3 (2) 3 3 3 3 3 3

3 3 3 (2) 3 3 3 3 3 3 3

3 3 (2) 3 3 3 3 3 3 3 3

3 (2) 3 3 3 3 3 3 3 3 3

(2) 3 3 3 3 3 3 3 3 3

The possibilities are endless, and you can see where you will end up with a bible full of rhythm permutations.

The rest of my clinics are in the form of books that I have on the market:

-*Mallet Chord Studies*, published by Hal Leonard

-*Music and Rhythm Permutations*, published by Hal Leonard

-*Sight Reading for Mallets*, published by Hal Leonard

The following books can be purchased at Steve Weiss Music   purchasing@steveweissmusic.com:

-*Fun Compositions For The Very Young and/or Unmusical*

-*Making Music around the Home Or Yard*

-*Tune In: Making More Musical Sounds*

-*Mallet Exercises for the Drummer*

-*Two and Four Mallet Chord Studies*

The following music is available for purchase:

For Marimba Quartet:

-*Celesta*

-*Celesta #2*

-*Underdog Rag*

-*What's the Costa Rica*

For Marimba Sextet:

-*My Friend Eileen*

-*On Hearing the First Cuckoo in Spring (Delius),*

-*Badabing*

Available CDs:

Wonderful World of Percussion

Calamari, Live at Rocco's

Emil Richards with the Jazz Knights

Luntana

Maui Jazz Quartet

Yazz Per Favore

APPENDIX 4: FILMS AND TV SHOWS I HAVE PLAYED IN
(Note: general release/airing dates shown –
some sessions may have been played the previous year)

8 Seconds AKA Lane Frost 1994
10 1979
13th Warrior 1999
14 Going On 30–(TV) 1988
21 Hours in Munich–(TV) 1976
48 Hours 1982
100 Rifles 1969
101 Dalmatians 1996
1941 1979
1969 1989
Absolute Power 1997
Abyss, The 1989
Academy Awards 1977
Academy Awards 1979
Academy Awards 1987
Academy Awards 1988
Academy Awards 1989
Academy Awards 1990
Academy Awards 1991
Academy Awards 1992
Academy Awards 1993
Academy Awards 1994
Academy Awards 1995
Academy Awards 1997
Academy Awards 1998
Academy Awards 1999
Academy Awards 2000
Academy Awards 2001
Academy Awards 2003
Academy Awards 2005
Academy Awards 2006
Academy Awards 2007
Academy Awards 2008
Academy Awards 2009

Ace Ventura, Pet Detective 1995
Ace Ventura: When Nature Calls 1995
Across 110th Street 1972
Addams Family–(TV) 1977
Adventures In Babysitting 1987
Adventures Of Freddie 1977
Adventures Of Huckleberry Finn–(TV) 1984
Adventures Of Pinocchio, The 1996
Adventures Of Pinocchio, The– (TV) 1975
Adventures Of Sheriff Lobo 1981
After Mash–(TV) 1983
Against All Odds 1984
Air Force One 1997
Airplane 1980
Airport 77 1977
Airport 79/The Concorde 1979
Airwolf #3 & #6 1980s
Alcatraz-The Whole Shocking Story 1980
Alex And The Gypsy 1976
Alex In Wonderland 1970
Alex In Wonderland 2011
Alice–(TV) 1976
Alice In Wonderland 2010
Alien 4: Resurrection 1997
A Little Sex 1982
Alive 1993
All God's Children–(TV) 1980
All My Darling Daughters–(TV) 1972
All Night Long 1981
All Of Me 1984
All the President's Men 1976
Almost An Angel 1990

Aloha Means Goodbye—(TV) 1974
Aloha Paradise—(TV) 1981
Along Came a Spider 2001
Altered States 1980
Alvin and the Chipmunks—(TV) 1983
Always 1989
Amazing Panda Adventure, The 1995
Amazing Stories—(TV) 1985
Amazon—(TV) 1999
Amazon AKA Minerva Files 1980
Ambassador, The 1984
Amber Waves—(TV) 1979
Ambushers, The 1967
Amelia Earhart—(TV) 1976
American Dad-(TV) 2005-08
American Dream, An 1966
American Dreams—(TV) 2002
American Dreams—(TV) 2004
American Flyers 1985
American Gothic 1988
American Idle—(TV) 2003
American Hot Wax 1978
America's Sweethearts 2001
Amerika—(TV) 1987
Amistad 1997
Amityville Horror 1979
Amsterdam Kill 1977
Anamaniacs—(TV) 1993
Andy Griffith Show—(TV) 1960s
An Eye For An Eye 1981
Angel Dusted—(TV) 1981
Angie—(TV) 1979
Angie 1994
Animal House 1978
Annie 1982
Another 48 Hours 1990
Another Woman's Child—(TV) 1983
Arctic 1981
Around The World And Under The Sea 1966
Article 99 1991

A-Team, The—(TV) 1983-86
At Ease—(TV) 1983
Atlantis, The Lost Empire 2001
Audrey Rose 1977
Austin Powers 1999
Autobiography Of Jane Pitman—(TV) 1974
Avengers—(TV) 1999
Awakening Land—(TV) 1978
Babe, The 1992
Baby: Secret of Lost Legend 1985
Baby It's You—(TV) 1990s
Baby-O 1983
Back To School 1986
Back Together—(TV) 1983
Backfire 1988
Bad Boys 1983
Bad Boy Two 1992
Bad Medicine 1985
Bad News Bears—(TV) 1970s
Bad News Bears: Breaking Training 1977
Bad Ronald—(TV) 1974
Badlands 1973
Ballad Of Cable Hogue 1970
Banacek: Project Phoenix—(TV) 1972
Bandolero 1968
Banning 1967
Barbarosa 1981
Barefoot In The Park 1967
Baretta—(TV) 1975-76
Barney And Friends—(TV) 1992
Batman 1997
Batman Returns 1992
Bat People, The 1974
Batteries Not Included 1987
Battle Of The Planets 1978
Battle Star Galactica—(TV) 1980s
Beach Boys: An American Family—(TV) 2000
Beach Red 1967

Beasts Are Loose- (Hanna/Barbera) 1978
Beau Geste (Last Remake Of) 1977
Beautiful Killers—(TV) 1990
Beauty And the Beast (Disney) 1991
Beauty And the Beast—(TV) 1987-89
Beavis And Butt-Head—(TV) 1993
Bedknobs and Broomsticks—(TV) 1987
Beer 1985
Bees 1998
Beetlejuice 1988
Beguiled, The 1971
Believe In Me 1971
Bella Mafia—(TV movie) 1997
Bell Jar 1979
Bell, Book And Candle—(TV) 1976
Beryl Markham: A Shadow On the Sun—(TV movie) 1989
Best Defense 1984
Best Little Girl In The World—(TV) 1981
Best Little Whore House In Texas 1982
Best Seller—(TV) 1970s
Betsy, The 1978
Betty Boop 1993
Beulah Land—(TV) 1980
Beverly Hillbillies, The 1993
Beware The Blob 1972
Bewitched—(TV) 1964
Beyond The Poseidon Adventure 1979
Big 1988
Big Bounce, The 1969
Big Brawl 1980
Big Bus, The 1976
Big Hand For The Little Lady, A 1966
Big Jake 1971
Big Mouth, The 1974
Big One, The Great Los Angeles Earthquake—(TV) 1990
Big Top Pee Wee 1988
Big Trouble 1986

Big Trouble 2002
Big Wednesday 1978
Billy Jack 1971
Billy Jack Goes To Washington 1977
Bing Crosby TV Christmas Special—(TV) 1979
Bionic Woman—(TV) 1976-78
Bite The Bullet 1975
Black Beauty—(TV) 1978
Black Cauldron. The 1985
Black Eye 1970
Black Hole, The 1979
Black Sunday 1977
Blacula, AKA Scream Blacula Scream—(TV) 2006
Blansky's Beauties—(TV) 1977
Blarney Cock 1976
Blindfold 1975
Blood Beach 1980
Blood In, Blood Out 1993
Blood Work 2002
Blue 1970
Blue Knight—(TV) 1975
Blue Lagoon 1980
Blues Brothers, The 1980
Boatniks, The 1970
Bob & Carol & Ted & Alice 1969
Bob Newhart Show, The—(TV) 1970s
Body Double 1984
Body Heat 1981
Bonanza—(TV) 1960s
Boss' Wife, The 1986
Boulevard Nights 1979
Bound By Honor—(TV) 1995
Bourne Identity—(TV) 1988
Boys On The Side 1995
Brady Bunch—(TV) 1960s-70s
Brainstorm 1965
Brainstorm 1983
Breakdown 1997

Breaking Away 1979
Breakout 1975
Breathless 1983
Brenda Starr 1989
Brennan—(TV) 1976
Bret Maverick—(TV) 1981
Bret Maverick (The Lazy Ace)—(TV) 1982
Brian's Song—(TV movie) 1971
Bridge Across Time—(TV) 1985
Bringing Down The House 2003
Brink's Job, The 1978
Broadcast News 1987
Broken Arrow 1996
Broken Chain—(TV) 1993
Broken Home—(TV) 1991
Bronk—(TV) 1975
Brother John 1971
Brotherhood, The/Wind River 1968
Brubaker 1980
Buck And The Preacher 1972
Buck Rogers—(TV) 1979
Buck Rogers In The 25th Century—(TV movie) 1979
Buddy Buddy 1981
Buddy System 1984
Bugs Bunny Looney Christmas Tales—(TV movie) 1979
Bunker, The—(TV movie) 1981
Bunny O'Hare 1971
Burbs, The 1989
Bus Riley's Back In Town 1965
Bustin' Loose 1981
Busting 1974
Busy Body, The 1969
Butch And Sundance-The Early Days 1979
Butch Cassidy And The Sundance Kid 1969
CSI—(TV) 2000
Cabe—(TV) 1976
Cactus Flower 1969

Cage Without A Key—(TV) 1975
Cagney And Lacey—(TV) 1980s
California Kid, The—(TV movie) 1974
Callie And Son—(TV movie) 1981
Candy 1968
Cannonball Run II 1984
Capricorn One 1977
Captain Eo 1986
Captains Courageous—(TV movie) 1977
Captured 1981
Car 54, Where Are You?—(TV) 1960s
Car Pool—(TV) 1993
Car, The 1977
Care Bears—(TV) 1980s
Carey Treatment, The 1972
Carny 1980
Cars 2 2011
Casey's Shadow 1978
Casino 1995
Castaway Cowboy, The 1974
Columbo: Murder, Smoke And Shadows—(TV) 1989
Castle Keep 1969
Casual Sex? 1988
Cat Ballou 1965
Celebrity 1984-86
Celtic Pride 1996
Centennial 1978
Chain Reaction 1996
Challenge, The AKA Sword of the Ninja 1982
Champions 1984
Charlene 1977
Charley 1970
Charley Varrick 1973
Charlie Chan—(TV) 1972
Charlie Chan And the Curse of the Dragon Queen 1981
Charlie's Angels—(TV) 1976-78
Charlotte's Web 2006
Charleston 1977

Charly 1968

Che 1969

Cheap Detective, The 1978

Cherokee Kid 1996

Chicago 2002

Chicago Story—(TV movie) 1981

China Beach—(TV Pilot) 1987

China Beach—(TV) 1988-79

Chinatown 1974

ChiPs—(TV) 1977-79

Choices of the Heart—(TV movie) 1983

Choirboys, The 1977

Christian Licorice Store 1971

Christmas Comes To Pacland—(TV movie) 1982

Christmas Lilies Of The Field—(TV movie) 1979

Christmas Lilies Of The Valley 1970

Chu Chu And The Philly Flash 1981

Chuka—(TV) 1970

Cincinnati Kid 1965

City Hall 1996

Clambake 1967

Clara's Heart 1988

Class 1983

Class Of '44 1973

Class Of '65—(TV) 1977

Cleopatra 1963

Cleopatra Jones 1973

Cleopatra Jones In The Casino of Gold 1975

Cleveland—(TV) 2008

Cliff Hangers—(TV) 1978

Clifford 1994

Close Encounters Of The Third Kind 1977

Club Paradise 1986

Club, The AKA Players 1980

Clueless 1995

Cocoon 1985

Cocoon: The Return 1988

Code Red—(TV) 1981

Colbys, The 1985-86

Cold Dog Soup 1990

Cold Turkey 1971

Collector, The 1965

Color Purple 1985

Columbo—(TV) 1971-74

Columbo Goes To College—(TV) 1990

Come Blow Your Horn 1963

Comedy Awards 1976

Comes A Horseman 1978

Comic, The 1969

Command 5—(TV movie) 1985

Commando 1985

Common Ground—(TV movie) 1990

Competition, The 1980

Conan The Barbarian 1982

Concorde (Airport '79) 1979

Condominium—(TV movie) 1980

Condorman 1981

Congo 1995

Conquest Of The Planet Of The Apes 1972

Constantine 2005

Contact 1997

Contender 1979

Coogan's Bluff 1968

Cool Hand Luke 1967

Cool Ones, The 1967

Coomba 1977

Cops and Robbersons 1994

Cougar: Ghost of the Rockies —(TV) 1990

Country Store 1978

Coupe De Ville 1990

Courage, The AKA Mother Courage 1986

Cousins—(TV movie) 1976

Cracker Factory—(TV movie) 1979

Crazy Horse—(TV movie) 1996

Crazy House—(TV) 1973

Crazy In Alabama 1999
Crazy Like A Fox—(TV) 1984
Crime Club—(TV pilot) 1975
Critical List, The—(TV) 1978
Crossings—(TV) 1986
Cruise Into Terror—(TV movie) 1978
Cry For Happy 1962
Culpepper Cattle Company, The 1972
Curly Sue 1991
Curse of K 1981
Cutter To Huston—(TV) 1983
Cutting Edge, The—(TV) 1990
D2-the Mighty Ducks 2 1994
Dad 1989
Dallas-Acceptance 1978-86
Damnation Alley 1977
Dances With Wolves 1990
Dancing With Danger—(TV) 1994
Dangerous Minds 1995
Danny Kaye TV Specials 1960s-70s
Danny Thomas Show 1976
Dante's Peak 1997
Daring Dobermans, The 1973
Dark Mirror—(TV movie) 1984
Dark Secret Of Harvest Home, The—
(TV) 1978
Darkwing Duck 1991
Darker Than Amber 1970
Darkman 1990
Dark Secret Of Harvest Home—(TV) 1978
Date Night 1986
Dave 1993
Davy Crockett—(TV) 1988
Dawnbreakers 1976
Dawn Of The Dead 2004
Day Of Reckoning: Wisdom Keeper—
(TV) 1994
Day Christ Died—(TV movie) 1980
Day Of The Evil Gun 1968
Dead And Buried 1981

Dead Heat On A Merry-Go-Round 1966
Dead Men Tell No Tales—(TV movie) 1971
Dead Poet's Society 1989
Deadly Blessing 1981
Deadly Business—(TV movie) 1986
Dealing 1980
Death Hunt 1981
Deep Rising 1998
Deep Sea AKA Denizens Of The Deep
2006
Deep, The 1977
Deer Hunter 1978
Defiance 1980
Delta House—(TV) 1979
Delvecchio—(TV) 1977
Dennis the Menace 1993
Descending Angel 1990
Desire, The Vampire AKA I Desire—
(TV movie) 1982
Detroit 9000 1973
Devil And Max Devlin 1981
Devil And Miss Sarah, The—(TV movie)
1971
Devil In A Blue Dress, The 1995
Devil's Advocate 1997
Devlin Connection—(TV) 1982
Dexter's Laboratory Ego Trip —(TV
movie) 1999
Diagnosis Murder—(TV) 1994
Dial M For Murder—(TV movie) 1981
Diana Ross TV Special 1977
Diary Of Anne Frank 1959
Dick Tracy 1990
Dick Van Dyke Show—(TV) 1971
Die Hard 1988
Die Hard 2 1990
Die Laughing 1980
Dime With A Halo 1963
Dinner Party—(TV movie) 2007
Dinosaur/Disney 2000
Dinosaurs—(TV) 1991

Dirty Harry 1971
Distant Thunder 1988
Disturbing Behavior 1998
Disturbing Behavior—(TV) 2001
Divorce American Style 1967
Doctor Detroit 1983
Doctor, You've Got To Be Kidding 1967
Doctor Zhivago 1965
Dog Soldier 1989
Dolores Claibourne 1995
Don Is Dead, The 1973
Don Knotts Show—(TV) 1970s
Donovan's Reef 1963
Don't Be Afraid of the Dark—(TV movie) 1973
Don't Cry, It's Only Thunder 1982
Don't Go To Sleep 1982
Don't Look Back—(TV movie) 1981
Don't Make Waves 1967
Don't Tell Mom The Baby Sitter's Dead 1991
Dorothy Hamill Special 1976
Double Exposure 1983
Double Indemnity—(TV movie) 1973
Down With Love 2003
Dragnet—(TV) 1967
Dreamcatcher 2003
Dream Lover 1986
Dream West—(TV) 1986
Dresser, The 1983
Dribble AKA Scoring 1979
Drowning Pool, The 1975
DuckTails 1987
Duel—(TV movie) 1971
Dukes of Hazzard—(TV) 1979-80s
Dune 1984
Dying Young 1991
Dynasty—(TV) 1976-89
ER—(TV) 2002
Eagle Has Landed, The 1976

Earth Star Voyager—(TV) 1980s
Earthquake 1974
Easter Sunday 1980
Easy Come, Easy Go 1967
Easy Money 1983
Edge, The 1997
Edward Scissorhands 1990
Eiger Sanction, The 1975
Eight Seconds To Glory 1994
Electro Man 1979
Ellery Queen—(TV) 1975-76
Ellis Hall 1981
Elvis—(TV movie) 1979
Emerald Bay 1983
Emergency—(TV) 1976
Empire Of The Ants 1977
Empire Of The Sun 1987
End Of The World 1977
End, The 1978
Enemies, A Love Story 1989
Ensenada 1970
Ensign Pulver 1964
Enter Laughing 1967
Enter the Dragon 1973
Enterprise—(TV film) 2003
Envy 1976
Epic 2013
Equalizer, The —(TV) 1985
Equals—(TV) 1984
Eric—(TV movie) 1975
Escape Artist, The 1982
Escape From Alcatraz 1979
Escape From the Planet Of The Apes 1971
Escape To Victory—(TV) 1981
Everybody's All American 1988
Evilspeak 1981
Evita Peron—(TV movie) 1981
Executive Decision 1996
Executive, The—(TV) 1963

Frighteners—(TV) 1996

Frisco Kid, The 1979

From Noon Till Three 1976

From The Earth To The Moon 1998

Fugitive, The 1993

Fun In Acapulco 1963

Funhouse, The 1981

Funny Farm 1988

Funny Girl 1968

Funny Lady 1975

Fun With Dick And Jane 1976

Future Cop—(TV) 1977

F/X/2 1991

Gable And Lombard 1976

Galactica—(TV) 1980

Gambit 1966

Gambler, Part 2—(TV) 1971

Game of Death 1978

Games 1967

Gang That Couldn't Shoot Straight 1971

Gangster Chronicles 1981

Gardens Of Stone 1987

Gauguin The Savage—(TV movie) 1980

Gauntlet, The 1977

Gene Kelly TV Special 1977

George Of The Jungle 1997

Geronimo: An American Legend 1993

Geronimo—(TV movie) 1993

Get Smart—(TV) 1960s

Ghost And Mr. Chicken, The 1966

Ghost Of Flight 401, The—(TV movie) 1978

Ghostbusters 1984

Ghostbusters II 1989

Gift Of Life—(TV movie) 1982

Gilligan's Island—(TV) 1960s

Gilmore Girls—(TV) 2001

Girl From Petrovka, The 1974

Girl Happy 1965

Glass Bottom Boat, The 1966

Glass Houses 1972

Gloria 1980

Glory 1989

Godfather: Part 3 1990

Gods Must Be Crazy II 1989

Godzilla 1998

Goin' South 1978

Going Berserk 1983

Going In Style 1979

Golden Child, The 1986

Golden Needles 1974

Goldie Hawn TV Special 1978

Goliath Awaits—(TV movie) 1981

Gomer Pyle—(TV) 1960s

Gong Show—(TV) 1977

Good Morning, Vietnam 1987

Goonies 1985

Gore Vidal's Lincoln—(TV) 1988

Gorillas In The Mist 1988

Gotcha 1985

Grammy Awards 1999

Grand Canyon 1991

Grand Prix 1966

Gravy Train AKA The Dion Brothers 1974

Gray Lady Down 1978

Great Bank Robbery, The 1969

Great Mouse Detective, The 1986

Great Northfield Minnesota Raid, The 1972

Great Race, The 1965

Green Acres—(TV) 1960s-70

Green Eyes—(TV movie) 1977

Gremlins 1984

Gremlins 2 1990

Grimm's Thanksgiving TV Special 1977

Guess Who 2005

Guess Who's Coming To Dinner 1967

Gumball Rally, The 1976

Guns Of Paradise—(TV) 1990

Gus 1976

Gypsy 1962
Gypsy Moths, The 1969
Halls Of Anger 1970
Hand, The 1981
Handle With Care AKA Citizen's Band 1977
Hang 'Em High 1968
Hanky Panky 1982
Hanna-Barbera Cartoons—(TV) 1970s
Happening, The 1967
Happiest Millionare, The 1967
Happy Birthday, Wanda June 1971
Happy Days 1975-80
Happy New Year 1987
Hard To Hold 1984
Hardy Boys/Nancy Drew—(TV) 1977-79
Harlem Nights 1989
Harlow 1965
Harry And Walter Go To New York 1976
Harry In Your Pocket 1973
Harry O—(TV) 1970s
Harry's Hong Kong—(TV movie) 1987
Hart To Hart—(TV) 1979
Harum Scarum 1965
Haunting, The 1999
Haunts of the Very Rich—(TV) 1972
Hawaii Five-O 1975-76
Hawaiians, The 1970
Hawk, The 1993
Hawmps! 1976
Haywire 1980
Head 1968
Heart Is A Lonely Hunter, The 1968
Heartbeat 1993
Heartbreak Ridge 1986
Hearts of the West 1975
Heaven Can Wait 1978
Heaven Help Us, AKA Catholic Boys 1985
Heidi 1975
Heidi's Song 1982

Hell in the Pacific 1969
Hell With Heroes, The 1968
Hello Down There 1969
Herbie Goes Bananas 1980
Herbie Goes To Monte Carlo 1977
Hero 1992
Hero At Large 1980
Hidalgo 2004
High Plains Drifter 1973
High Risk 1981
High Road To China 1983
Highway To Heaven—(TV) 1985-86
Hindenburg, The 1975
History Tour 1996
Hit! 1973
Hitchhike! 1974
Hoffa 1992
Hogan's Heroes—(TV) 1960s-71
Holiday 1978
Hollywood Wives—(TV) 1985
Hombre 1967
Home Alone 1990
Home on the Range—(TV) 1978
Homeward Bound: The Incredible Journey 1993
Honeymoon Hotel 1964
Hong Kong Phooey—(TV) 1974
Honky Tonk Freeway 1981
Hook 1991
Hook, Line And Sinker 1969
Hopscotch 1980
Hot Rock, The 1972
Hot Rods To Hell 1967
Hot Shots! Part Deux 1993
Hot To Trot 1988
Hotel—(TV) 1983
House Calls 1978
House Of Mouse -(TV) 2000
House Where Evil Dwells 1982
How The West Was Won—(TV) 1978

How To Frame A Figg 1971

How To Save A Marriage And Ruin Your Life 1968

How To Steal A Million 1966

Howard the Duck 1986

Huckleberry Hound—(TV movie) 1988

Hud 1963

Hudson Hawk 1991

Hulk, The 2003

Hunt For Red October 1990

Hunter, The 1980

Hurricane, The 1979

Husbands, Wives And Lovers—(TV) 1978

Hysterical 1983

I Dream of Jeannie—(TV) 1960s

IFR 7000 1978

I Love My Wife 1970

I Love Trouble 1994

I Love You, Alice B. Toklas! 1968

I Sailed To Tahiti With An All Girl Crew 1968

I Spy—(TV) 1960s

I, the Jury 1982

Ice Castles 1978

Ice Station Zebra 1968

Iceman 1984

If He Hollers, Let Him Go 1968

Ike: The War Years—(TV) 1979

I'm Gonna Git You Sucka 1988

Immigrants, The—(TV movie) 1978

Impostor—(TV movie) 1984

In Cold Blood 1967

In Country 1989

In Harm's Way 1965

In The Best Interest Of The Children 1992

Incredible Hulk, The—(TV) 1977-83

Incredible Journey Of Dr. Meg Laurel, The—(TV) 1979

Incredible Machine-The Human Body 1975

Incredibles, The 2004

Independence Day 1996

Indiana Jones And The Temple Of Doom 1984

Indiana Jones And The Last Crusade 1989

In Harm's Way 1965

Inner Space—(TV) 1974

Instinct 1999

Institute For Revenge—(TV movie) 1979

Intimate Strangers—(TV movie) 1986

Invasion Of The Body Snatchers 1978

Invictus 2009

Invitation To A Gunfighter 1964

Ironclads—(TV movie) 1991

Iron Eagle 1986

Ishi: Last Of His Tribe—(TV movie) 1978

Island At The Top Of The World 1980s

Island, The 1980

It Could Happen To You 1994

It Isn't Easy Being A Teenage Millionaire-(TV) 1978

It's Only Money 1962

J. D.'s Revenge 1976

Jabberjaw—(TV) 1970s

Jack 1996

Jackson County Jail 1976

JAG—(TV) 2001-04

Jake And The Fatman 1987-91

James And The Giant Peach 1996

James Dean: First American Teenager—(TV movie) 1976

Jaws 1975

Jaws: The Revenge 1987

Jaws Of Satan 1981

Jeffersons—(TV) 1970s

Jerk, The 1979

Jerk. Too, The—(TV movie) 1984

Jesse Owens Story, The—(TV movie) 1984

Jigsaw John—(TV) 1970s

160

Jo Stafford, Paul Weston TV Specials 1970s
Joe Dirt 2001
Joe Panther 1976
Joe Versus the Volcano 1990
John And Mary 1969
John Carter Of Mars 2011
Journey Of Natty Gann, The 1985
Journey Of The August King 1995
Judge Dee—(TV) 1960s
Judy Garland TV Specials 1970s-80s
Judy Moody And The Not Bummer Summer 2011
Junior 1994
Jurassic Park 1993
Juror, The 1996
Just Cause 1995
Just You And Me, Babe 1979
Just You And Me, Kid 1979
Kane And Abel—(TV) 1985
Karate Kid 1984
Karate Kid, The, Part II 1986
Karate Kid, The, Part III 1989
Kay O'Brien—(TV) 1986
Kelly's Heroes 1970
Kennedy—(TV) 1983
Kennedys Of Massachusetts, The—(TV) 1990
Key West—(TV movie) 1973
Kicks—(TV movie) 1985
Kill Me If You Can—(TV movie) 1977
King Cobra 1999
King Kong 1976
King Kong 2005
King Of The Gypsies 1978
King Of The Hill—(TV) 1997-2002
King Ralph 1991
Kingston: Confidential—(TV) 1976
Klute 1971
Knight Rider—(TV) 1982-83
Knots Landing—(TV) 1979-86

Kojak—(TV) 1973-76
Kolchak—(TV) 1972-74
Kung Fu—(TV) 1972-75
Kung Fu Panda 2008
Kung Fu: The Movie 1986
LA Confidential 1997
LA Law—(TV) 1986-87
Lady Blue—(TV) 1985
Ladybugs 1992
Laguna Heat—(TV movie) 1987
Land Of The Lost 2009
Land Of The Lost—(TV) 1974-77
Lanigan's Rabbi—(TV) 1977
Last Action Hero 1993
Last American Hero, The 1973
Last Angry Man, The—(TV movie) 1974
Last Boy Scout, The 1991
Last Castle, The 2001
Last Days of Disco, The 1998
Last Detail, The 1973
Last Dragon, The 1985
Last Giraffe—(TV movie) 1979
Last Hard Men, The 1976
Last Married Couple In America, The 1980
Last Ninja, The—(TV movie) 1983
Last Of His Tribe—(TV movie) 1992
Last Of Sheila, The 1973
Last Of The Good Guys—(TV movie) 1978
Last Of The Secret Agents, The 1966
Last Remake Of Beau Geste, The 1977
Last Resort, The 1986
Last Samurai 2003
Last Starfighter, The 1984
Late Show, The 1977
Laverne And Shirley—(TV) 1979
Law And Disorder 1974
Law And Order 1980s
Lawyer, The 1970

Lazarus Syndrome—(TV) 1979

Legal Eagles 1986

Legend Of Lylah Clare, The 1968

Legend Of Walks Far Woman—(TV movie) 1982

Legs—(TV movie) 1983

Leonard Part 6 1987

Lethal Weapon 1987

Lethal Weapon 2 1989

Lethal Weapon 3 1992

Lethal Weapon 4 1998

Life TV Documentary—(TV) 1986

Life Goes To War—(TV) 1977

Lilly 1987

Limbo 1972

Lincoln—(TV) 1989

Lindbergh Kidnapping Case, The—(TV movie) 1976

Lipstick 1976

Little House On The Prairie—(TV) 1975-82

Little Rascals Christmas Special—(TV movie) 1979

Little Red Riding Hood 1995

Little Sweetheart 1989

Little White Lies—(TV) 1989

Lives of Ben Franklin: The King's Rebel 1974

Lock Up 1989

Logan's Run 1976

Lolly-Madonna XXX 1973

Lonesome Dove—(TV) 1989

Long Escape, The 1978

Long Goodbye, The 1973

Longest Night, The—(TV) 1972

Lonely Guy, The 1984

Lookalike—(TV movie) 1990

Look Alive 1990

Look What's Happened To Rosemary's Baby 1976

Look Who's Talking Too 1990

Looney Tunes Comedy Hour—(TV) 1985

Lord of the Rings 1978

Losin' It 1983

Lost—(TV) 2004-08

Lost Horizon 1973

Lost In The Stars 1974

Lost Man, The 1969

Lou Grant—(TV) 1977-78

Love And Betrayal: Mia Farrow Story—(TV movie) 1995

Love And Bullets 1979

Love Boat—(TV) 1979-81

Love God, The 1969

Love Has Many Faces 1965

Love Lives On—(TV) 1985

Love On The Run 1979

Love With The Proper Stranger 1963

Lovers And Other Strangers 1970

Loving 1970

Lucan—(TV) 1978

Luv 1967

M*A*S*H—(TV) 1972-83

Mac And Me 1988

MacArthur 1977

MacGyver—(TV) 1986

Mackenna's Gold 1969

Mad Bull—(TV movie) 1977

Made In Paris 1966

Madigan 1968

Madness Within, The—(TV) 1977

Maggie 1981

Magic Statue, The 1980

Magnificent Ambersons, The—(TV) 2002

Magnum Force 1973

Major Effects—(TV) 1979

Makin' It—(TV) 1979

Making Love 1982

Making The Grade—(TV) 1982

Malice In Wonderland—(TV movie) 1985

Mallory: Circumstantial Evidence—(TV movie) 1976
Maltese Bippy, The 1969
Mame 1974
Man Called Flintstone, The 1966
Man Called Gannon, A 1968
Man Eaters Are Loose 1978
Man From Atlantis—(TV) 1977
Man Of Honor, A 1981
Man On A Swing 1974
Man Who Loved Cat Dancing, The 1973
Mandingo 1975
Manitou, The 1978
Mannix—(TV) 1968-75
Man's Favorite Sport? 1964
Marathon Man 1976
Marcus-Nelson Murders—(TV) 1973
Marcus Welby, MD—(TV) 1972-73
Marian Rose White—(TV movie) 1981
Mario Puzo's The Last Don—(TV) 1997
Married To It 1991
Mars Attacks 1996
Marvin And Tige 1983
Marvin The Martian In The Third Dimension 1997
Mary Tyler Moore—(TV) 1973-76
Masada 1981
Masquerade 1988
Massacre 1976
Massarati And The Brain—(TV movie) 1982
Master, The—(TV) 1984
Master Gunfighter 1975
Mastermind 1976
Matchstick Men 2003
Matlock—(TV) 1980s-90s
Matt Houston—(TV) 1982
Maverick 1994
Max Dugan Returns 1983
Maxie 1985
McClain's Law—(TV) 1981

McCloud—(TV) 1980s
McHale's Navy 1964
Mean Girls 2004
Mean Season, The 1985
Medical Center—(TV) 1976
Meet Joe Black 1998
Meet The Parents 2000
Meet The Robinsons 2007
Megaforce 1982
Melinda 1972
Memorial Day—(TV movie) 1983
Men in Black 1997
Men in Black II 2002
Men in Black 3 2012
Men Of Honor 2000
Mephisto Waltz 1971
Mercury Rising 1998
Merv Griffin TV Shows 1971-72
Metamorphosis—(TV movie) 1987
Meteor 1979
Metro 1997
Mexican, The 2001
Michael 1996
Mickey Mouse Works—(TV) 1999
Micki + Maude 1984
Midnight In The Garden Of Good And Evil 1997
Midway 1976
Mighty Ducks, The 1992
Mighty Ducks 2 1994
Million Dollar Duck 1 And 2—(TV) 1974
Milton Berle TV Special 1978
Miracle On 34th Street—(TV movie) 1973
Mirage 1965
Mission: Impossible—(TV) 1966-73
Mission: Impossible 1996
Mission: Impossible 3 2006
Mission: Impossible 4 2011
Mississippi Masala 1991
Mister Buddwing 1966

Mod Squad–(TV) 1968-72
Modern Problems 1981
Molly Maguires, The 1970
Money Talks 1997
Money Trap, The 1965
Mongo's Back In Town–(TV movie) 1971
Monkey Shines 1988
Monte Walsh 1970
Moon Over Parador 1988
Moonlighting–(TV) 1986
Moonshine War, The 1970
Mork And Mindy–(TV) 1979
Morning 1983
Mountain Men, The 1980
Mouse And His Child, The 1977
Moving Violation 1976
Mr. And Mrs. Smith 2005
Mr. Baseball 1992
Mr. Destiny 1990
Mr. Ed–(TV) 1960s
Mr. Horn–(TV movie) 1979
Mr. Jones 1993
Mr. Mom 1983
Mr. Smith 1983
Mrs. Doubtfire 1993
Mulan 1998
Mulholland Falls 1996
Mumford 1999
Munsters–(TV) 1960s
Munsters' Revenge, The–(TV movie) 1981
Muppet Show–(TV) 1970s
Muppet's Wizard of Oz, The
Murder Among Friends–(TV movie) 1985
Murder By Death 1976
Murder Me, Murder You–(TV) 1983
Murder, She Wrote–(TV) 1985-94
Murderer's Row 1966
Murph The Surf 1975
Muscle Beach Party 1964
Muzak 1980

My Best Friend's Wedding 1997
My Blood Runs Cold 1965
My Favorite Martian–(TV) 1960s
My Giant 1998
My Girl 1991
My Kingdom For A Horse–(TV) 1991
My Life 1993
My Old Man–(TV movie) 1979
My Science Project 1985
My Stepmother Is An Alien 1988
My Three Sons–(TV) 1960s
Mysterious Monsters, The 1976
Mystery Of The Haunted House–(TV) 1977
Mystic River 2003
Nacho Libre 2006
Naked Gun: From The Files Of Police Squad 1988
Namu the Killer Whale 1966
Napoleon And Josephine: A Love Story–(TV) 1987
Nat'l Geographic (TV): Amazon Land Flooded 1990
Nat'l Geographic (TV): Australia's Animal 1980
Nat'l Geographic (TV): Bushman Of The Kalahari 1974
Nat'l Geographic (TV): Creatures Of Namib Desert 1986
Nat'l Geographic (TV): Dr. Leakey And Dawn 1976
Nat'l Geographic (TV): Great Whales 1977
Nat'l Geographic (TV): Great White Sharks 1980
Nat'l Geographic (TV): Grizzlies 1980
Nat'l Geographic (TV): Incredible Human 1975
Nat'l Geographic (TV): Mysteries Of Mankind 1988
Nat'l Geographic (TV): Mysterious Mind 1980

Nat'l Geographic (TV): Save The
Panda 1983
Nat'l Geographic (TV): Save The
Whales 1980
Nat'l Geographic (TV): Search For The
Great Apes 1975
Nat'l Geographic (TV): Serengeti 1989
Natural, The 1984
Navy AKA Emerald Point–(TV) 1983
Necessary Roughness 1991
Neighbors 1981
Neptune Factor, The 1973
New Adventures Of Heidi, The–(TV
Movie) 1980s
New Adventures Of Wonder Woman,
The 1977-78
New Centurions, The 1972
New Kind of Love, A 1963
New Leave It To Beaver–(TV) 1986
New Maverick–(TV) 1978
New World 1976
Newhart–(TV) 1984-85
Newman 1980s
Newman's Law 1974
Next Karate Kid, The 1994
Next of Kin 1984
Next Step Beyond, The–(TV) 1978
Nickel Ride, The 1974
Nightbreed 1990
Night Gallery–(TV) 1971-73
Nightingales 1988
Nightmare 1976
Nightmare Before Christmas, The 1993
Night Stalker 1987
Nobody's Perfect–(TV) 1980
North And South–(TV) 1984-85
Northern Exposure–(TV) 1991-92
Not With My Wife, You Don't 1966
Nothing But Trouble 1991
Notorious Landlady 1962
Now And Then 1995

Now You See Him, Now You Don't 1972
Nude Bomb, The 1980
Nunzio 1978
Nutcracker: Money, Madnes
& Murder–(TV) 1987
Nutty Professor, The 1963
Oceans of Fire–(TV movie) 1986
Off Beat 1986
Off Limits 1988
Oh. God! 1977
Oh, God! You Devil 1984
Oklahoma Crude 1973
Old Gringo 1989
Olly, Olly, Oxen Free 1978
O'Malley–(TV movie) 1983
On Deadly Ground 1994
On the Ropes 2001
On Wings Of Eagles–(TV) 1986
Once An Eagle–(TV) 1976
Once Around 1991
Once Upon A Brothers Grimm–(TV
movie) 1977
Once Upon A Crime 1992
Once You Kiss A Stranger 1969
One And Only, The 1978
One Crazy Summer 1986
One From the Heart 1982
One Little Indian 1973
One More Saturday Night 1986
One More Train To Rob 1971
One Of My Wives Is Missing–(TV
movie) 1976
One On One 1977
One Or The Other 2004
Onassis: The Richest Man In The
World–(TV movie) 1988
Oregon Trail–(TV) 1976-77
Organization, The 1971
Original Sin–(TV movie) 1989
Oscar 1991
Oscar And Lucinda 1997

Osterman Weekend, The 1983
Other, The 1970
Our World-(TV) 1986
Outbreak 1995
Out Of Africa 1985
Out Of Sight 1994
Out Of Time 2003
Out On A Limb-(TV movie) 1987
Outfit, The 1973
Outland 1981
Outlanders, The 1978
Outlaw Cats Of Colossal Cave, The-(TV) 1975
Outlaw Josey Wales, The 1976
Over the Edge 1979
Oz The Great And Powerful 2013
P. J. 1968
Pack, The 1977
Package, The 1989
Paint Your Wagon 1969
Pale Rider 1985
Panache-(TV movie) 1976
Pancho Barnes-(TV movie) 1988
Paper Chase, The 1973
Paper, The 1994
Papillon 1973
Paris When It Sizzles 1964
Partridge In A Pear Tree 1980
Passenger 57 1992
Paternity 1981
Patsy, The 1964
Patton 1970
Paw Paws-(TV) 1985
Pearl Harbor 2001
Pee-wee's Big Adventure 1985
Pee-wee's Playhouse-(TV) 1980s
Pen 'N' Inc. -(TV movie) 1981
Pentagon Papers, The-(TV movie) 2003
People's Choice Awards 1978
Perfect Murder, A 1998

Perfect World, A 1993
Peter And Paul-(TV movie) 1981
Peter Pan 2003
Pieces of Dreams 1970
Pink Floyd The Wall 1982
Pioneer Woman-(TV movie) 1973
Pipe Dreams 1976
Pirate, The-(TV movie) 1978
Pirates Of The Caribbean 2003
Planet Of The Apes 1968
Planet Of The Apes 2001
Play Misty For Me 1971
Pleasantville 1998
Plutonium Incident, The-(TV movie) 1980
Pocahontas II: Journey To A New World 1998
Point Blank 1967
Point Pleasant-(TV) 2005
Police Squad-(TV) 1982
Police Story, The Cut Man Caper-(TV) 1975
Pollock 2000
Poltergeist 1982
Poltergeist II 1986
Pope Of Greenwich Village, The 1984
Poseidon Adventure, The 1972
Posse 1975
Possessed, The-(TV movie) 1977
Postman, The 1997
Postman Always Rings Twice, The 1981
Practice -(TV) 1997
Prayer For The Dying 1987
Predator 1987
Prep & Landing 2-(TV) 2010
President's Analyst, The 1967
Pretty In Pink 1986
Pretty Maids All in A Row 1971
Pretty Poison 1968
Pretty Woman 1990
Primal Fear 1996

Prince And The Pauper–(TV movie) 1996
Prince Of Central Park–(TV movie) 1977
Prince Of Tides 1991
Princess And The Cabbie, The–(TV movie) 1981
Princess Daisy–(TV movie) 1983
Prison For Children–(TV movie) 1987
Private Eye: War Buddy–(TV) 1987
Prize Winner Of Defiance, Ohio 2005
Prizzi's Honor 1985
Problem Child 2 1991
Professionals, The–(TV) 1970s
Project X-(Fox) 1987
Project X-(Paramount) 1968
Project X-(Universal) 1978
Promise–(TV movie) 1986
Promises In The Dark 1979
Proof of Life 2000
Prophecy 1979
Protocol 1984
Proud Bird From Shanghai 9, The–(TV) 1973
Psycho II 1982
Punky Brewster–(TV) 1984-85
Pure Luck 1991
Pursuit–(TV movie) 1972
Pursuit of D.B. Cooper 1981
Pursuit Of Happiness, The 1971
Quarterback Princess–(TV movie) 1983
Queen Of The Damned 2002
Questor Tapes–(TV movie) 1974
Quigley Down Under 1990
Quincy–(TV) 1977
Rabbit, Run 1970
Race For Survival–(TV) 1978
Race With the Devil 1975
Radioland Murders 1994
Rafferty–(TV) 1977
Raggedy Man 1981
Raid On Entebbe 1977

Raid On Rommel 1971
Raise The Titanic 1980
Rambo: First Blood, Part II 1985
Rape Of Richard Beck, The–(TV movie) 1970s
Ratatouille 2006
Ravagers 1979
Rawhide–(TV) 1960s
Real Ghostbusters–(TV) 1988
Real Steel 2011
Real World–(TV) 1992
Rebels, The–(TV movie) 1979
Red Dawn 1984
Red Dragon 2002
Red Heat 1988
Red Skelton Show–(TV) 1970s
Red Sky At Morning 1971
Redwood Curtain–(TV movie) 1995
Reggie–(TV) 1983
Reincarnation Of Peter Proud 1975
Reivers, The 1969
Remington Steele–(TV) 1982-85
Remo Williams–(TV) 1988
Rented Lips 1988
Resurrection 1980
Return Of Jafar, The 1994
Return Of Sherlock Holmes, The–(TV) 1986
Return To Earth–(TV movie) 1976
Return To Lonesome Dove–(TV) 1993
Return To Me 2000
Return To The Blue Lagoon 1991
Revenge of the Nerds 1984
Revenge of the Stepford Wives–(TV movie) 1980
Rhinemann Exchange 1980s–(TV movie) 1977
Rich Man, Poor Man–(TV) 1976
Rig, The 1986
Right Stuff, The 1983
Ringer–(TV) 1996

Rio Conchos 1964

Rio Lobo 1970

Riot 1968

Ripley's Believe It Or Not–(TV) 1982

Rita Hayworth, The Love
Goddess–(TV movie) 1983

River Wild, The 1994

Road House 1989

Robert Kennedy And His Times–(TV) 1985

Robin And The Seven Hoods 1964

Robin Hood, Prince of Thieves 1991

Robocop 2 1990

Robocop 3 1993

Rock, The 1996

Rocky III 1982

Rocky IV 1985

Rocky–(TV) 1990

Roger Rabbit, Tummy Trouble–(TV)
1989

Rollercoaster 1977

Roman Grey: The Fine Art Of
Crime–(TV movie) 1975

Rookie Of The Year 1993

Rookie, The 1990

Rooster 1975

Rooster Cogburn 1982

Roots–(TV) 1976-79

Roots: The Gift AKA Roots Christmas–
(TV movie) 1988

Roses Are For The Rich–(TV movie) 1983

Roswell–(TV) 1999

Rough Cut 1980

Roustabout 1964

Rover Dangerfield 1990

Roxanne: Prize Pulitzer, The–(TV
movie) 1989

Ruby Cairo/Deception 1993

Rudy 1993

Rumor Of War 1980

Run Buddy Run–(TV) 1966

Run Down, The 2003

Runaway Bride 1999

Runaway Father–(TV movie) 1991

Runner, The 1999

Running Brave 1983

Running Hot 1984

Rush Hour 1998

Rush Hour 2 2001

Rush Hour 3 2007

SAG Awards 1996

Salem's Lot 1979

Salvage–(TV) 1979

Salzburg Connection, The 1972

Same Time, Next Year 1978

Sam Whiskey 1969

Sammy Davis Jr.–(TV Specials) 1970s

Samurai–(TV movie) 1979

Sand Pebbles 1966

Sanford And Son–(TV) 1970s

Sarah T: Portrait Of A Teenage Alco-
holic- (TV movie) 1975

Satan's School For Girls–(TV movie)
1973

Saturday Night Fever 1977

Savages 1972

Scarecrow, The 1973

Scavenger Hunt 1979

Scene Of The Crime–(TV) 1984-85

Scooby Doo–(TV) 1970s

Scout, The 1994

Scream 1996

Scream Blacula Scream 1973

Scream Pretty Peggy–(TV movie) 1980s

Scrooged 1988

Search For The Great Apes–(TV) 1976

Seconds 1966

Second Thoughts 1983

Secret Of Old Glory Mine–(TV movie)
1976

Secrets Of A Mother And Daughter–
(TV movie) 1983

Seekers–(TV movie) 1979

Spaceballs 1987
Sparkle 1976
Special Delivery 1976
Specialist, The 1994
Speed 2: Cruise Control 1997
Speed Racer 2008
Spell, The–(TV movie) 1977
Spider-Man 2002
Spider-Man 2 2004
Spider-Man–(TV) 2003
Spin City 1997-98
Spinout 1966
Split Image 1982
Split, The 1968
Spongebob–(TV) 1999
Sprague 1983
Spy Hard 1996
Squaw, The 1975
Squids (IMAX) 1993
St. Ives 1976
St. Valentine's Day–(TV) 1977
St. Valentines Day Massacre 1967
Star Chamber 1983
Starcrash AKA Stella Starr 1978
Star Is Born, A 1976
Star Trek 1979
Star Trek II: The Wrath of Khan 1982
Star Trek III: The Search For Spock 1984
Star Trek IV: The Voyage Home 1986
Star Trek TNG: We'll Always Have Paris–(TV) 1988
Star Trek V: The Final Frontier 1989
Star Trek VI: The Undiscovered Country 1991
Star Trek: First Contact 1996
Star Trek: Insurrection 1998
Star Trek: TNG 2000
Star Trek: Enterprise—(TV) 2002
Star Trek: The Prelude 2009
Star Trek 2013

Starflight: The Plane That Couldn't Land–(TV movie) 1983
Stark–(TV movie) 1985
Stars Fell On Henrietta 1995
Starship Troopers 1997
Starsky And Hutch–(TV) 1975-79
Star Wars–(TV Special) 1978
State of Grace 1990
Statesman, The–(TV) 1975
Steel 1997
Steel Magnolias 1989
Sterile Cuckoo, The 1969
Steve Allen–(TV shows) 1980s
Stewardess School 1986
Stick 1986
Stickin' Together AKA Wonderland Cove—(TV movie) 1978
Strange And Deadly Occurrence, The–(TV movie) 1974
Streets of Fire 1984
Streets Of San Francisco–(TV) 1972-76
Strike Force–(TV) 1981
Stripes 1981
Striptease 1996
Stunt Man, The 1980
Sudden Impact 1983
Sugarland Express 1974
Summer of '42 1971
Sunchaser. The 1996
Sunset 1988
Super Cops 1974
Superdome/Disney Orlando 2002
Super 8 2011
Superhuman Syber-Squad AKA SSSS-(TV) 1994
Survive the Savage Sea–(TV movie) 1992
Suspect Behavior–(TV) 2000
Swashbuckler, The 1976
S.W.A.T. –(TV) 1975-76
Sweepstakes–(TV) 1979
Sweet Charity 1969

Sweet Ride. The 1968
Sweet November 1968
Swinger, The 1966
Switch–(TV) 1976-77
Switching Channels 1988
Sword Of Justice–(TV) 1978
Sybil–(TV movie) 1976
Sylvester And Tweety–(TV) 1995
Sylvia 1965
Synanon 1965
T. W. A. T., Cheech And Chong 1976
Taffy And The Jungle Hunter 1965
Taking Of Pelham 1 2 3, The 1965
Tales Of The Unexpected–(TV) 1977
Tank 1984
Tap 1989
Taps 1981
Target Risk–(TV) 1975
Tarzan, The Ape Man 1981
Tattoo 1981
Taxi–(TV) 1978
Taxi Driver 1976
Tecumseh: The Last Warrior–(TV movie) 1995
Teenage Ninja Turtles–(TV) 1990s
Telefon 1977
Tell Them Willie Boy Is Here 1969
Tender Warrior 1971
Tenth Man, The–(TV movie) 1988
Terror On The 40th Floor–(TV movie) 1974
Terror On The Beach–(TV movie) 1973
Testimony of Two Men–(TV) 1977
That Championship Season 1982
That's Dancing 1985
That's Life 1986
They Call Me Mister Tibbs 1970
They Might Be Giants 1971
Thieves Like us AKA Gang 1974
Thin Red Line, The 1998

Things Are Tough All Over 1982
Thomas Crown Affair, The 1968
Thomas Crown Affair, The 1999
Thorn Birds, The–(TV) 1983
Three Amigos! 1986
Three Days Of The Condor 1975
Three Musketeers, The 1993
Three On A Couch 1966
Thursday Game–(TV movie) 1974
Thursday's Child–(TV movie) 1983
THX 1138 1971
Tickle Me 1965
Tide Is High, The 1970
Tiger Makes Out, The 1967
Tightrope 1984
Time For Killing, A 1967
Timon And Pumbba—(TV) 1995-96
Tiny Toons–(TV) 1990-92
To Find My Son—(TV movie) 1980
To Race the Wind—(TV movie) 1970s
Tom And Jerry: The Movie 1992
Tony Rome 1967
Topaz 1969
Tortilla Soup 2001
Toy Story 1995
Toy, The 1982
Trade Winds–(TV) 1993
Trader Horn 1973
Train Robbers, The 1973
Trauma Center—(TV) 1983
Treasure Planet 2002
T-Rex 1995
Trial Of Billy Jack, The 1974
Trial Of Lee Harvey Oswald, The—(TV movie) 1977
Triple Cross 1967
Triumph Of The Spirit 1989
Trouble Man 1972
True Crime 1999
True Identity 1991

Try To Find A Spy 1964
Tummy Trouble 1989
Turnabout—(TV) 1979
Twilight Zone—(TV) 1985-86
Twilight Zone: The Movie 1983
Twins 1988
Twister, Bull From The Sky—(TV) 1976
Two Bits 1995
Two Of A Kind 1983
Two Of A Kind—(TV) 1998
Two Of Us—(TV) 1981
Two On A Guillotine 1965
Two People 1973
Two Worlds, The 1990
Ultimate Impostor, The—(TV movie) 1979
Ultimate Warrior 1975
Ulzana's Raid 1972
Unaccompanied Minors 2006
Uncle Joe Shannon 1978
Uncommon Valor 1983
Unconditional Love 1999
Under Siege 2: Dark Territory 1995
Under The Rainbow 1981
Under The Volcano 1984
Underwater City 1962
Unfaithfully Yours 1984
Unforgiven 1992
Unmarried Woman, An 1978
Up 2009
Up the Sandbox 1972
Used Cars 1980
Users, The—(TV movie) 1978
U. S. Marshals 1998
V—(TV movie) 1983
Valdez Is Coming 1971
Valley Of The Dolls 1981
Vanilla Sky 2001
Vanishing, The 1993
Vega$—(TV) 1978
Vegas Vacation 1997

Velvet—(TV movie) 1984
Venetian Affair, The 1967
Vengance Unlimited—(TV) 1998
Vertical Limit 2000
Victims, The—(TV movie) 1969
Victory AKA Escape To Victory 1981
Vigilante Force 1976
Villa Rides 1968
Villain, The 1979
Violets Are Blue 1986
Vital Signs AKA Crisis 1990
Voyage Of The Damned 1976
Voyagers—(TV) 1982
V—(TV movie) 1983-84
WUSA 1970
Wackiest Ship In The Army—(TV) 1965
Walk, Don't Run 1966
Walk On The Moon, A 1999
Walk Proud 1979
Wall Street 1987
Waltons, The—(TV) 1977
Wanted 2008
War At Home, The 1996
War Of The Roses 1989
Waterworld 1995
Weapons Of Mass Distraction—(TV movie) 1997
Weather Man, The 2005
Welcome Home AKA Passage 1989
West Wing, The 2002
Whatever Happened To Aunt Alice? 1969
What Women Want 2000
What's Love Got To Do With It 1993
What's So Bad About Feeling Good? 1968
What's the Matter With Helen ? 1971
Wheels—(TV) 1978
When Dreams Come True—(TV movie) 1985

When Hell Was in Session—(TV movie) 1979
When The Boys Meet the Girls 1965
When You Comin' Back, Red Ryder? 1979
Where Angels Go...Trouble Follows 1968
Where Love Has Gone 1964
Where The Buffalo Roam 1980
Where The River Runs Black 1986
Where Were You When the Lights Went Out? 1968
Whiffs 1975
Whirlwind, The—(TV movie) 1974
White Buffalo 1977
White Dawn, The 1974
White Fang 1991
White Hunter Black Heart 1990
White Lighting 1973
White Mama—(TV movie) 1980
Who'll Stop the Rain 1978
Wholly Moses! 1980
Who's Been Sleeping In My Bed? 1963
Who's Got The Action? 1962
Who's Minding The Mint? 1967
Wild Bill 1995
Wild Bunch, The 1969
Wildcats 1986
Wild Rovers 1971
Wild, Wild West 1999
Wilder Napalm 1993
Wildfire 1986
Wilds Of Ten Thousand Lakes 1977
Wildside—(TV) 1985
Will And Grace—(TV) 2002
Will Penny 1968
Will There Really Be A Morning?—(TV movie) 1983
Willard 1971
Willie and Phil 1980
Willie Dynamite 1984
Wind 1992

Winter Kills 1979
Witchcraft 2000
Witches Of Eastwick 1987
Wolfman, The 2010
Wolfen 1981
Won Ton Ton: The Dog Who Saved Hollywood 1976
Wonder Woman—(TV) 1979
Wonderful World Of Disney—(TV) 1970s
Word, The 1978
World According To Garp, The 1982
World War III 1982
World's Greatest Athlete, The—(TV) 1983
Wrath Of God, The 1972
Wrongfully Accused 1998
Wyatt Earp 1994
X-Men 2000
Yakuza, The 1974
Year Of The Comet 1992
Year Of The Dragon 1985
Yellow Rose—(TV) 1983
Yes, Georgio 1982
Yesterday's Child—(TV movie) 1977
Yogi Bear—(TV) 1980s
Yogi's All-Star Comedy Christmas Caper 1982
You Are the Jury—(TV) 1984
You'll Like My Mother 1972
Young At Heart—(TV movie) 1995
Young Doctors In Love 1982
Young Harry Houdini—(TV) 1987
Young Joe, The Forgotten Kennedy—(TV movie) 1977
Young Lust 1984
Young Pioneers—(TV) 1976-78
Zacharia 1971

APPENDIX 5:

RANGE FINDER

For The

PERCUSSION

Seeker

A List Of
Six Hundred and Fifty
Percussion Instruments
With Their Ranges
By
EMIL RICHARDS

The Percussionist's Standard Equiptment

I Mallet Instruments

Marimba
Orchestra Bells
Xylophone

II Chimes

III Vibraphone

IV Timpani

V Percussion Instruments

Anvil, Bamboo Wind Chimes, Bell Plate, Bird Whistles, Boat Whistles, Brass Wind Chimes, Bulb Horn, Concert Bass Drum (Gran Cassa), Concert Snare Drum, Cow Bell, Cricket Clicker, Cymbal(s), Duck Call, Field Drum, Fire Bell, Fight Bell, Glass Wind Chimes, Jingle Sticks, Piatti (Pair of Cymbals), Piccolo Snare Drum, Pop Gun, Ratchet, Ship's Bell, Siren Whistle, Slap Stick, Sleigh Bells, Slide Whistle, Tabor (Tabour), Tambourine, Tam Tam (Gong), Temple Blocks, Tom Tom, Triangle, Washboard, Wood Block.

Latin Instruments

Au-Go-Go, Bongos, Cabasa, Castanets, Cencerro (Latin Cow Bell), Chocalho (Snaker), Claves Conga Drums, Cuica, Guiro (Scratcher), Jawbone (Quijada), Maracas, Maraca Sticks, Pandero (Brazillian Tambourine), Puelli Sticks,Reco Reco (Scratcher), Sand Blocks, Timbales, Vibraslap.

Chromatic Percussion

Anvils Tune

Two octaves of Anvils are arranged in Keyboard
fashion. Played with hard Bell or Xylo mallets
Range-highest two Chromatic octaves of the piano.

Anvils Tuned

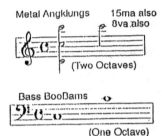

(Two Octaves)

Ang Klungs (Metal)

Triple Octave Chimes.
Each note strikes in triple octaves.
Played by shaking one in each hand.
(Two Octaves)

Metal Angklungs   15ma also
                   8va also

(Two Octaves)

Bass Doo Dams

Played with palm of open hands, as
tuned congas, or with soft mallets.
(One Octave)

Bass BooBams

(One Octave)

Bass Chimes

The extension of eight chimes begin
at (B) just below middle (C), where
the regular chimes end. They go down
chromatically to (E) below middle (C),
and are on a rack with a sustain pedal.

Bass Chimes   **Standard Chimes**

(8 Tone Extension)

Bass Gamelon

Individual metal bars are suspended
over box resonators and played as a
low metal-a-phone. One and a half octaves.

Bass Gamelon

(One and a half Octaves)

Bass Marimba

Played with large, soft or medium
mallets. This instruments. starts lower
than most known marimbas.
(Two Octaves)

Bass Marimba

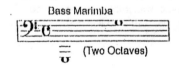

(Two Octaves)

176

Chromatic Percussion

Bass Vibraphone

The top note of the Bass Vibe is the
lowest note of the standard Vibe. (F)
below middle (C), and extends down-
ward to Two (C's) below middle (C).
It has a sustain pedal, no vibrato.
(One Octave and a Fourth)

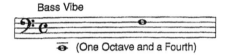

Bass Vibe

(One Octave and a Fourth)

Bell Lyre

Portable Glockenspiel in the
form of a lyre. Played with
hard rubber or brass mallets.
(Two Octaves and a Fourth)

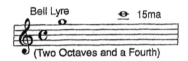

Bell Lyre   15ma

(Two Octaves and a Fourth)

Boo Bams

Tuned Bongoes played with
hands and fingers, or with soft
mallets.(Two Octaves)

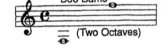

Boo Bams

(Two Octaves)

Bottles Tuned

Thirteen, half- magnum sake bottles
can be tuned, by adding water to their
contents. Played with hard rubber mallets.
(One Octave)

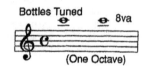

Bottles Tuned   8va

(One Octave)

Brass Tube Gamelon

Brass, hollow tubes are cut and
tuned to sound like Metal-a-phones
of Javanese and Balinese Gamelon.
Played with rubber or hard vibe
mallets. (Three Octaves).

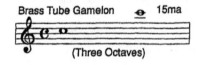

Brass Tube Gamelon   15ma

(Three Octaves)

Chromatic Percussion

Boom Whackers Tuned

Three octaves of chromatic tuned plastic tubes are arranged
Keyboard fashion. The sound is similar to a muffled BooBam.
Played with hard Xylo, or soft Vibraphone mallets

Boom Whackers

(Three Octaves)

Bulb Horns-(Tuned)

Each bulb can be "honked" by
squeezing the rubber bulb
attached to each tone.
(Two Octaves).

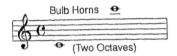

Bulb Horns

(Two Octaves)

Buzz Marimba

By placing onion skin paper under each bar, over
each resonator, the authentic "buzz" tone of the
South American and African Marimbas can be produced.
Played with Mallets.(Four Octaves).

Buzz Marimba   8va

(Four Octaves)

Buzz Marimba (Buzzimba)

A membrain of monkey intestine
is placed at the base of each
resonator, to produce a loud buzzing
sound when played with medium
marimba mallets.(Three Octaves)

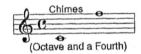

Buzzimba

(Three Octaves)

Chimes (Tubular Bells)

Struck with raw hide hammers
muted hammers, or cluster bars.
sustain and dampening pedal attached.
(One Octave and a Fourth)

Chimes

(Octave and a Fourth)

Chimes Bass - See (Bass Chimes).

Cimbalon-(Cimbalum)

Three to four strings per note, are
struck with cotton wound, or wooden
stick mallets to produce piano-like
tones. A sustain pedal is attached.
(Four Octaves) and one lower tone.

Cimbalum

(Four Octaves)

Chromatic Percussion

Cow Bells

Played with soft or hard rubber mallets
and mounted in keyboard fashion.(Two Octaves).

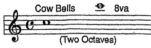

Cow Bells (Extended Range)

Same as above set with wider range.
(Two and a half Octaves).

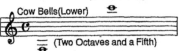

Crotales

Tuned finger cymbal-like disks
are played with brass or hard rubber
mallets to produce striking brilliant,
bell-like tones. (Two Octaves).

Crotales (Bowed)

Same as above; they also are suspended
so that each disk can be bowed to produce
high string harmonic-like tones.
(Two Octaves)

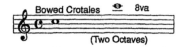

Dulcimer

Strings are struck with padded hammers
or wood mallets. (Three Octaves)

Electronic Vibraphone

Electronic pick-ups are mounted under
each bar and can be in-put into any existing
electronic devise. Played with all styles
of mallets (Three and a Quarter Octaves).

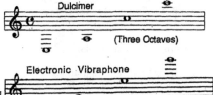

Chromatic Percussion

Flapamba

The bars of this Marimba-like instrument are suspended at one end rather than at the nodal points, producing an unusual "liquid" woody sound when played with very soft mallets or fingers, A hard mallet will produce a "slap-tongue" effect. (Two Octaves)

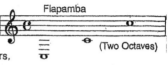

Flapamba

(Two Octaves)

Flapamba (New) Extended Range

This instrument was built in mid 2007.
Like the Flapamba, it has a very liquid, mellow quality.
It's range goes lower and higher than the original Flapamba.

Flapamba (New)

(Three and a quarter Octaves)

Gamelon -See -"Brass Tube Gamelon" See - " Pipe Gamelon" See-Gongs,Tuned Nipple Gongs

Giant Thumb Piano

Known as ARRAY M'BIRA, this instrument was built by theorist, William Wesley. It has Five Octaves of unisons on each note. Arranged in cycles of Fifths, it's range starts on C, Two octaves below middle C, and can play as much as 5 Octaves of each note. The whole sequence repeats in a horizontal row, Three times Chromatically.

Giant Thumb Piano

Etc. moving in 5ths back up to (C)

Glasses - (Tuned)

Crystal Glasses are filled with water, for tuning. Played by bowing with string bow, over rims. (Two Octaves)

Glasses   8va

(Two Octaves)

Glass Marimba

The sound of this glass bar instrument is soft, clear, and resonant. There is an unusual water-like quality to it's tone. Played with soft mallets. (Two Octaves)

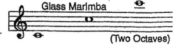

Glass Marimba

(Two Octaves)

Glockenspiel - See - Orchestra bells

Chromatic Percussion

Glock Tree

(Chromatic Wind Bells)
Three sets of Orchestra Bells are suspended
in wind chime fashion. Glisses can be repeated
3 times by passing over them with sweep of hand,
or hard rubber mallet. (Two and a Half Octaves).

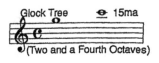

Glock Tree   15ma
(Two and a Fourth Octaves)

Gongs (Tuned Nipple Gongs)

Tuned tone Gongs are bossed with a sound center. They are all tuned to
chromatic pitches. They are played with specific gong beaters, and struck on
their bossed centers to produce pure sustaining pitches. The Gongs are arranged
on seperate racks, and are listed below to show the physical hanging of each
octave. The Gongs in the lowest octave are 3 Ft. in diameter and require three
racks to hold them. They graduate in size as they ascend in pitch untill the
highest rack holds an octave and a fourth, and are 6 inches in diameter.
Range (Four Octaves and a Fourth)

Gong Rack#1,2,3. Two Octaves below Middle "C"

Rack#1 (C2)(C#2)(D2)(D#2)

Tuned Gongs (Rack1)

Rack#2 (E2)(F2)(F#2)(G2)

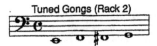

Tuned Gongs (Rack 2)

Rack#3 (G#2)(A2)(A#2)(B2)

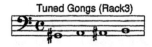

Tuned Gongs (Rack3)

Tuned Gongs (Rack 4)

Rack#4 (C3)(C#3)(D3)(D#3)(E3)(F3)

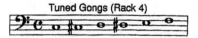

Chromatic Percussion

Gong Rack#4,5 One Octave below Middle"C"

Rack#5 (F#3)(G3)(G#3)(A3)(A#3)(B3)

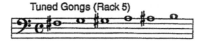

Tuned Gongs (Rack 5)

Gong Rack#6 Middle"C"Octave

Rack #6 (C4)(C#4)(D4)(D#4)(E4)(F4)(F#$)(G4)(G#4)(A4)(A#4)(B4)

Tuned Gongs (Rack 6)

Gong Rack#7 One Octave above Middle"C"to 3 F's above Middle "C"
Rack#7 (C5)(C#5)(D5)(D#5)(E5)(F5)(f#5)(G5)(G#5)(A5)(A#5)(B5)(C6)(C#6)(D6)
(D#6)(E6)(F6)

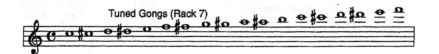

Tuned Gongs (Rack 7)

Harmonium

Although the actual keyboard range extends
two and a half octaves, the stops can extend
the range upward and downward 5 octaves. The
feet must be employed pumping while playing
the keyboard.(Five Octaves)

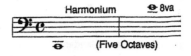

Harmonium   8va

(Five Octaves)

Chromatic Percussion

Jaltarang (Tuned Bowls)

Porcelain rice bowls, tuned by amounts of
water poured into them. Played with wooden
sticks.(One Octave and a Fourth).

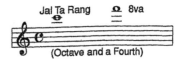

Kalimba

South African Thumb Piano, played with thumbs,
and thumb Nails.Tuning can be altered by moving
metal tongues. (Two Octaves)

Kelon Marimba

Marimba with bars made of a kelon plastic. The
sound is warm and resonant, with extended range.
Played with soft and hard mallets.
(Four and a half Octaves).

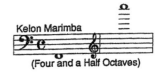

Kettle Drums - See - Timpani

Keyboard String Harp

One hand strums the unison strings with a guitar
pick, while the other hand depresses the keyboard
arrangement of keys. (Two Octaves)

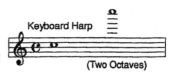

Log Drums Tuned

Wood bars are suspended over individual
box resonators, so that specific tones can be
used as rhythm accents. Played with soft mallets.
(One and a half Octaves)

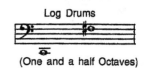

Marimba (Standard)

Played with soft to loud wound
mallets.(Four Octaves)

Chromatic Percussion

Octa Marimba (Octave Marimba)

Each bar of this instrument has two bars
side by side. One bar sounds an octave higher
than the bar next to it. When struck with
special soft or hard double-headed mallets,
each bar sounds in octaves. The instrument is
physically 3 octaves, but plays the range
of a standard marimba. (Four Octaves)

Octave Marimba

(Four Octaves)

Octa Vibe (Octave Vibraphone)
Same as Octa Marimba above. One bar sounds
an octave higher than the bar next to it. The same
principle as the twelve string guitar. Regular vibe range.

Octa Vibe

Three Octaves)

Orchestra Bells (Glock)

Glockenspiel with miniature piano keyboard,
played with hard rubber or brass mallets.
(Two Octaves and a Fourth.)

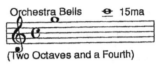

Orchestra Bells   15ma

(Two Octaves and a Fourth)

Orchestra Bells (Extended Range)

Made especially for music that requires
a larger range. Played with hard rubber,
or brass mallets. (Three Octaves and a Semi-Tone)

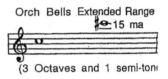

Orch Bells Extended Range
15 ma

(3 Octaves and 1 semi-tone

Parcifal Bells

Same range as orchestra bells with resonators
under each tone bar. Formerly used in symphonic
writing. (Two octaves and a Fourth)

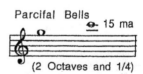

Parcifal Bells
15 ma

(2 Octaves and 1/4)

Piccolo Boo Bams (Plastic Xylophone)

Tuned plastic golf club protector tubes have
been cut and tuned in keyboard fashion. Played
with soft or hard mallets.
(Two Octaves)

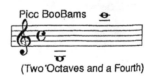

Picc BooBams

(Two Octaves and a Fourth)

Chromatic Percussion

Piccolo Wood Blocks

Hollow Wood Blocks in high range.
Played with hard rubber or wood mallets
(Two Octaves)

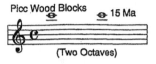

Pipe Gamelon

Made out of one and a half inch galvanized
pipe. Set up in keyboard fashion. The pipes
produce unusual overtones with the funda-
mental pitch creating the sound of Gamelon
found in Bali and Java. (Three Octaves)

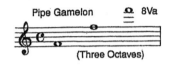

Roto Toms

There are seven different sized Roto
Drums.Each can be readily tuned, by
rotating the rims,to change the pitch
tension on the drum.Played with soft
mallets or drum sticks.The seven pitches
encompass a (Three and a half Octave Range)

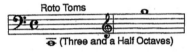

Rub Rods (Round)

Round solid aluminium tubes are suspended
in tubular chime like fashion. A pair of gloves
are worn and rubbed with rosen. When the
gloved fingers stroke the rods, high,string-
like, long sustaining harmonics are produced.
(One Octave)

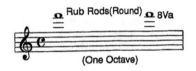

Rub Rods (Square)

Square hollow aluminium tubes. Same as above
with slightly different range. Played by stroking
rods with rosened gloves.long sustaining.
(One Octave)

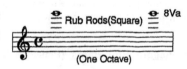

Chromatic Percussion

Satellite Cans

These are tuned hollow metal pans. There is a metal rod welded across the middle of each pan, where the instrument is struck, to produce steel drum-like tones, with it's own unique quality of sound and over-tones. (Two Octaves)

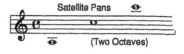

Sleigh Bells (Tuned)

Small groups of tuned sleigh bells are strung on individual straps. Each player can hold one pitch in each hand (Swiss Hand Bell) style. The bells are hand held and shook. (Two Octaves)

Song Bells

The Song Bells are in the full bodied range of the Celesta. They play lower than orchestra bells, and are played with hard or soft yarn covered mallets. (Two Octaves and a Fourth)

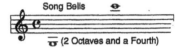

Stone Marimba

The slate stone's ,inherently low vibration, gives it an unusual timbre ,not found in other materials. The low notes are gusty and rich in overtones,while the upper notes are sharp and clear.(Two Octaves)

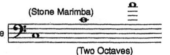

Steel Drums (Melody Pan)

Oil Drum with hammered grooves are tuned to chromatic pitches. Played with soft wound , rubber mallets.(Two Octaves)

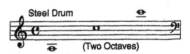

Chromatic Percussion

Steel Marimba

It has the quality of lower pitched song bells
or celesta, played with soft mallets, or can have
the sound of tuned Gamelon with hard mallets.
(Three Octaves)

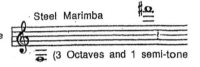

Steel Marimba

(3 Octaves and 1 semi-tone

Swiss Hand Bells

These are tuned bells. Each bell is on a handle.
Each player holds one bell in each hand and plays
their individual notes, to correspond to the song
being played, by the whole ensemble. There is a
knocker in each bell, that has a soft or hard striker.
Each bell is hand held and shook, producing one
strike for each bell-shake. (Two Octaves)

Swiss Hand Bells

(Two Octaves)

Thumb Piano(Tuned) see **Kalimba / Giant Thumb Piano**

Timpani (Timpany) (Kettle Drums)
The modern Timpani can be tuned by means of a pedal very quickly. Standard
drum sizes are 32"- 30"- 29"-28"-26"-25"-23".(One Octave and a Sixth)

Standard Timpani Drum Sizes

32"-30"   29"-28"   26"-25"   23"

(Range Perfect Fifth-Possible Sixth)

TOY PIANO

One of the better made toy keyboards.
It has a three octave range, played like
a real piano with a good toy sound.

TOY PIANO

(Three Octaves)

Tube Bells (Viscount Bells)

These hollow steel/aluminium tubes are tuned
to the highest two octaves of the regular
orchestra bells, and add a high, sparkle-like
tone to a glock sound. Played with hard rubber
or brass mallets.(Two Octaves)

Tube Bells

(Two Octaves)

Chromatic Percussion

Tubolo

This instrument is made of hollow cardboard tubes, mounted in keyboard fashion. When slapped on their top ends with flat rubber shower thongs, the sound is like a louder set of Boo Bams,or a slap-toungue effect.(Three Octaves)

Tubular Bells See-(Chimes)

Vibraphone (Vibraharp)

A standard instrument with variable vibrato, sustain and damper pedal. Played with soft to hard wound mallets. (Three Octaves)

Vibraphone-(Soprano)

Range is Higher than standard Vibe, with sustain,damper pedal, and vibrato.

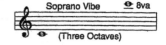

Woodblock-Xylorimba

Tuned wood blocks, with individual tone resonators placed under each block, give this instrument two unique sounds, when played with hard rubber or soft wound sticks. (Three Octaves)

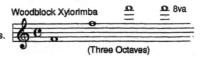

Xylophone

Standard instrument with wood or kelon bars. Played with hard rubber or wooden mallets. (Three and a half Octaves.)

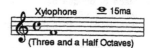

Xylorimba

Covers full Xylophone and Marimba range.One to four players can be employed on this instrument, with soft marimba mallets in lowest register, to hard xylo mallets in upper register.(Five Octaves)

TONAL PERCUSSION

NOTE: Many of the instruments found in this section do not always correspond to A-440 pitch. All of the **(MICROTONAL)** instruments are listed in this section.

African Marimba (Balafon) (Congo)

Five tone scale, repeating upward of three and a half octaves. Gourd resonators; played with mallets.

(African Marimba 5 Tone)

(3 1/2 Octaves)

African Marimba (West) (Curved)

Seven tone scale. One and a half octaves on curved frame with gourd resonators. Played with Mallets.

(African Marimba 7 Tone)

(Two Octaves)

African Marimba (Amadinda)

Five tone scale, made of spruce wood. Derivative of the Ugandan Marimba. Twelve pitches, Pentatonic. Played with padded sticks on ends of bars.

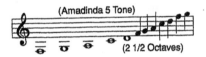

(Amadinda 5 Tone)

(2 1/2 Octaves)

Aluminiaphone (Micro-Tonal)

Thirty Five tones per octave. Made of conduit pipe. 3 1/3rd octave range. Played, or glissed with medium to hard mallets.

(Aluminiaphone) 15ma

(3 1/3 Octaves)

Ang Klungs (Bali Laos Thailand

Bamboo rattles played by holding one or two in each hand, and shaking. Each rattle plays in one or two octaves.

Ang Klungs

TONAL PERCUSSION

CLAY Marimba

The bars, and trough,(which
act as a resonator), are both
made of clay.The tuning is
pentatonic. Bars are long
sustaining. Played with   mallets.

(Upper Clay Bars)

8va

(Lower Clay Bars)

Clay Cup Bells

These are long ringing cups
of clay, tuned to the same five
tone pentatonic scale as the Clay
Marimba, mentioned above.It's six
pitches correspond to the highest six of
the clay marimba. Played with chop sticks.

(Clay Cup Bowls)

8VA

(One Octave)

Cup Chime Cymbals

The seven graduated cymbals start
small, as they have been cut down near
the bell of each cymbal so that the tone
of each is as pronounced as the crash sound.

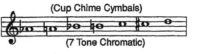

(Cup Chime Cymbals)

(7 Tone Chromatic)

Death Knell

Four foot tall steel and aluminum
bar is suspended over wooden box
chamber, with six metal resonators,
that amplify the different harmonics,
sounding from the bar. Soft mallet or
chime hammer produces the knell of the final hour.

(Death Knell)

Devil Chasers

Single toned drone, Jew's Harp-like,
bamboo sticks.Each player can hold
one in each hand, hitting the buzzing
bamboo against the knee, while activat-
ing the opening with the thumb, to
produce (wa wa) effects.

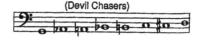

(Devil Chasers)

TONAL PERCUSSION

Dharma Bells (MICRO-TONAL)

Chineese Temple bells, usually found in sets
of 3, 5, or 7, have been all mounted together
on a rack, graduating from large to small, in a
28 tone to the octave scale. Struck with soft
mallets or glissed with wrapped sticks.

Flex A Drum

Drum has pedal which presses a bowl
against the under side of the drum to
produce upward and down-ward glisses.
Played with sticks.

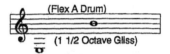

Flex A Tone Giant (Bowed)

Long piece of spring steel with handle, can
be struck or bowed. Pitches gliss two octaves.

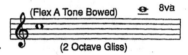

Gendere (Bali Metal a Phones)

Four Instruments make up this ensemble.Each instrument contains the
traditonal five tone scale repeated twice on each instrument.#1 and #3
are tuned the same.#2 and #4 are tuned microtonally apart, to create
vibrato, "beats," when they are played together.

TONAL PERCUSSION

Gongs African Double Bells

Non sustaining bell gongs
used as rhythm keepers.The
set of four have two pitches each.

Gong Bells (Congo)

Gongs (Bali)

Ringing gongs played with
soft mallet on bossed center.

Gongs (Bali)

Gongs (Balinese Gamelon)

Non sustaining gongs played
as rhythm keepers,played with
covered mallets, hit on bossed center,

Gongs Gamelon (Bali)

Gong (Burma)

Ringing gong played with soft mallet,
hit on bossed center.

Gong (Burma)

Gongs Cambodia

Non sustaining gongs played
with soft mallet.

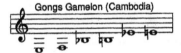

Gongs Gamelon (Cambodia)

Gong (Japan)

Long ringing, played with hard mallet,or used
as rhythm keeper. Played with bone mallet.

Gong (Japan)

Gongs (Java)

Sustaining gongs played
with soft mallet, hit on
bossed centers.

Gongs (Java)

TONAL PERCUSSION

Gongs (Korea)

Sustaining gongs played with soft
mallet, hit on bossed centers.

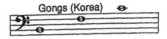

Gongs (Thailand)

Sustaining gongs played
with soft mallets, hit on
bossed centers.

Gongs (Tibet)

Sustaining gongs played with soft
mallets,hit on bossed centers.

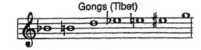

Hand Harmonium (India)

Hand pumped drone box pushes air
through the reed openings for any
combination of 1 to 8 pitches.

Japanese (Buddah Bell)

Large long sustaining bell, played by rubbing,
or striking the rim with leather covered club.
Produces many over tones.

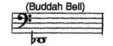

Japaneese Temple Bells

Bells are played by rubbing or
striking the rims with leather
covered stick. Bells can also be
bowed on timpani while depressing
timp pedal to gliss the pitches.

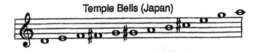

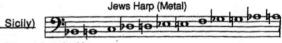

Jew's Harp (America. India. Sicily)

One tone (predominant) drone. Played by plucking
metal tongue while placing instrument in mouth,
against the open teeth,to form resonating cavity.

TONAL PERCUSSION

Jew's Harp (Bali)

One tone drone. Played by
plucking bamboo tongue.

Jew's Harps (Bali)

Kalimba (Bass)

Seven metal and seven bamboo
tongues can be readily tuned to
any seven tone scale. Played
by plucking tongues with fingers.

Kalimba (Bass)
(7 Tone Scale)

Lujons (Metal)

Six metal squares are suspended
over bamboo resonators and struck
with fingers or soft mallets.

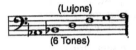
(Lujons)
(6 Tones)

Mandala Harp (India)

Strings are strummed and can be
tuned to scales within it's range.

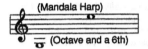
(Mandala Harp)
(Octave and a 6th)

Marimbula (Afro-Cuban)

Played by plucking metal tongues,
(with fingers) which are secured
over box resonator.Two sizes.

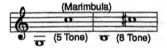
(Marimbula)
(5 Tone)   (8 Tone)

Marx A Phone

Played by depressing keys, which
strike spring steel mallets against
strings, in rapid, sustained motion.

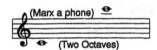
(Marx a phone)
(Two Octaves)

Mello Drum

Drum has pedal, which presses a bowl against
the under side of the skin. This causes the drum
to gliss upward. By striking the drum with sticks
in different areas, many different sounding glisses
can be made.

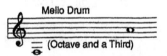
Mello Drum
(Octave and a Third)

TONAL PERCUSSION

Micro-Tonal   See: Alumin-a-Phone
                        Dharma Bells
                        Quarter Tone Xylophone
                        Thirty One Tone Bells
                        Trans-Celeste
                        Tubalong
                        Water Chimes

Quarter Tone Xylophone (Micro-Tonal)

Redwood bars are mounted together in
a single row to form a quarter tone scale.
Played by rolling in atremolo gliss fashion
with medium hard mallets.

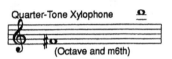

Roto Pedal Drum

Remo calls this the Timp Tom. You now have
the luxury of using both hands on the drum,
while your foot controls the ascending and
descending glisses, in a two octave spread.

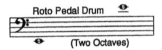

Santur (Iran.Persia)

Three octaves, diatonic, with four
strings per note. The strings are
struck with wood or cotton covered
sticks.Tuned to any 7 tones.

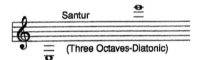

Slide Whistle (Bass)

Trombone like slide, moves up or
down, while blowing, to create
glissing tone bends.

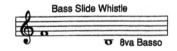

Slide Whistle (Tenor)

Smaller slide moves up or down while
blowing, to create glissing tone bends.

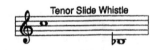

TONAL PERCUSSION

Stamping Tubes

Hollow bamboo tubes are stamped
on hard ground surface. One (unison)
pitch in each hand stamps out rhythm
and tone. Most effective with two or more players.

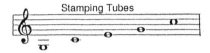

Sound Stone Sculptures

Two very large Rocks have been cut to produce a multitude of
arbitrary pitches, when glissed by rubbing 2 smaller stones against
them. The sounds are somewhat like striking a waterphone with a mallet.

Tabla (India)

Pair of tuned hand drums of north India
comprised of a treble drum (tabla), and
kettle drum (baya). A hammer is used to
tune the drums, which usually plays the
root of a scale. Played with fingers.

Tambura (India)

Four string drone is plucked, to produce
nasal like drone, to compliment sitar
or tabla players. Tuning pegs make it
possible to tune any four tones.

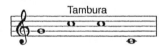

Thirty One Tone Bells (Micro Tonal)

31 tones in a one octave configuration.
Each bell has it's own individual tuned
resonator. Played with hard vibe mallets.

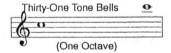

(One Octave)

Trans Celeste (Micro Tonal)

Fashioned after the east Indian sruti scale,
with twenty two tones to the octave. There
are two octaves, played or glissed with hard
vibe mallets.

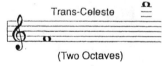

(Two Octaves)

Tubalong (Micro Tonal)

Three octaves of brass tubes are tuned to
thirty one tones to the octave. Played or
glissed with hard mallets.

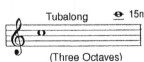

(Three Octaves)

TONAL PERCUSSION

Udu Drums (Nigeria)

Set of four pottery drums, the
sides are struck with fingers, for
high pitched sounds, while the
palms press against the holes in
the pots, to create low glisses,
boings, and deep, haunting sounds.

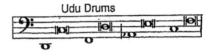
Udu Drums

Vibra-Tone

Struck with mallet. Long sustain tone.
By thumbing the sound hole,the sound
can be changed to a "wah wah" effect.

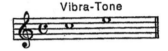
Vibra-Tone

Water Chimes (Micro Tonal)

Four brass discs are struck with
soft or hard mallets. The discs can
be lowered into a water trough by
means of a foot pedal,to lower each
tone approximately a minor third in pitch.

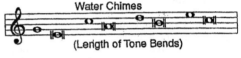
Water Chimes
(Length of Tone Bends)

Whale Drum (Bass Lujon)

Made from large water heater.
Eight indefinite pitches create
the low metalic sounds of being
under water. Played with soft mallets.

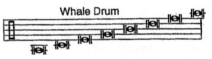
Whale Drum

Xylophone (Chinese)

Large rosewood bars are suspended
over bamboo resonators in a pentatonic
(five tone) scale. Played with hard mallets.

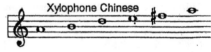
Xylophone Chinese

NON DISTINCT PITCHED

BELLS

African Double Bells	2 Pitch rhythm keeper struck with wood or metal.
Ankle Bells (India)	Shake pitches, small bells on leather straps.
Ankle Bells (Syria)	Shake pitches on braclets.
Aluminum Bells	5 Pitches long sustain struck with soft beater.
American Indian Bells	Shake pitches, jingles on leather straps.
Aporo (Africa)	2 Pitched bells struck with wood or metal beaters.
Au Go Go	2 Pitched bells struck with wood or metal beaters.
Balinese Gong Bell	1 Pitch rhythm keeper struck with wooden beater.
Bell Plate	1 Pitch long sustain struck with metal beater.
Bell Tree	30 Pitches glissed or struck with metal beater.
Big Ben Bells	4 Pitches long sustain struck with vibe mallets.
Bike Bell	1 Pitch pressed with thumb.
Boat Bell	1 Pitch struck with metal mallet.
Bobati (Africa)	Wood rhythm bell played with wood beater.
Bowed Temple Bells	Pitch glisses while bowing on pedaled timpani.
Buddah Bell (Japan)	Large temple bell rubbed for long sustain.
Burmese Bells	1 Pitch struck with hard beater and spun.
Brake Drum Bells	Long ring when struck with mallet on inside rim.
Camel Bells (India)	Multi pitched, can be struck or shook.
Camel Bell (Egypt)	1 Pitch struck with hard wound beater.
Cencerro	1 Pitch latin cow bell struck with wood or metal.
Chap (Thailand)	2 Finger bells struck together for keeping time.
Chinese Water Bells	3 Pitches struck with bell mallet for glissed tone.
Chinese Temple Bells	1 Pitch struck with padded beater.
Church Steeple Bell	1 Pitch struck with padded knocker.
Clay Bells (Mexico)	3 Pitches shook.
Clay Bells	12 Pitches struck or glissed with hard mallet.
Clock Chimes	4 Pitched glisses, while struck on pedaled timpani.
Cow Bell	1 Pitch, struck with beaters for effect or rhythm.
Crank Bell	1 Pitch with prolonged ring when cranked.
Crank Siren	Glissed long ring when cranked
Crotale Bell	1 Pitch struck with hard beater or bowed.
Crystal Bell	1 Pitch very long ringing. Struck with soft beater.
Dinner Bells	3 Pitches struck with vibe mallet.
Dinner Bells	1 Pitch shook
Fight Bells	1 Pitch struck with hammer.
Finger Bell	1 Pitch tapped with index finger.
Finger bells	2 Pitches struck together.
Fire Bell	1 Pitch struck with metal beaters.

NON DISTINCT PITCHED

BELLS

Foot Bell(India)	2 Pitches, 1 when depressed, and 1 when released.
Flower Pot Mold Bells	1 Pitch, 8 large pots played with soft mallet.
Ghug Hura Bells(India)	Small bells on leather straps, shake pitches.
Glass Bells	1 Pitch, shake or strike.
Glock Tree	80 Pitches,glissed with hand or mallet.
Jingle Bells	Shake pitches, held together on wooden handle.
Jingle Sticks	Bells on broom sticks used for rhythm playing.
Kyeezee Bell	1 wavered pitch, spin after striking with mallet,
Mark Tree Bells	Multi pitched brass tubes glissed or struck.
Manjira	Finger bells, clapped together for rhythm.
Mission Bell	Large cast bell struck with padded beater.
Mission Bells	Clay pitched bells, glissed or shook.
Mixing Bowl Bells	Stainless steel bowls, hit on inner rims, long ring.
Phone Bell	Hand cranked.
Porcelain Bells	20 Pitches struck with soft wooden chop sticks.
Persian Temple Bell	1 Pitch, struck with soft Beater.
Roto Rim Bell Tree	9 Pitches, struck or glissed with metal beaters.
Saw Blade Bells	1 Pitch, struck with metal beater,long ring tone.
Ship's Bell	1 Pitch, struck with metal beater.
Sleigh Bells	Shake pitches, large or small.
Stainless Steel Bells	Bowls, hit on inner rims, with padded stick.
Tap Bell	1 Pitch, tapped with index finger.
Taxi Bell(India)	2 Pitches, foot or hand operated.
Telephone Bell	1 Pitch, hand crank, long or short ring.
Temple Bells(Japan)	1 Pitch, rubbed with stick or bowed.
Temple Bells(Korea)	1 Pitch, struck with soft or hard beater.
Thailand Bells	26 Pitches, glissed or struck.
Tin Can Bell	1 Pitch, shook.
Train Bell	1 Pitch, with metal knocker.
Tree Bells(Camel)	12 Pitches,shook or glissed.
Tree Bells(Chinese)	70 Pitches, glissed with padded sticks.
Tree Bells(Clay)	17 Pitches glissed with beebees thrown over them.
Tree Bells(Glock)	80 Pitches of orchestra bells glissed or struck.

NON DISTINCT PITCHED

BELLS

Tree Bells(Japan)	17 Pitches,glissed or struck with metal beater.
Tree Bells(Mission)	40 Pitches,glissed with hands.
Tree Bells(Pakistan)	30 Pitches, chromatic, glissed or struck.
Tree Bells(Roto Rim)	10 Pitches,glissed or struck with metal beater.
Tree Bells(Thailand)	37 Pitches, glissed with hands.
Triangle Bells	3 Or more pitches, struck with metal beaters.
Water Bells(China)	3 Pitches, struck with mallet and glissed.
Water Chimes)	4 Pitches,struck with mallets and glissed.
Wind Bells	80 Pitches,glissed with hands.
Wood Bells(Japan)	Shake pitches.
Yak Bells(Thailand)	2 Pitches, shake or strike.
ZuZu Bells(Japan)	Sistrum jingles on stick,shook.

NON DISTINCT PITCHED

BLOWERS

(African)Horn Trumpet	Crow Call	Sheng (China)
African Mating Flute	Duck Call	Sho (Japan)
American Indian Flute	Fish Horn	Shofer (Israel)
Bamboo Flute(Persia)	Fog Horn	Siren Whistle
Bamboo Horn (Thailand)	Frog Call	Slide Whistle (Bass)
Bass Flute(Bolivia)	Hiss Whistle	Slide Whistle Piccolo
Bird Calls	Jay Call	Slide Whistle (Standard)
Bird Whistles	Jew's Harp (Bali)	Slide Whistle (Tenor)
Boat Whistle	Jew's Harp India)	Steam Whistle
Bolivia Flute	Jew's Harp (Sicily)	Thai Reed Mouth Organ
Bolivia Pan Pipes	Jew's Harp (U S A)	Water Bird Chirp
Brazilian Bird Whistle	Kazoo	Warbler Whistle
Buffalo Horn Trumpet	Ma Ma Cry	Yugoslav Double Flute
Bulb Horn	Mardi Gras Whistle	Zulu Mating Whistle
Cricket Call	Microphone Neck Flute	
Conch Horn (Hawaii)	Nose Flute (Hawai)	
Conch Horn (Tibet)	Police Whistle	
Cow Scream Horn	Shanka Trumpet	

NON DISTINCT PITCHED

CYMBALS AND GONGS

Aluminum Bowl Gongs	1 Pitch, played with soft mallets.
Buddhist Temple Gong	1 Pitch, many overtones, played by rubbing rim.
Bowed Gong	Varied pitches, played with bow in hole.
Castanet Cymbals(Morroco)	1 Pair held in each hand, struck together.
Chang Chang(Bali)	5 cymbals struck with 2 others held in hand.
Chap Cymbals(Thailand)	Finger cymbals used as rhythm keepers.
Chinese Cymbals	Large and small, struck with various sticks.
Chinese Opera Gong	Bending Pitches, played with mallet.
Chinese Piatti Cymbals	Struck together.
Chinese Roar Cymbals	Rubbed together for roaring sound.
Chinese Water Cymbals	Struck with hard mallet, glissed pitches.
Crystal Bowl Gong	1 Pitch, played by rubbing stick on rim of bowl.
Coca Cola Gong	1 Pitch, played with gong mallet.
Cup Cymbals	7 Pitches,played with sticks or mallets.
Cymbal Tree	14 Pitches glissed with metal beater.
Fight Gong	1 Pitch, struck with metal or wood hammer.
Finger Cymbals	Struck together.
Gamelon Gongs (Bali)	1 Pitch, struck with soft mallets.
Great Gong (Bali)	1 Pitch, many overtones, with soft mallet.
Hi Hat Cymbals	2 Cymbals struck together.
Korean Bending Gong	Bending pitch, played with mallet.
Keyeeze Gong (Burma)	Varied pitch, twirl while striking with mallet.
Pelong Gong (Bali)	1 Pitch, struck with mallet.
Rhythm Gong(Bali)	1 Pitch,to keep time, struck with wood beater.
Roto Disk Gong	1 Pitch, struck with stick while twirling disc.
Roto Rim Gong	1 Pitch, struck with triangle beater.
Saw Blade Gong	1 Pitch, struck with metal beater.
Scraped Cymbals	Scraped with coin or metal beater.
Scraped Gong	Scraped with metal beater.
Sled Gongs	1 Pitch, struck with mallet.
Slendro Gong (Bali)	1 Pitch, played with mallets.
Super Ball Cymbal	Rubbed with super ball for moan effects.
Super Ball Gong	Rubbed with super ball for moan effects.
Tam Tam	1 Pitch, multi overtones, struck with mallet.
Tibetian Cymbals	Struck together.
Tree Cymbals	Glissed with metal beater.
Water Bell Plate Gong	Glissed pitch, struck with mallet, in water.
Water Cymbals	3 Pitches struck and glissed.
Water Gong	Glissed pitch, struck with mallet, in water.
WaWa Cymbals	Struck and shook for (wa wa) type sound.

NON DISTINCT PITCHED

DRUMS

African Bass Talking Drum	Glissed pitches, played with hands.
African Barrel Drum	1 Pitch played with sticks.
African Clay Bongoes(Morroco)	2 Pitches,many sizes,played with hands.
African Djembe (Large)	1 Pitch on stand, played with hands
African Djun Djun	3 Pitches, 3 sizes, played with sticks.
African Dune Dune(Deeper)	3 Pitches, 3 sizes, played with sticks.
African Giant Drum	2 Pitches, played with sticks.
African Hair Drum	1 Pitch played with stick or mallet.
African Oil Drum	2 Pitches, played with sticks.
African Pedal Talking Drum	Pedal glissed pitches, play with sticks.
African Power Dunes	3 Pitches, played with sticks, mallets.
African Pottery Drums(Egypt)	1 Pitch, 2 tones, played with hands.
African Talking Drum	Glissed pitches, played with stick.
African Tom Toms	3 Pitches, played with sticks, mallets.
African Conga Drum	1 Pitch, played with hands.
African Gourd Drum	1 Pitch, played with hands or sticks.
African Goblet Drum	1 Pitch, played with sticks.
African Kettle Drums	1 Pitch, played with sticks.
African Snare Drum	1 Pitch, played with hand and stick.
African Squeeze Drum	Glissed pitches, played with stick.
Africn Walking Drum	1 Pitch with jingles,played with hands.
African Water Drums	Gourds played in water with mallets.
African Zebra skin Drum	1 Pitch, played with sticks.
Afro-Cuban Bata Drum	2 Pitches, played with hands.
Afro-Cuban Cajon	Wood drum, played with hands.
American Indian Giant Drum	1 Pitch, played with mallets.
American Indian Pow Wow Drum	Played by many players with sticks.
American Indian Tom Tom	(Apachi) 1 pitch, played with sticks.
American Indian Tom Tom	(Chippewai) 1 pitch, played with sticks.
American Indian Tom Tom	(Hopi) 1 pitch, played with sticks.
American Indian Tom Tom	(Navaho) 1 pitch, played with sticks.
American Indian Tom Tom	(Sioux) 1 pitch, played with sticks.
American Indian Tom Tom	(Zuni) 1 pitch, played with sticks.
American Indian Tom Toms	3 Pitches, played with sticks.

NON DISTINCT PITCHED

DRUMS

Basque Drum	Small snare drum with one gut, played with sticks.
Barrel Drums	(See) African, Chinese, Japanese.
Bodrun (Ireland)	1 varied pitch, played with stick.
Bomba (Argentina)	1 Pitch, played with stick and hand.
Bongoes	2 Pitches, played with hands.
Boo Bams	Multi Pitches, played with palms.
Buddhist Drum	1 Pitch, struck with stick, and shook.
Chinese Barrel Drum	1 Pitch, played with sticks.
Chinese Bongoe	1 Pitch, Played with stick.
Chinese Opera Drum	1 Pitch, played with sticks.
Chinese Snake Drum	1 pitch, struck with stick and shook.
Chinese Spring Drum	1 pitch, struck with stick while spring rattles.
Chinese Temple Drum	1 Pitch, played with mallets.
Chinese Tom Tom	(Ton Ku) 1 pitch, struck with sticks.
Chinese Tom Tom	(Ying Ku) 1 pitch, struck with sticks.
Concert Bass Drum	1 Pitch, played with various beaters.
Concert Tom Toms	1 Pitch, 8 sizes, played with sticks or mallets.
Concert Snare Drum	Played with or without snares, struck with sticks.
Conga Drums	1 Pitch, played with hands.
Cuica (Brazil)	Vary pitch, by rubbing stick, to vibrate skin head.
Daiko-Chu (Japan)	Medium drum, 2 pitches, played with sticks.
Daiko-O (Japan)	Large drum, 2 pitches, played with sticks.
Darabuka (Turkey)	1 Pitch, played with hands.
Drum Table	Extra large table drum, 1 pitch, played with mallets.
Eskimo Drum	Struck on rim with stick, and shook to vibrate head
Field Drum	1 Pitch, snares on or off, played with sticks.
Flex-A-Drum	Glissed pitches with pedal, played with sticks.
Frame Drum	i Pitch, played with fingers.
Friction Drum (Brazil)	Vary pitches by rubbing stick, to vibrate skin head.
Friction Drum(Bark)	Rubbing string, creates short dog barks.
Friction Drum(U S A)	Rubbing string, creates long growls.
Galvanized Drums	1 Pitch, played with bass drum beaters.
Goblet Drum	1 Pitch, played with hands.
Gourd Drum	1 Pitch, played with hands.

NON DISTINCT PITCHED

DRUMS

India Darmu	Glissed pitches, shake and squeeze.
India Dolak	2 Pitches, played with hands.
India Elephant Drum	1 Pitch, played with sticks.
India GoopGupi	Glissed pitches, pluck string, attached to drum.
India Kanjira	1 Pitch with jingle, played with fingers.
India Kettle Drum	1 Pitch, played with sticks.
India Khol	2 Pitches, played with hands.
India Mirdangam	2 Pitches, played with hands.
India Monkey Drums	Glissed pitches, shake and squeeze.
India Tabla	1 Pitch drone,1 pitch glissed, played with fingers.
Japanese Chu Daiko	1 Pitch, 2 sided, played with sticks.
Japanese Gagaku	1 Pitch played with sticks.
Japanese Kabuki Drum	1 Pitch, played with sticks.
Japanese Uchiwa Daiko	1 Pitch, pancake drum, hit with stick and shake.
Japanese O Daiko	1 Pitch, 2 sided, played with sticks.
Kettle Drums	1 Pitch played with mallets,pedal changes pitch.
Korea Chang ko	Glissed pitches, played with stick, squeeze ropes.
Korea Ko	1 Pitch, hand held, played with stick.
Korea Temple Drum	1 Pitch, played with sticks.
Korea Tom Tom	1 Pitch, played with sticks.
Long Drum(Thailand)	1 Pitch played with hands.
Morrocan Bongoes	2 Pitches, played with fingers.
Morrocan Snare Drum	1 Pitch hand held, played with fingers.
Mello Drum	Glissed pitches with pedal, played with sticks.
Pandeiro(Brazil)	With Jingles, played with hands.
Pedal Roto Tom	Glissed pitches with pedal, played with sticks.
Pedal Tom Tom(Italy)	Glissed pitches with pedal, played with sticks.
Piccolo Snare Drum	1 Pitch, played with drum sticks.
Pow Pow Drum	1 Pitch, played with sticks or mallets.
Revolutionary Drums	Replica bass and snare from Civil War era, sticks.
Rope Drums	Bass drum and deep snare drum tune by the ropes.
Roto Toms	Glissed pitches, played with mallets or sticks.

NON DISTINCT PITCHED

DRUMS

Scottish Snare Drum	Very high pitched, crisp authentic snare sound.
Surdo(Brazil)	1 Pitch, played with 1 mallet, and pressed hand.
Steel Drum	See: Chromatic Percussion.
Tabla	Pair, called Tabla and Baya, played with fingers.
Tabor	With or without snares, played with sticks.
Tabour	With or without snares, played with sticks.
Taiko	See: (Daiko) or (O Daiko)
Tambour	With or without snares, played with sticks.
Tambourine(American)	With or without jingles, played with hands.
Tambourine (Brazil)	Without Jingles, played with 1 stick, press head.
Tambourine (China)	With metal rings, played with fingers.
Tambourine (France)	With jingles, played with hands.
Tambourine (Greece)	With jingles, played with hands.
Tambourine (Iraq)	With jingles, played with hands.
Tambourine (Italy)	With jingles, played with hands.
Tambourine (India)	With jingles, played with hands.
Tambourine (Turkey)	With jingles, played with hands.
Tambourine (Syria)	With jingles, played with hands.
Tahitian Conga	1 Pitch, played with hands.
Tahitian Pahu	1 Pitch, played with sticks.
Tibetian Prayer Drum	Glissed pitch, played with 1 stick, and shook.
Tibetian Tabla	2 Pitches, played with fingers.
Timbales	2 Pitches, played with sticks.
Timpani	1 Pitch played with mallets,pedal, to change pitch.
Timpany (India)	1 Pitch, played with sticks.
Telephone Book Drums	2 Pitches, can be tuned, played with mallets.
Tom Toms	See: African, American Indian,Chinese.
Trinidad Drum	1 Pitch, played with hands.
Tsin ku	1 Pitch, played with sticks.
Tumbak Metal)	1 Pitch with jingles, played with fingers.
Tumbeg (Middle East)	1 Pitch, played with fingers.
Tumbuk (Clay)	1 Pitch, played with fingers.
Udu Drums	Glissed pitches, played with hands.
Voo Doo Drum	1 Pitch, played with hands.
Water Gourd Drum	1 Pitch, played in water, struck with mallet,gourd.
Water Drum (Kaluba)	1 pitch, played with fingers,
Water Drum (New Guinea)	Glissed Pitches, played by slapping on water.
Whale Drum	8 Arbitrary tones, played with soft mallets.

NON DISTINCT PITCHED

METAL AND STRING INSTRUMENTS

African Thumb Piano	Large metal tounges are played with thumbs.
African Thumb Piano	Medium metal tounges are played with thumbs.
African Thumb Piano	Small metal tounges are played with thumbs.
Anvil	2 Pitch metal bar, struck with metal mallet.
Anvil (Blacksmith's)	Used for horse shoeing, struck with hammer.
Anvil (Mounted)	2 Pitches, dull, ringing, on stand, hard mallet.
Au Go Go	2 Pitch, used for Afro, latin rhythms; metal beater.
Bell Plate	1 Pitch, long ringing, struck with hard mallet.
Birimbao(Brazil)	(String) Pitch bends played with coin,stick,rattle.
Blank Gun	A 38 blank, six shot pistol , very loud,
Boing Box	(String) Pitch bends, with pick, and bending neck.
Boing Pots	Pitch bends, played with soft mallets on bottoms.
Brake Drums	2 Pitches, Dull, ringing, played with metal beater.
Cencerro	Latin cow bell used for rhythm, with metal beater.
Cimbalum	(String) See Chromatic Percussion.
Clappers	Played with 1 in each hand, hit against knee.
Clock Chime	Gliss pitch, placed on timp head, hit with mallet.
Clock Chime Harp	Made with finger cymbal,played in palm of hand.
Crashers	Metal on metal, struck with mallet.
Cricket Clicker	Clicked by squeezing between thumb & forefinger.
Dulcimer	(String) See: Chromatic Percussion.
Ektara (India)	(String)Glissed Pitches, plucked,squeeze neck.
Flex A Tone	Glissed pitch, struck with mallet while bending.
Fry Pan Au Go Go	2 Pitches used for rhythm keeping, hit with metal.
Garbage Can	1 Pitch, struck with bass drum mallet.
Giant Flex A Tone	Glissed pitches, played with bow.
Guitarron	(String) Tuned like bass fiddle, played pizzicato.
Gutt Bucket	(String) 1 String plucked, while bending neck.
Hand Crank Siren	Long sustain prison siren,crank handle.
Jew's Harp (Metal)	1 Tone, played by plucking metal tongue on teeth.
Kalimba	See Chromatic Percussion.
Log Drum Metal	Multi pitched, play with soft mallets.
Lujons	Multi pitched, play with soft mallets.

NON DISTINCT PITCHED

METAL AND STRING INSTRUMENTS

Marinzano	Metal jew's harp from Sicily.
Marimbula	See: Tonal Percussion.
Marx A Phone	See: Tonal Percussion.
Mbira	Metal tongues are played with thumbs.
Metal AngKlungs	See: Chromatic Percussion.
Metal Castanets	Played in pairs with hands.
Metal Cluster	Metal bar struck on orchestra chimes.
Metal Notched Stick	Scraped with triangle beater.
Metal Notched Triangle	Struck or scraped with triangle beater.
Mouth Bow	(String)Played with pick using mouth as resonator
Murching	Metal Jew's harp from India.
Music Box	Hand crank, plays a tune.
Musical Saw	Glissed pitches, played with bow.
Oil Can	Played as rhythm keeper, with hands or sticks.
Oil Can Poppers	Played by pressing thumb on bottom of cans.
Oop Gupi	(String) Played with pick, glissed pitches.
Pop Gun	Loud pop, push handle forward to release cork.
Rhythm Log (Metal)	Multi pitches, played with soft rubber mallets.
Roto Rim Tree	Discs on stand, played with triangle beater.
Santur	(String) See Tonal Percussion.
Spoons (Metal)	Played as rhythm keeper on palms and knees.
Starter Pistol	6 Shots,used as sound effect.
Steel Drum	See: Chromatic Percussion.
Steel Mixing Bowls	2 Pitches,bell like, soft mallet, boings on bottoms
Tambura	(String) See: Tonal Percussion.
Tap Shoes	Pair, played with hands to simulate dance rhythm.
Thumb Piano	Metal Tounges, played with fingers.
Thunder Sheet	Shook to duplicate cracking thunder sound.
Tin Can Marimba	Hit with mallets on can bottoms.
Triangle	Played with beater for rhythm, or high accents.
Water Phone	Wobbled pitches, played with mallet or bow.
Whale Drum	8 Pitches played with soft mallets.

NON DISTINCT PITCHED

SCRAPERS SHAKERS RATTLES WHIRLERS

African Axatsi	Strike, Shake
African Bamboo Rattles	Shake, Rattle
African Basket Rattle	Shake
African Giant Pod Shakers	Shake, Rattle
African Gourd Shaker	Strike, Shake
African Jingle Sticks	Shake
African Pod Rattles	Shake, Rattle
African Sea Shell Belt Rattles	Shake, Rattle
African Spider Coccon Rattle	Shake, Rattle
African Sistrum (Ethiopia)	Shake
African Sistrum (Morroco)	Shake
African Wood Scratcher	Scrape
American Indian Ankle Belts	Shake, Rattle
American Indian Antelope Horn Rattle	Shake, Rattle
American Indian Buffalo Hide Rattle	Shake, Rattle
American Indian Cocoon Rattle	Shake, Rattle
American Indian Dancing Belt Rattle	Shake, Rattle
American Indian Deer's Hoof Rattle	Shake, Rattle
American Indian Deer Skin Rattle	Shake, Rattle
American Indian Elm Bark Rattle	Shake, Rattle
American Indian Fish Skin Rattle	Shake, Rattle
American Indian Hoof Belt Rattle	Shake, Rattle
American Indian Leg Belt Rattle	Shake, Rattle
American Indian Pea Pod Rattles	Shake, Rattle
American Indian Pepper Can Rattle	Shake, Rattle
American Indian Peyote Rattle	Shake, Rattle
American Indian Rattle Snake Rattles	Shake, Rattle
American Indian Seal Skin Rattle	Shake, Rattle
American Indian Sleigh Bell Rattle	Shake, Rattle
American Indian Spider Cocoon Rattle	Shake, Rattle
American Indian Turtle Body Rattle	Shake, Rattle
American Indian Turtle Shell Rattle	Shake, Rattle
Ang Klong Rattles (Bali)	Rattle
Ang Klong Rattles (Chordal)	Rattle
Ang Klong Rattles (Laos)	Rattle
Ang Klong Rattles (Metal)(U S A)	Rattle
Ang Klong Rattles (Thailand)	Rattle
Aztec Maracas	Shake

NON DISTINCT PITCHED

SCRAPERS SHAKERS RATTLES WHIRLERS

Bamboo Rattles	Rattle, Shake
Basket Maracas	Shake
Bean Bag	Shake, Tap
Bean Can Shaker	Shake
Beer Can Maracas	Shake
Bin Zasara (Japan) Wood Scrap	Scrape
Bones	Click Together
Bottle Cap Jingles	Shake
Bottle Cap Sticks	Shake, Stomp
Brazilian Scraper	Scrape
Bird Roarer	Whirl
Bull Roarer (Africa)	Whirl
Bull Roarer (American Indian)	Whirl
Bull Roarer (Australia)	Whirl
Buzz Roarer	Whirl
Cabasa	Shake, Rub
Caxixi (Brazil)	Shake
Chicken Clucker	Rub
Chimta (India) Jingle Stick	Shake, Stomp
Ching A Ring	Shake, Stomp
Chocalho	Shake
Cricket Clicker	Click
Cricket Rattle	Shake
Eskimo Rattle	Shake
Fishing Reel Ratchet	Crank
Flex-A-Tone	Shake
Giant Pipe Shaker	Shake, Swish
Ghunghara Stick	Shake, Stomp
Gourd Rattle (Africa)(Senpo)	Shake
Gourd Rattle (Brazil)	Shake
Gourd Maracas (Africa)	Shake
Gourd Maracas (Mexico)	Shake
Guiro (Costa Rica)	Scrape
Guiro (Cuba)	Scrape
Guiro (Mexico)	Scrape
Ivory Coast Rattle	Shake
Ivory Coast Shells	Shake
Ivory Coast Vibraslap	Strike to Vibrate

NON DISTINCT PITCHED

SCRAPERS SHAKERS RATTLES WHIRLERS

Jangle Sticks	Strike, Shake
Jaw Bone (Mexico)	Strike to Vibrate
Jhanjhana Maracas (India)	Shake
Jingle Sticks	Stomp, Shake
Kartal (India)	Stomp, Shake
Maracas (Africa)	Shake
Maracas (America)	Shake
Maracas (India)	Shake
Maracas (Italy)	Shake
Maracas (Mexico)	Shake
Metal Cabasa	Shake, Rub
Metal Guiro	Scrape
Metal Maracas (India)	Shake
Metal Maracas (Mexico)	Shake
Metal Notched Pipe	Scrape
Metal Scraper	Scrape
Metal Scratcher	Scrape
Metal Shaker	Shake
Musical Hose	Whirl
Notched Stick	Scrape
Nsenge Reed Shaker	Shake
Pepper Shaker	Shake
Peyote Rattle	Shake
Pea Pod Shakers	Shake
Piccolo Cabasa	Shake, Rub
Pod Ankle Belts (Africa)	Shake
Pod Ankle Belts (Eskimo)	Shake
Pod Ankle Belts (Mexico)	Shake
Puelli Sticks (Hawaii)(Cold Weather)	Strike
Quijada	Strike to Vibrate
Rain Stick (Bamboo)	Swish
Rain Stick (Metal)	Swish
Ratchet (Metal)	Crank
Ratchet (Wood)	Crank
Rattan Shaker	Shake
Rattles (Gourd)	Shake
Rattle Mallets	Shake
Reco Reco (Bamboo)	Scrape Reco Reco (Wood)

NON DISTINCT PITCHED

SCRAPERS SHAKERS RATTLES WHIRLERS

Sand Blocks	Scrape
Scraper	Scrape
Scratcher	Scrape
Sea Shell Rattles	Shake
Shaker	Shake
Shaker Sticks	Shake
Shekeri	Shake
Siren	Crank
Sistrum (Africa)	Shake
Sistrum (Egypt)	Shake
Sistrum (Ethiopia)	Shake
Sistrum (Japan)	Shake
Slap Stick Rattle	Shake
Snail Shell Rattle	Shake
Spoons (Wood, Metal)	Clap
Spring Scratcher (Brazil)	Scrape
Spring Scratcher Hub Cap	Shake
Tambourine Jingles	Shake
Temple Sticks (Australia)	Strike
Temple Sticks (Korea)	Strike
Thunder Stick	Whirl
Thunder Sheet	Shake
Timp Rattle Mallets	Shake
Toilet Ball Maracas	Shake
Tree Bark Maracas	Shake
Tubo	Shake
Tubolo	Shake
Turtle Body Rattle	Shake
Turtle Shell Rattle	Shake
Vibra Slap	Strike to Vibrate
Washboard (American)	Scrape
Washboard Vest (Zideco)	Scrape
Whale Skin Rattle	Shake
Wilmurra	Whirl
Wind Machine	Crank
Wind Wand	Whirl
Wobble Board	Wobble
Wood Scratcher	Scrape
Wood Shaker	Shake

NON DISTINCT PITCHED

WIND CHIMES

Absydian Wind Chimes   (ALL GLISSED WITH HANDS OR STICKS)
Aeolian Cristallaphone
Bamboo Wind Chimes
Bolt Wind Chime
Brass Wind Chime
Clay Bell Wind Chime
Chinese Temple Bell Wind Chime
Cymbal Tree Wind Chime
Drum Stick Wind Chime
Fork and Spoon Wind Chime
Glass Ball Wind Chime
Glass Wind Chime
Glock Wind Chime
Ice Crystal Wind Chime
Jar Top Wind Chime   (ALL GLISSED WITH HANDS OR STICKS)
Key Tree Wind Chime
Locksmith Wind Chime
Mark Tree Wind Chime
Microtonal Bell Wind Chime
Microtonal Glass Wind Chime
Microtonal Tube Wind Chime
Microtonal Pipe Wind Chime
Rim Tree Wind Chime
Rock Salt Wind Chime
Rose Wood Wind Chime
Rim Tree Wind Chime
Scrap Iron Wind Chime
Screw Wind Chime   (ALL GLISSED WITH HANDS OR STICKS)
Sea Shell Wind Chime
Silverware Wind Chime
Thai Bell Wind Chime
Teak Wood Wind Chime
Tin Can Wind Chime
Valve Wind Chime
Volcanic Glass Wind Chime
Wood Stick Wind Chime
Wrench Wind Chime

NON DISTINCT PITCHED

WOOD INSTRUMENTS

African Slit Drums	Struck
African Slit Logs	Struck
Back Beat Clappers	Struck
Bamboo Slit Logs (Bali)	Struck
Bones	Clicked
Cajon	Slapped
Castanets (Wood)	Clicked
Chinese Wood Blocks	Struck
Chinese Wood Drum	Struck
Clappers	Struck
Claves	Struck
Coconut Shells	Struck
Daka De Bello	Struck
Devil Chasers	Struck
Ebony Claves	Struck
Eucalyptus Claves	Struck
Gourd (Dried, Whole)	Slapped
Grape Stake Puelli	Struck
Horses Hooves	Struck
Ipu	
Kabuki Clappers	Struck
Korean Clappers	Clapped
Korean Temple Blocks	Struck
Log Drums	Struck
Log Drum Bass (Red Wood)	Struck
Log Drum Bass (New Guinea)	Struck
Marching Machine	Stomped
Piccolo Wood Blocks(China)	Struck
Piccolo Wood Blocks (Japan)	Struck
Prayer Sticks (Australia)	Struck
Puelli Sticks	Struck

NON DISTINCT PITCHED

WOOD INSTRUMENTs

Rhythm Logs	Struck
Slap Stick	Struck
Slit Logs (Africa)	Struck
Slit Logs (Bali)	Struck
Slit Logs (Mexico)	Struck
Slit Logs (New Guinea)	Struck
Slit Logs (Polynesia)	Struck
Slit Logs (Tahiti)	Struck
Spoons (Wood)	Clapped
Stamping Tubes	Stomped
Telephone Books	Struck
Temple Blocks	Struck
Tap Shoes	Stomped
Turtle Shell	Struck
Touetti	Struck
Water Log (New Guinea)	Struck
Wobble Board	Wobbled
Wood Blocks	Struck
Wood Shakers	Shook
Wood Table	Struck
Wood Tambourine (Sicily)	Struck
Wooden Bongos	Struck

INDEX

ABOUT THE CO-AUTHOR

om Di Nardo is a Philadelphia-based journalist who has written on the arts since 1970. After eight years of reviews and feature stories in the *Philadelphia Evening Bulletin*, his interviews and articles on classical music, opera and ballet have been published regularly in the *Philadelphia Daily News* since 1982.

His articles have also appeared in *Symphony, Music Makers, Attenzione, Stagebill, Playbill*, the *Chautauqua Daily, Accent on Music, Applause* and many other magazines, as well as in the *New Grove Dictionary of Music and Musicians*.

He has also written widely on film music, and published film reviews in books entitled "On The Set" and "Movies On Tape."

He first met Emil Richards, then playing with the George Shearing Quintet at George Wein's Storyville Club in Boston, in 1957, beginning a friendship which has lasted for over 55 years.

EMIL RICHARDS WEBSITE LINKS

EMIL RICHARDS WEB SITE, LESSON BOOKS AND DVD'S AVAILABLE
http://www.emilrichards.com/

EMIL RICHARDS CDs
http://www.cdbaby.com/cd/emilrichards1
http://www.cdbaby.com/cd/emilrichards2
http://www.cdbaby.com/cd/emilrichards3
http://www.cdbaby.com/cd/emilrichards4
http://www.cdbaby.com/cd/emilrichards5

EMIL RICHARDS BOOKS FOR ADULT AND CHILDREN PLAYERS
INCLUDING STUDIO TECHNIQUES, MUSIC & RHYTHM PERMUTA-
TIONS, MALLET EXERCISES, ESSENTIAL SIGHT READING, AND FUN
FOR KIDS
http://emilrichards.com/music-store/books.php
emilvibes@gmail.com to order
http://www.halleonard.com/product/viewproduct.do?itemid=6620134&lid=0&
keywords=EMIL%20RICHARDS&subsiteid=1&
http://www.halleonard.com/product/viewproduct.do?itemid=6620133&lid=1&k
eywords=EMIL%20RICHARDS&subsiteid=1&
http://www.halleonard.com/product/viewproduct.do?itemid=6620135&lid=2&
keywords=EMIL%20RICHARDS&subsiteid=1&
http://www.halleonard.com/product/viewproduct.do?itemid=6620132&lid=3&
keywords=EMIL%20RICHARDS&subsiteid=1&

A LIST OF MANY RECORD SESSIONS EMIL HAS PLAYED ON
http://www.hammerax.com/artists_emil_richards.htm

172 ALBUMS WITH EMIL RICHARDS IN THE LINER NOTES
Http://www.cduniverse.com/sresult.asp?HT_Search=ALL&HT_Search_Info=emi
l+richards&style=music

MORE LINER NOTES WITH EMIL RICHARDS
http://www.cduniverse.com/sresult.asp?HT_Search=ALL&HT_
Search_Info=emil+radocchia&style=music

ORAL HISTORY PROGRAM INTERVIEW ABOUT FILM WORK/ VIDEO
http://www.namm.org/library/oral-history/emil-richards

MANY PAGES OF BILLBOARD MAGAZINE ARTICLES WITH EMIL
RICHARDS DATING BACK TO 1958
http://www.google.com/search?tbo=p&tbm=bks&q=EMIL+RICHARDS&tbs=,b
kt:m,bkms:1168684103302644149

ALLMUSIC GUIDE DISCOGRAPHY
http://www.allmusic.com/artist/emil-richards-mn0000819595

IN DEPTH EMIL INTERVIEWS / VIDEO/ AUDIO AND WRITTEN
http://www.npr.org/2011/02/27/134053797/emil-richards-timekeeper-of-tinseltown
http://www.newyorker.com/online/blogs/alexross/2010/05/giacchino-out-
takes-ii-emil-richards.html
http://www.jakefeinbergshow.com/2011/05/the-emil-richards-interview/

A GREAT ARTICLE WITH SOME UNUSAL EMIL STORIES AND INSIGHT
http://www.headheritage.co.uk/unsung/thebookofseth/beaver-and-krause-
rocksampler

INSTRUMENTS AND HARRY PARTCH LETTERS EMIL RICHARDS HAS
DONATED TO THE PAS MUSEUM
http://rhythmdiscoverycenter.org/?s=EMIL+RICHARDS

PAS HALL OF FAME ARTICLE WITH EMIL QUOTES ON SESSIONS AND
COMPOSERS
http://www.pas.org/experience/halloffame/RichardsEmil.aspx
EMIL RICHARDS AND THE PRO DRUM SHOP
http://www.youtube.com/watch?v=wCR9F4Dhmkg
THE WRECKING CREW
http://www.youtube.com/watch?v=uhYGKTsfGeo
http://www.wreckingcrewfilm.com/premiumemilrichards/
EMIL RICHARDS BRIEF HISTORY
http://www.lastudiomusicians.info/emilrichards.htm

EMIL RICHARDS LA TIMES ARTICLE
http://articles.latimes.com/1994-07-01/news/va-10719_1_emil-richards

MICHAEL GIACCHINO TALKING ABOUT WORKING WITH EMIL RICHARDS
http://www.nytimes.com/2006/05/07/movies/07burl.html?_r=0
http://www.scpr.org/programs/offramp/2012/03/01/22748/behind-the-
scenes-composer-michael-giacchino-score

EMIL RICHARDS COLLECTION AND DETAILS ON FILM SCORES
CLICK EMILRICHARDS COLLECTION FOR THE LISTS
http://www.lapercussionrentals.com
http://www.lapercussionrentals.com/infopage_erc.html#fla

AUDIO OF UNUSUAL EMIL RICHARDS ALBUMS
http://www.youtube.com/watch?v=13QKmJE1stk
http://www.youtube.com/watch?v=z3zKHd2Sot0
http://www.youtube.com/watch?v=8h8JvQ11yUc
http://www.youtube.com/watch?v=1J4RZOaYdxo

REVIEWS OF "WONDERFUL WORLD OF PERCUSSION" ALBUM
https://groups.google.com/forum/?fromgroups=#!topic/rec.music.bluenote/d
12Ht1Bn8RE

EMIL RICHARDS BIG BAND VIDEOS
http://www.youtube.com/watch?v=COM7u5OnFJo
http://www.youtube.com/watch?v=6PQEqNYGTlg
http://www.youtube.com/watch?v=lC4Akh_88L4

EMIL RICHARDS CHARITY WORK WITH MR HOLLANDS OPUS
http://www.mhopus.org/

EMIL RICHARDS MALLETS BY MIKE BALTER
http://www.mikebalter.com/emil_richards_sound_of_the_studio_series.htm

EMIL RICHARDS AND PAISTE
http://www.paiste.com/

EMIL RICHARDS AND THE REMO PADDLE DRUM
http://www.remo.com/portal/products/6/123/266/pd_paddle_drum_2pack.htm

EMIL RICHARDS AND YAMAHA
http://www.yamaha.com/artists/emilrichards.html

VIDEO OF EMIL RICHARDS HAVING FUN AT NAMM
http://www.youtube.com/watch?v=Cx23A9k4G9A

VIBES WORKSHOP
http:www.vibesworkshop.com

EMIL RICHARDS IS PASSIONATE ABOUT MUSICIANS HAVING RIGHTS
http://www.promusic47.org/

IMDB EMIL RICHARDS
http://www.imdb.com/name/nm0724079/

EMIL RICHARDS WORKING WITH DANNY ELFMAN
http://www.scoringsessions.com/news/100/

EMIL RICHARDS AND THE CONTRA BAND
http://www.youtube.com/watch?v=LQF8XiEZuXA

38 PAGES OF EMIL RICHARDS AS A PLAYER
http://www.discogs.com/search?q=emil+richards&type=all

EMIL RICHARDS ON THE FILM "THE OMEGA MAN"
http://www.filmscoremonthly.com/notes/omega_man_02.html

INTERVIEW WITH EMIL RICHARDS AT THE GRAMMY MUSEUM
http://www.grammymuseum.org/interior.php?section=exhibits&page=tthirdfloor

TYPE IN EMIL RICHARDS AND SEE HOW MANY SONGS YOU FIND
albumlinernotes.com

FOR CLINICS INCLUDING STUDIO TECHNIQUES, CREATING NEW
SOUNDS, MAKING INSTRUMENTS, ODD TIME RYTHMS, JAZZ IMPROV,
MASTER MALLET CLINICS, CONTACT EMIL RICHARDS AT
emilvibes@gmail.com

CPSIA information can be obtained
at www.ICGtesting.com
Printed in the USA
FSHW010759120720
71555FS

9 781593 932657